EXPLORING
TheIBM® PC/Jr.™
HOME COMPUTER

EXPLORING
The IBM® PC/Jr.™
HOME COMPUTER

Peter Norton

Illustrated by Mits Katayama

MICROSOFT®
PRESS

PUBLISHED BY
Microsoft Press
A Division of Microsoft Corporation
10700 Northup Way, Bellevue, Washington 98004

Library of Congress Cataloging in Publication Data
Norton, Peter, 1943-
Exploring the IBM PCjr Home Computer
Includes Index.
1. IBM PCjr (Computer) I. Title.
II. Title: Exploring the I.B.M. P.C.jr home computer
QA76.8.I2593N67 1984 001.64 84-3828
ISBN 0-914845-02-0

Printed and bound in the United States of America

1 2 3 4 5 6 7 8 9 DODO 8 9 0 9 8 7 6 5 4

Distributed to the book trade in the United States and Canada
by Simon and Schuster, Inc.

CompuServe® is a registered trademark of CompuServe Information Services, Inc. Digital Research® is a registered trademark of Digital Research. Epson® is a registered trademark of Epson America, Inc. IBM®, PC*jr*™, and XT™ are trademarks of International Business Machines Corporation. Intel® is a registered trademark of Intel Corporation. Microsoft®, Microsoft® Word, Microsoft® Flight Simulator, and Microsoft® Multiplan™ are trademarks of Microsoft Corporation. Motorola® is a registered trademark of Motorola, Inc. Texas Instruments® and TI® are registered trademarks of Texas Instruments, Inc. THE SOURCE[SM] is a service mark of Source Telecomputing Corporation, a subsidiary of The Reader's Digest Association, Inc. The Norton Utilities™, DiskLook™, UnErase™, SecMod™, FileHide™, FileFix™, SSAR™, Hard-Look™, and Hard UnErase™ are trademarks of Peter Norton. UCSD Pascal® is a registered trademark of the Regents of the University of California.

CONTENTS

ACKNOWLEDGMENTS

A book like this is the result of many talents. To start with, we all can express our thanks to IBM for creating the PCjr. Larry Goldstein started me writing books about computers in the first place; since writing books has turned out to be lots of fun and a nice way to make a living, I'm personally grateful to Larry for that. Nahum Stiskin got the whole project for a series of books on the PCjr going. Tracy Smith helped keep things on track. Salley Oberlin and her editorial staff wrestled me to the ground in order to get this book into readable prose. Karen de Robinson was responsible for the art direction of the wonderful book design. Larry Levitsky made sure that this book reached its many readers.

Essential help with technical information came from IBM's Jeanette Maher and Jill Liscom.

Eileen Harris provided aid and comfort. Hi, Mom.

JUNIOR MAGIC
AT HOME

There is nothing more magical than a
computer, and this book is about how
the IBM Personal Computer Junior
performs its magic.

Ever since they were invented, computers have impressed even the people who make them with the speed and power of what they can do. Never before has mankind been able to create such a flexible tool—one we can interact with and that seems, almost, to take on a life of its own. Even to their creators, computers have always seemed like magic. And how much more magical they become now, when ordinary folks can have the power of computers in their homes.

The IBM® Personal Computer Junior—known as the PCjr™ or, simply, Junior—isn't the first computer inexpensive enough to become a home appliance, but it represents a major advance in home computing for two simple and compelling reasons. First, the PCjr is significantly more powerful than earlier home computers, with more speed, more memory, more and better ways to display both pictures and information, and more general ability to perform the magic that only computers can perform. Second, the PCjr is a very close relative of the IBM Personal Computer.

The IBM Personal Computer—which most people just call the PC—had a dramatic impact on the world of small computing when it appeared in 1981. In the few years since then, the PC has become the center of the small-computing world. Most of the important, powerful, and useful software programs that have been developed since its introduction have either been created specifically for the PC, or have been adapted so that the PC can use them. Now there is a large library of wonderful software, all focused on IBM personal computers. The vast majority of the programs written for the PC run perfectly on the more affordable PCjr. In fact, the only PC programs we can't expect to use are the few that require more memory, or more disk storage capacity, than Junior provides.

The inexpensive IBM Personal Computer Junior can handle practically every important computing task that used to be within the abilities only of much more expensive machines. Before the PCjr, the magic of computing had already come into the home; but now, with Junior, the magic of IBM PC software comes home as well.

A QUICK LOOK AT THIS BOOK

This book will take us exploring under the covers of the IBM Personal Computer Junior, so that we can come to understand its inner workings. Why would we want to explore the PCjr?

One reason is to satisfy our curiosity about how Junior works and to take up the intellectual challenge of mastering the concepts buried inside. The PCjr is probably the most powerful tool that we have at our command. To make the most of this tool, we need some understanding of the principles behind it.

Even if we have no immediate practical use for the inside scoop on how the PCjr works, this knowledge is interesting in itself and potentially very useful.

The second reason for exploring the PCjr is to become able to move on to more advanced uses of the machine. If we want to write programs for Junior, the more we understand this computer, the better the programs we are going to produce.

But whatever our reasons for wanting to know more, here is the place to get into the real workings of this remarkable computer. Before we start, though, let's settle on a little bit of groundwork. Every book has to make some assumptions about its readers; otherwise, it could end up trying to please the world, but satisfying no one.

I'll be assuming that you have had your PCjr long enough to have become comfortable using it. Especially if you are fairly new to computers, I hope that you have read the first book in this series, *Discovering the IBM PCjr Home Computer.* This second book is complete in itself, but it does build on the information presented in *Discovering,* so many of you will probably find it helpful to read these books in order.

It will also be helpful, though again not necessary, for you to know a little about the BASIC programming language. I'll be presenting a few programming examples to illustrate certain features of the PCjr, but for those of you who don't yet know BASIC, we'll move from simple programs to more complex ones. Since BASIC uses very English-like language and I'll be explaining what's going on, you should have very little difficulty following the logic of these program examples.

Some authors of books about the inner workings of computers assume that you already understand enough to know what does what and how everything fits together. In this book, I'll try to provide that framework. Of course, I present lots of information that will be of special interest to computer professionals and hobbyists, but, as much as I can, I'll make it accessible to those of you who are unfamiliar with the concepts and the terminology.

More than anything else, this book bridges the gap between beginner's material, which helps you start out, and technician's material, which lays out the facts coldly and with little or no explanation. You will probably find most, or all, of what you want to know about Junior in this book, but in case you need to know where to look for more information, I have included a list for further reading as an appendix.

In this book, we will take a complete tour of the PCjr. First, in Chapter 1 we'll take a look at the IBM personal computer family; then, in Chapters 2 through 5, we'll look at the basic parts of the PCjr and see how the computer does its thinking and its work. Then we will move on in Chapter 6 to the PCjr's elementary education, which is embodied in its ROM-BIOS programs. We will take a look at a little assembly language in Chapter 7, and examine the cartridges in Chapter 8.

For the PCjr's higher education, Chapter 9 will explain the disk operating system, called DOS, which adds special layers of sophistication. The key to an operating system is disk storage, so in Chapter 10 we'll delve into the mysteries of disks.

When the computer shows us its stuff, it uses a display screen. So Chapters 11 through 13 will cover the many aspects of Junior's displays.

Lots of other pieces of magic are also incorporated into the PCjr. We'll cover the telephone connection in Chapter 14, sounds in Chapter 15, the keyboard in Chapter 16, and some odds and ends in Chapters 17 and 18. More mysteries of the built-in ROM-BIOS will be covered in Chapter 19, and we'll end in Chapter 20 with the secrets of programming access to the PCjr.

That's the magic we will find here, as we go exploring the IBM Personal Computer Junior.

1
THE IBM PC FAMILY

Part of what makes the IBM PCjr
so interesting, useful, and important
is that it is part of a family,
the family of IBM personal computers.

To help you understand the PCjr, we'll take a short look at the history of the entire IBM PC family and at the strengths of each family member.

THE FAMILY TREE

The original member of the family is the IBM Personal Computer, belovedly called the PC, a fairly complete and powerful computer for home and office use. While it is perfectly adequate for many uses, the PC lacks high-capacity disk storage, meaning that its programs and data are not immediately available for use. PC users have to insert the program and data diskettes appropriate for the type of work they are doing (for example, a word-processing program and a diskette containing files of letters) and then change the diskettes when they switch to another kind of work (for example, to a spreadsheet program).

During periods of heavy use, a great deal of time can be saved if all the programs and data normally used with the computer are always on tap, so the second member of the family, the IBM Personal Computer XT™, was introduced. (XT is an abbreviation of the word "extended.") The XT contains a built-in storage disk capable of holding 10 million characters, and another 10-million-character disk can be added.

Original PCs can now be upgraded to be functionally equivalent to the XT, by adding an expansion unit that contains the same high-capacity disk the XT uses. This means that a wealth of programs can be on tap at one time, and a large amount of information can be used at once. With 10 or 20 million bytes of disk storage, many businesses and professional workers can now have all their records and data ready to use. As a personal example, the PC that this book is being written on contains, in its one 10-million-byte expansion disk, every program I have bought, every program I have developed for sale, and the text of every book and article I have written about the IBM personal computers. Even with all that information, I still have about 20 percent of the PC's disk space left over for growth. That means that everything I do with my computer I can do with minimal fuss.

The original IBM Personal Computer represented IBM's entry into the area of personal computing, with a very powerful computer. The XT and the expansion unit for the PC model took care of the one shortcoming of the original PC—complete disk storage. These developments set the stage for the IBM Personal Computer Junior.

Many people wanted to take advantage of the marvelous software and computing power of the IBM personal computers but could not afford the cost of either the PC or XT. IBM's answer to that problem was to develop the Personal Computer Junior, commonly called the PCjr.

Naturally, to hold down the cost of the PCjr, something had to be given up. A modest fraction of the speed—the computing power—was sacrificed to make it possible to eliminate some costly parts. Also, much of the expansion capability of the PC and the XT was lost, again to save the cost of the circuitry that makes expansion possible. But on the whole, the main parts of the PC and XT were left intact in Junior, so that this little system could have most of the capabilities and be able to use most of the programs of the first two models.

Although some speed and much of the expansion capability were given up, many wonderful features were added to the PCjr—features that aren't available on the original PC and XT. These are features that are particularly nice in home computers but of much less use or interest in business and professional computers. They include improved color graphics and much richer sound-making ability, both important for educational and entertainment programs.

As we explore the PCjr in this book, I will mention topic-by-topic how it differs from its bigger brothers; I'll talk about where it has more, where it has less, and where it is just plain different. The main fact, though, and the most important thing to remember, is that the PCjr really is a full-fledged IBM personal computer. It may be the baby of the family, but it is a full-blooded family member.

And now, on with the show, and into exploring the magic of the IBM Personal Computer Junior.

2

A TOUR THROUGH
THE HARDWARE STORE

In this chapter we'll take a brief
look at the main physical parts of the
IBM Personal Computer Junior:
the *hardware,* as opposed to the
software or programming parts.

Figure 2-1. A complete PCjr system

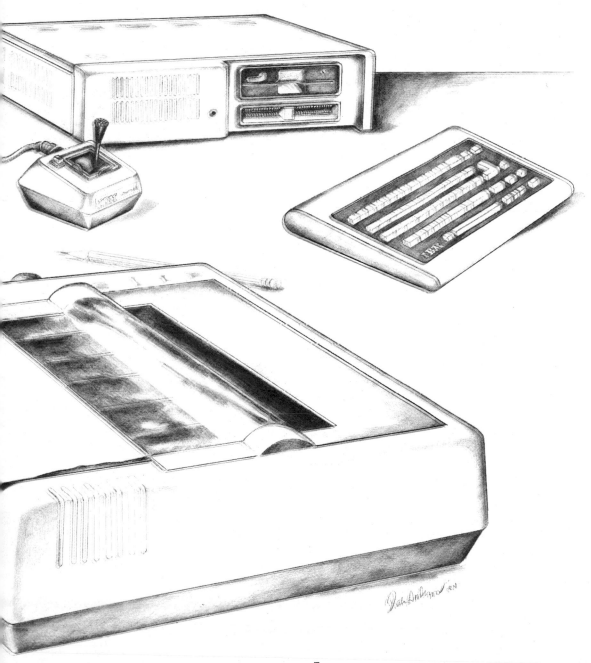

A QUICK TOUR

The design of the PCjr is based on the same simple philosophy that guided the design of its two bigger brothers, the PC and the XT. In essence, this design puts all the key working components into one integrated cabinet called the *system unit*. The system unit contains the working heart of the computer, and also critical parts such as the diskette drive.

For the convenience and ease of the person using the computer, the *keyboard* is provided as a separate detached unit, which can be freely moved around. This is a real advantage over computer designs that have the keyboard as an integral part of the system unit. In the case of the PCjr (but not the PC and XT models), we have a choice of two ways of connecting the keyboard to the system unit. One is by a cable—as for the PC—and the other is by infrared light. The infrared connection makes the keyboard even more movable.

To allow the greatest flexibility, the *display* is not built into any of the three IBM personal computers. Instead, the display is a separate unit, and this helps us in two ways: It gives us a freer choice as to the kind of display we use, ranging from an ordinary TV set to a high-quality color monitor; it also allows us to move the screen and position it for comfortable viewing without having to move or reorient the system unit. Figure 2-1 shows the three components that make up a complete PCjr system.

ONCE AROUND THE OUTSIDE

Now let's take a tour around the outside of Junior's system unit, looking at all the openings and connections.

The Front

On the front of the PCjr there are three openings, plus ventilation slots and a light sensor for the infrared keyboard. As Figure 2-2 shows, the biggest opening, on the top right, is for the optional diskette drive. Below it are two openings to accommodate software cartridges.

The Diskette Drive

The *diskette drive* is a standard type used in the microcomputer industry and is not anything specially developed or made for the PCjr or IBM. The type of diskette drive that is used in the PCjr is known as a half-high, 5¼-inch, double-sided, double-density, floppy diskette drive. Let's march through that word by word.

8

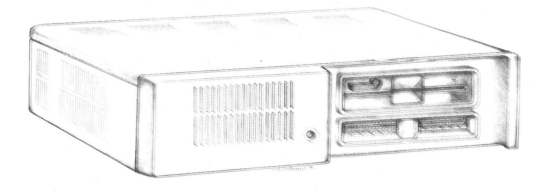

*Figure 2-2. The front of the PCjr system unit showing
the diskette drive, two cartridge slots,
and infrared light sensor*

The drive is half-high because it only takes up half as much vertical space as the diskette drives used on the PC and XT. Those older, standard-size diskette drives are about 3½ inches high and 6 inches wide (9 by 15 centimeters). Through improvements in design and materials, it has now become possible to make inexpensive and reliable diskette drives that are only half the height of the old units, or about 1¾ inches (4.5 centimeters) high; the width stays the same, though, since it fits the size of the diskette. These new drives are made half the height of the older design so that two can be installed in the space allotted to one full-height drive—a useful feature for upgrading older computers. In the case of the PCjr, which was designed from scratch, either height diskette drive could have been used. The half-high drive was chosen to help make the system unit lighter and more compact.

The next part of the diskette drive description specifies that it uses 5¼-inch *diskettes*. Although some computers use a larger, 8-inch-diameter diskette, most popular microcomputers, including all the IBM personal computers, use the 5¼-inch size. Using the same diskette size and the same way of storing information on the diskette are key factors in the PCjr's ability to use nearly all of the software developed for the PC and XT.

While we are on the subject, we ought to make note of one bit of terminology that might cause some confusion. Because the 8-inch size is called a diskette, our 5¼-inch size is sometimes called a mini-diskette. So, if you are ordering supplies from a computer catalog and see a listing for mini-diskettes, don't be confused—that's what you need for your PCjr. There are also several kinds of micro-diskettes, which are about 3 or 4 inches in diameter; our PCjr doesn't use them.

Our diskettes are also double sided. This means that our Junior's diskette drive can use both sides of the diskette's recording surface. This gives us twice the storage capacity of single-sided diskettes. Our double-sided drives can work with diskettes that are single or double sided. Unlike a record player, where you have to flip the record to use both sides, the disk drive has two heads, one for each side of the diskette; so you never have to flip the diskette.

When we buy programs for our IBM personal computers, they usually come on single-sided diskettes, simply so they can be used on those older PCs that don't have double-sided drives. Our PCjrs can use either format, but we're usually better off transferring our programs onto double-sided diskettes.

The term double density is the next part of the diskette drive specification. Density refers to how much information is packed into a given space on the diskette, and particularly to how many tracks of data are written onto the diskette. (A track on a diskette is roughly comparable to a track of music on a phonograph record.) Double density is the standard format for IBM computers, and it provides 40 tracks per diskette. Our PCjr uses these 40-track, double-density drives.

The Cartridges

Besides the diskette-drive opening, there are two other slots on the front of the PCjr. These accommodate software memory *cartridges*. A cartridge plugged into either of these slots provides the computer with additional, prerecorded read only memory (ROM) that can be used, but not changed, by the computer. Normally, the cartridges contain such programs as the advanced BASIC program, or they contain game programs. When a program cartridge is plugged into a PCjr, the program can then be executed and used directly.

The Back

Moving to the back of the PCjr, we find 13 different plugs and sockets that are used to connect all sorts of equipment. They are labeled with letters, molded into the cover, to help us identify them and use the right ones. We will go through them from right to left, as seen from the back. Figure 2-3 shows you the sockets and the letters that identify them.

The first socket, labeled A, is a low-voltage, audio output jack. This jack is for connecting the PCjr to a hi-fi system to allow high-quality reproduction of the many sounds that the PCjr can generate.

Like the other IBM personal computers, the PCjr has a built-in speaker to create the sounds that it generates. Unfortunately, this speaker is about as low-quality as you can get, and so it does a very crude job of producing sounds. Since sound generation is one of the special features of the PCjr, the quality of

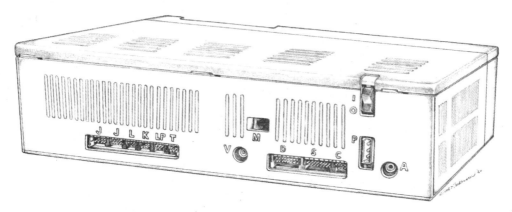

Figure 2-3. The back of the PCjr system unit showing the 13 sockets

these sounds is partly wasted if we use its built-in speaker.

All the sound signals that go to the speaker, though, also go to the audio output jack, and some of the PCjr's sounds *only* go to the audio jack. When a hi-fi cable is plugged into this audio jack, the PCjr's built-in speaker is automatically shut off so that it will not interfere with the better-quality sounds coming from the hi-fi. The electrical signals sent to this jack are adjusted to the level needed for input into a hi-fi amplifier. They are not strong enough to be used directly with a loudspeaker. Ordinarily, this jack will be connected to the AUX, or auxiliary input of an amplifier. The better sound quality that can be produced through a hi-fi system can be very valuable for entertainment programs, and it is nice for any program that creates sounds.

The next connection on the system unit's back is the power input, labeled P; this is where we plug in Junior's *power transformer.* The PCjr has a two-stage power supply. The first stage is the transformer, which converts our high-voltage, AC household current down to a safer 17 volts, still AC. The 17-volt power that comes out of Junior's transformer plugs into this P socket on the back of the system unit. The step-down transformer is outside the PCjr's system unit for two main reasons: First, it makes the PCjr safer, since there is nothing but low voltages inside the system unit; and second, it separates the heat-sensitive circuitry inside the system unit from the heat-generating transformer. The second stage of the power supply is inside the system unit, and we'll cover it shortly.

Next comes the cassette recorder outlet, labeled C. This socket is used to connect an ordinary cassette tape player to the computer. Cassette tapes have been used as a way for very low-priced home computers to store programs and data. Cassette recording is similar to disk data storage, but it is cheaper and also much slower and clumsier. The PCjr's BASIC programming language gives all the commands necessary to store and retrieve cassette data. The original PC model also came with a cassette connection, but it was hardly ever used; the higher-powered XT model doesn't even have a cassette outlet. We probably won't see much use of the cassette connection with our PCjrs, but it is nice to know that it is there, if we have a use for it.

After the cassette plug comes the *serial port,* labeled S. The serial port is designed to transmit signals following a widely used computer standard known as *RS-232C.* You'll find this facility commonly called RS-232, or a serial port, or a serial connection; all these terms refer to the same thing. The serial port can be used for many things, but two are most common: to connect the computer to a telephone (to talk to other computers), or to a printer.

To use the computer with a telephone, the computer's signals have to be converted into telephone signals, which is done with a *modem.* To do this converting, we can either plug a modem into the serial port and then connect the modem to a telephone, or we can use an optional internal modem that fits inside the PCjr's system unit and connect it to a telephone. When we use the internal modem, the serial port socket is bypassed.

To connect the serial port to a *printer,* we must have a printer that is designed to work with the RS-232 serial format, such as the IBM Compact Printer. Some computer printers use this serial format, while others use another format, known as parallel, or Centronics. Before you plan to connect a printer to Junior's serial port, be sure that you have the right kind of printer.

The next socket is labeled D, for direct-drive *RGB video.* This is one of the three outlets for connecting the PCjr to different types of display screens. To get the highest-quality picture possible, this outlet provides separate signals for each of the three colors that are used to make color video images: red, green, and blue—the initials of these colors give RGB its name. The RGB signal can be connected to an RGB monitor, which is the highest-quality computer display screen. The IBM Color Display is an RGB monitor. Many of the new component-type TV sets can also use the RGB signal, although ordinary TVs can't.

Next along is the modem output, labeled M. As we mentioned, to use the computer with a telephone, the computer's serial signal must be converted by a modem. If we use a separate external modem, it connects to the PCjr's S, or serial, plug. But if we install Junior's optional smart modem, then the serial signal comes out of this M socket, already converted to telephone format. This modem outlet takes a standard, modular-type telephone cord.

After the modem outlet comes the second of the three video outlets, the *composite video* signal, labeled V. While the D connection is for use with expensive RGB monitors, this V connection is for cheaper composite display monitors. The composite signal combines the three color signals into one, which is what gives it the name composite. There are two types of composite display monitors that we can plug into this outlet. One is a composite color monitor, which will show the PCjr's color capabilities; the other is a composite monochrome display, which shows everything in one color (usually green or amber), but which works with the same composite video signal. Composite color displays produce the same kind of picture as RGB monitors, but with not quite the same crisp quality; these displays are excellent for programs that use color and graphics. Composite monochrome displays usually are fine for text work (such as word processing) and poor with programs that use color or graphics.

Next is the third and last of the video outputs, labeled T for television. This is the plug that is used to connect the computer to an ordinary TV set. A TV set needs a special form of video signal, which must include what is called radio-frequency, or RF, modulation. This T outlet provides the basic signal, and the PCjr's TV adapter cord has an *RF modulator* to finish getting the signal ready for our TV sets. TVs, of course, produce both sound and picture, and this outlet is designed to include the PCjr's audio signal (which also goes out the audio socket, labeled A) along with the picture signal. That lets our TVs give us the complete sound and picture output from the computer.

The next item is the plug for a *light pen*, labeled LP. A light pen is a special, hand-held probe. When we touch it to the computer's display screen, our programs can tell exactly where on the screen the pen is. With the right programs, we can use the pen to draw on the screen, and do other things.

Next is the keyboard socket, labeled K. While we can have our PCjr's keyboard talk to the system unit by infrared light, we might want a wired connection instead. A wired connection makes it possible to have several Juniors in the same room, or to have the keyboard out of sight of the system unit's light sensor. When we use the keyboard cable, it plugs into this K socket.

The next socket is labeled L, and IBM says that it is for a use that will come later.

The last two connections, both labeled J, are for plugging in *joysticks*, which are used with games and graphics programs. There are two joystick connections, so that two players can use a program at once.

And that finishes our tour across the back of the PCjr. There is only one thing left, and that is the hidden connection on the system unit's right side.

The Side

Hidden behind a panel on the right side of the system unit is the PCjr's *I/O channel connector.* This connector is a general-purpose connection to the circuitry of the computer. It is the equivalent of the *expansion sockets* that are inside the PC and XT models. IBM's only use for this I/O channel connector is as the place to connect the parallel printer adapter, but we can use it for many things. Much of the non-IBM equipment that can be added to a PC or XT can also be added to the PCjr through this connection. Our PCjr doesn't provide a physical space for additions, which the PC and XT do with expansion slots. Any add-on equipment for the PCjr either will have to be self-contained—like the IBM Printer Adapter—or will have to fit into some kind of expansion component specially designed to plug into the PCjr's I/O channel connector. IBM left the physical accommodation of add-on equipment for others to create; but the electronic accommodation of add-ons is taken care of with this I/O channel.

A LOOK INSIDE

Now we're ready to explore the insides of the PCjr. You might want to pry off the top of the system unit so you can look at the parts as we discuss them. It's simple and safe to do; just twist a screwdriver in the slots in the back. You'll find official directions in the PCjr's *Guide to Operations*.

The System Board

Within the cabinet of the system unit is the main circuitry that makes the computer go. All the key electronic parts are mounted on a single circuit board called the *system board*. The system board is also sometimes called the *motherboard*, and some of the IBM literature refers to the system board as the *planar*. If you run across any of these terms, remember that they all mean the same thing.

The system board is built up of several layers, so that the many interconnecting wires can crisscross without touching each other. The system board serves two purposes: It provides the physical framework to hold the electronic components in place, and it makes nearly all the electrical connections needed among the parts, doing so through the wires embedded in the board itself.

The system board contains virtually all the electronic parts that make the PCjr go. These include the Intel® 8088 *microprocessor* (the brains of the computer), the *memory*, and several other particularly sophisticated parts, including a programmable interrupt controller, a programmable peripheral interface, a special sound generator, and a timer. We'll take a look at these components now.

The Memory

A computer needs memory to function, and the system board contains two different kinds of memory. Ordinary computer memory, commonly called

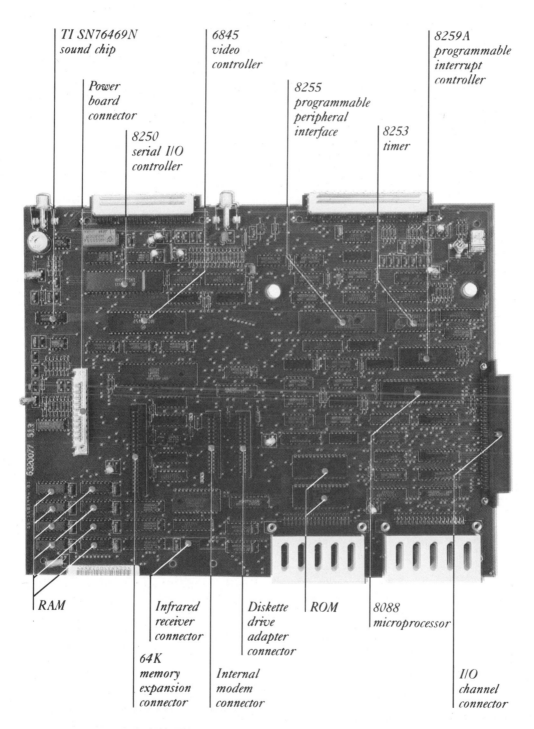

TI SN76469N
sound chip

Power
board
connector

8250
serial I/O
controller

6845
video
controller

8255
programmable
peripheral
interface

8253
timer

8259A
programmable
interrupt
controller

RAM

Infrared
receiver
connector

Diskette
drive
adapter
connector

ROM

8088
microprocessor

64K
memory
expansion
connector

Internal
modem
connector

I/O
channel
connector

Figure 2-4. The PCjr system board

15

RAM or *random access memory*, can be read and modified, and the computer uses it like a working notepad. The RAM used by the PCjr is provided in the form of 64K *memory chips*. The PCjr contains 64K (65,536) bytes, or characters, of RAM on its system board, and another 64K of working RAM can be added.

A little confusion in terminology creeps in here. When computer folks talk about a computer's memory, they usually talk in terms of bytes. A byte is the amount of memory needed to store one character, such as the letter A, and is made up of eight bits, or binary digits. But when these same folks talk about memory chips, they talk in terms of bits. So, to get 64K of working memory, in 8-bit bytes, we need to use eight separate 64K (bit) memory chips.

To guard against errors, most computers have one additional *parity bit* for each byte; the parity bit is set based on the eight data bits on the byte. While the PC and XT models have parity bits, our PCjr's memory doesn't. That sounds serious, but it isn't, for two reasons. First, today's memory chips are very reliable, so errors almost never occur. Second, the PC and XT don't make very good use of parity checking anyway. Leaving out parity checking helped IBM keep the cost of the PCjr low.

The second kind of memory installed on the PCjr's system board is *ROM*, or *read only memory*. A computer cannot do anything without programs to tell it what to do, and the most essential and fundamental programs for controlling the PCjr are stored in the ROM. Since the information stored in ROM cannot be changed, having the control programs in this type of memory eliminates the danger of accidentally erasing them. Also, they are always there, ready and able to perform the fundamental logic operations necessary to control the computer.

There are two separate kinds of programs stored in the PCjr's ROM. The first is called the *ROM-BIOS*, or *Basic Input/Output System*. The ROM-BIOS programs are truly the most fundamental to the operation of the computer, and they are responsible for such things as responding to our touch on the computer's keyboard and keeping track of the time of day.

In addition to the ROM-BIOS, the PCjr's ROM also contains the programs necessary to provide us with the BASIC programming language; this is called the *ROM-BASIC*. (Let's pause to avoid some confusion; the letter B in ROM-BIOS stands for basic, meaning fundamental; when we say BASIC in capital letters, we mean the *programming language* whose name is BASIC.)

Any programming language requires some supporting programs in order to work. The core programs needed to operate BASIC are built into the PCjr's ROM-BASIC. More sophisticated aspects of BASIC are provided by programs that are kept either in the BASIC cartridge or on diskettes. For the full glory of the BASIC programming language, we need these extra parts of BASIC; but for ordinary BASIC use, the permanently built-in ROM-BASIC is enough. This means that we can do BASIC programming on our Juniors without needing any additional cartridges, disks, or equipment.

The PCjr's system board includes a lot of other circuitry, but we are going to concentrate on the really interesting parts: the memory, which we've already discussed, the smart chips, about which we'll learn more soon, and our next topic, the plug-in sockets.

The System-Board Sockets

All sorts of things must plug into our PCjr's system board. Lots of these plug-in connections are located around the edge of the system board—they are the connections to the outside world, such as the video outputs and the keyboard socket discussed in the last section. But in addition, there are four special sockets, located in the middle of the PCjr's system board, for four special connections.

The first of these four brings power, in various forms, to the system board. The PCjr's power supply is responsible for providing specially groomed, DC power. The complete power supply for the PCjr is in two stages. The first stage, as we've mentioned, is an external transformer that lowers the AC voltage to a safe 17 volts. The second stage is a *power supply board* that fits inside the system unit cabinet and plugs into this special socket. It converts AC current into DC current and adjusts and grooms the voltage. This power supply is on a separate board, and not part of the system unit, for easier maintenance. It provides 33 watts of power, compared to the 64 watts provided to the original PC and the 130 watts to the XT. This smaller power supply is part of what makes it possible for Junior to be smaller, lighter, and less expensive than its big brothers.

The second of the special internal sockets accommodates a *memory board* that can provide the PCjr with its second 64K of memory. Without this extra memory, all PCjrs have 64K of RAM located on the system board; with the memory expansion, the PCjr has 128K of usable memory. The most memory that can normally be attached to a PCjr is 128K, while the PC and XT models can take up to 640K, or five times as much. This memory limitation is one of the main distinctions that sets the PCjr apart from its bigger relatives.

The third special socket is designed to accommodate a special intelligent modem, or telephone adapter. This modem attachment provides all the computer hardware needed to connect the PCjr to a telephone line, so that we can talk computer-talk with other computers. Using the modem attachment and appropriate programs, we can communicate with other Juniors, with mainframe computers, and with timesharing information services such as THE SOURCE℠ and CompuServe® which offer up-to-the-minute news and business reports.

The fourth and last of the special sockets on the system board is used to plug in the *diskette-drive adapter.* This adapter is needed when a diskette drive is part of the system. The diskette-drive adapter is specially designed for the PCjr, and it is not the same as that used on the PC and XT models. The adapter for the PC and XT is much more complicated and expensive; it can control up to four diskette drives and it operates independently of the rest of the computer. In contrast, the PCjr's inexpensive adapter is intended to control only one diskette drive, and the features it lacks are balanced by a more complicated ROM-BIOS program that provides special support for the PCjr's diskette. In effect, expensive diskette circuitry is replaced by cheap ROM programs in the PCjr. This reduces its performance compared to the PC and XT, but it is an important factor in making it so affordable.

One of the most noticeable differences between the PCjr and the other IBM personal computers is Junior's lack of the general-purpose expansion slots found in the PC and the XT, which can accommodate add-on equipment: more memory, display adapters, disk controllers, or whatever. In the PCjr, things are quite different. Each of its four internal sockets has its own dedicated use. In the place of expansion slots the PCjr has the single I/O channel connector on the right side of the PCjr's cabinet. However, IBM has largely made up for Junior's lack of expansion slots by anticipating the needs of most users and building in those features people are most likely to want.

Another important difference between the PCjr and the PC and XT models is that the latter two can use either or both of two different *display adapters:* the monochrome (black-and-white) adapter and the color/graphics adapter. This gives the PC and XT greater flexibility, but it means that a display adapter must be bought for each computer. With our PCjr, the equivalent of the color/graphics adapter is built into the system unit. This design feature reduces the cost of the PCjr and eliminates the need for expansion slots to accommodate display adapters.

The Brain—the 8088

The brain of the PCjr is the Intel 8088 microprocessor. It is exactly the same as the one used in the PC and XT models, meaning that Junior starts out with exactly the same computing brainpower as its bigger relatives.

We'll learn about the logical inner workings of the 8088 microprocessor later; this chapter is devoted to computer hardware, so let's look at the hardware aspects of the 8088.

The 8088 is a member of a family of microprocessors designed and built by the Intel Corporation. A close relative of the 8088 is the very similar 8086, and a lot of discussion that concerns our microprocessor goes on under the name of the 8086. For example, one of the reference sources mentioned in the appendix of further reading is *The 8086 Book.*

Computer microprocessors grow in capacity by expanding the amount of data they can work with at one time—which is called the *bus size*. The larger the *bus*, the larger the amount of information that the microprocessor can sling around at one time. The size of the bus is also referred to as the microprocessor's bit size.

The first microprocessor, a very primitive creature indeed, was the Intel 4004. It had only a 4-bit bus; it could only transfer four bits of data at a time. The first microprocessor to see widespread use was an outgrowth of the 4004 called the 8080. It had an 8-bit bus, and it could do arithmetic eight bits at a time. While the 8080 (and some of its competing offshoots, such as the Z80 microprocessor) was very successful, it suffered from the 8-bit limitation, which held down both the amount of memory it could use, and its operating speed.

To break out of those limitations, Intel produced its 16-bit microprocessor, the 8086. The 8086 could sling numbers around 16 bits at a time; it also talked to the world around it (to its memory, for example) 16 bits at a time. The internal capacity was a real advantage, but the 16-bit external bus did have one drawback: It couldn't use the cheap and readily available 8-bit circuitry that had become popular with 8-bit computers. The solution to that problem was the 8088 microprocessor. The 8088 is internally exactly the same as the 8086: It uses the same programs, handles the same data, and has the same computing power. But when the 8088 talks to the outside world, it uses an 8-bit external bus so that it can work with inexpensive 8-bit parts. (The 8086's 16-bit external bus makes it slightly faster than our 8088.)

All of the first three IBM personal computers share the 8088 micro-processor, with its 8/16-bit split personality.

The 8088 and the 8086 are designed to work with other processors in three different ways. First, they include features that make it possible to wire together several 8088s (or several 8086s), so that they can act as one closely cooperating team. The IBM personal computers do not use this feature of the 8088 design, but it is interesting to know about. The other two ways that our microprocessor can get assistance are with either of two special co-processors. Two different kinds of computing workload can be moved out of the main microprocessor and into a specialized co-processor. One is the 8089 I/O pro-cessor, which can take on the work of talking to peripheral devices; none of the IBM personal computers use the 8089. The other is the 8087 arithmetic co-processor. The 8087 is designed to do complicated arithmetic at lightning speed, and it has remarkably sophisticated features.

Both the PC and the XT models have the circuitry and a socket needed to accommodate an 8087. When the 8087 is plugged in, and appropriate software is used, the PC and XT can do arithmetic ten times faster or more. Our PCjr, though, cannot take an 8087 chip. This is one of the several ways in which the PCjr is a reduced-performance model of IBM personal computer. The simple fact is, though, that very few PCs and XTs use the 8087; although the 8087 can enhance almost any computing work, it is mostly good for high-intensity engineering calculations—what is called "number-crunching." The PCjr is not a number-cruncher's computer, and so we lost very little when the 8087 was not included in the PCjr's design.

The Helpers—the Other Smart Chips

In a sense, everything that is connected to the computer's system board is there as a helper to the microprocessor; but there are a few circuit elements that are particularly strong helpers. These are the other smart chips that are themselves key parts of the workings of the computer, including:

■ *The Intel 8259A programmable interrupt controller* (PIC). Interrupts can be thought of as electronic "attention getters." A key part of the success of a microprocessor like our 8088 is the use of interrupts to help manage the processor's relationship with the world around it, including the devices to which it is connected. The 8259A PIC is used to control when and how interrupts from the computer's external devices are presented to the micro- processor. Although the 8259A is programmable, such programming is complex and best left to experts. We have little need for details about how the PIC works, but it is interesting to know who the main friends of the family are.

■ *The Intel 8253 timer.* Many of the most important functions of the PCjr require the use of a timer that can be controlled. For example, the cassette interface uses the timer for the cassette tape signals, and sounds on the PCjr's speaker can be generated with the 8253 timer as well.

■ *The Intel 8255 programmable peripheral interface* (PPI) helps control the various peripheral devices that work with Junior by supervising the ports through which the peripherals talk.

■ *The Motorola® 6845 video controller chip* provides the signals and control needed by a cathode ray tube (CRT) display screen.

■ *The Intel 8250 chip* takes care of supplying communications control bits, modem control functions, and similar operations needed by the RS-232 serial port.

■ *The Texas Instruments® SN76496N sound chip* is used for the PCjr's more sophisticated sound production. (For simple sound generation, all IBM per- sonal computers make use of the 8253 timer.) The sound chip is designed to produce the kinds of sounds needed by the better game programs. It has three voices that can produce three different notes or musical tones. Each voice has its own separate attenuation, which is used to make sounds fade in and out. In addition to the three voices, the sound chip also has a fourth noise channel that can be used for nonmusical sounds, such as explosions.

Apart from the TI® sound chip, all of the helpers mentioned are common to the PC and XT as well as our PCjr.

And that completes our basic tour through the PCjr's hardware.

3
NUMBERS, NUMBERS EVERYWHERE

The IBM Personal Computer Junior, or more properly the processing unit inside the computer, is a general-purpose, logical machine that can be made to do just about any task that can be described in complete detail.

The most important thing about a computer is that it has the ability to carry out a set of instructions. These instructions are a computer *program*. If the program is written in the correct form and describes a specific task, the computer can perform that task and give us some useful or interesting result. This ability to carry out instructions is the heart of what computers and computing are all about.

BRIDGING THE GAP—PROGRAMMING LANGUAGES

The computer program must, in the end, be expressed in what is called *machine language*. This is the most detailed form of program, and it is completely unintelligible to most human beings because it is full of so many niggling details, all expressed in numbers. To make computer programming easier, all sorts of *programming languages* have been developed. The computer, however, cannot work with these programming languages directly—one way or another, they first have to be translated into machine language.

One form of programming language is called *assembly language*. Assembly language is very close to machine language; it restates the computer's machine language in terms programmers can understand. Its main advantage is that it uses meaningful words, such as ADD, to represent incomprehensible machine-language codes, such as hex 83C207. Assembly language is more or less the exact equivalent of machine language, but translated into a more readable form. In fact, whenever people write about machine language, they usually express it in assembly language. That's what we'll do in this book.

Translating computer programs into a form that the computer can work with is the job of an *assembler* (in the case of assembly language), an *interpreter* (in the case of ordinary interpreted BASIC), or a *compiler* (in the case of Pascal, COBOL, FORTRAN, or compiled BASIC). The terms—assemble, interpret, and compile—are different; the mechanics of the process are different; but the result is the same: a machine-language program in one form or another.

Computer programs work with data that have to be represented in a form that the computer can accept. Data vary as to how appetizing they are to computers. Computers like numbers very much, especially small whole numbers such as 1, 2, and 3. Other kinds of data, such as people's names, addresses, and telephone numbers, are a little harder for computers to swallow; but with a little encouragement computers can handle anything.

COUNTING LIKE COMPUTERS

In the next chapters we are going to look at the details of computer operations. We will often have to speak in the computer's terms, especially where numbers are concerned. To make sure that you are familiar with the terms and notations that we'll be discussing, let's take a quick look at them here.

To a computer, everything is numbers; numbers are numbers, programs are numbers, and even letters of the alphabet are numbers. There are many ways to write numbers, some of them oriented to people and some oriented to computers.

We all learned in school to work with numbers in *decimal* notation, which means that our numbers are based on powers of ten. Some people think that decimal is the most common notation because we have ten fingers. Decimal numbers are written with ten different symbols, the digits 0, 1, 2, and so on, to 9; past 9, the digit symbols are used in combinations to express larger numbers, so that the next number after 9 is written as 10. For example, if we write a number like 123, we mean 100 (or one times ten squared) plus 20 (or two times ten) plus 3; the total is the value 123. But there are other notations that would write the same value in other ways.

Binary

Now let's base a number system on only two of our ten fingers, say our index fingers. This number system would be *binary*—based on powers of two. Binary numbers are written with only two symbols, 0 and 1.

Computers don't have fingers, of course, but in their heart of hearts they like to be binary and the reason is very simple. In the electronic circuitry that makes computers function, it is very easy to represent the two binary values either by the presence or absence of electrical power or by two voltages, one higher and one lower. It is much easier and more reliable to build electronic circuits that have only two values (that are binary) than it is to build circuits that represent more than two values.

While binary numbers inside the computer are represented as high and low voltages, when they are written out for us to see, they appear as a string of zeros and ones. Each zero or one is a binary digit, which we call a *bit*. Here is an example of a binary number made up of eight bits:

01111011

This particular combination of bits, interpreted as a binary number, represents the value written earlier in decimal: 123.

Binary notation, though, has some real disadvantages: It is lengthy, and it hides some of the structure that often underlies numbers inside the computer. To avoid those shortcomings, another notation is usually used with computer numbers; this notation is called *hexadecimal*, or often just *hex* for short.

Hexadecimal

Hexadecimal uses 16 as a base, whereas decimal uses ten, and binary uses two. Hex notation is widely used in the computer world. It was first popularized by IBM itself in the early 1960s, when the corporation introduced the 360-series of computers.

Why base a number system on 16? If you take four binary digits—four bits—and see how many numbers you can make with them, you get 16 combinations—16 values. Since hexadecimal numbers are based on 16, each hex digit can represent four binary digits. This means that numbers that are actually binary can be written in one-fourth as many symbols in hexadecimal notation. The numbers are the same, but the way of writing them is more compact.

Compactness isn't the only reason for using hex notation instead of binary, though. As we'll see when we learn more about how computer numbers and memory work, bits are usually used in multiples of four or eight. So hex notation helps us see some of the structure that underlies binary numbers.

How are hex numbers written? With a base of 16, we need 16 symbols to write in hex. The symbols start out with the same ten we use for decimal numbers: 0 through 9. After 9, we need six more symbols to represent the values 10 through 15. For this, hex uses the letters of the alphabet: A represents the value 10, B represents 11, and so on through F, which represents 15. As with decimal, binary, or any other notation, higher numbers are represented by combinations of symbols. So the decimal value 16 is written in hex as 10.

Here are some examples. The sample number, 123, that we used earlier is 7B in hex (seven times 16, plus 11). The decimal number 1492 is 5D4 in hex, while 1776 in hex is 6F0.

A moment's thought will show you that 10 represents the value of the base in any number system. In decimal notation, ten is written as 10; in binary notation, two is written as 10; and in hexadecimal notation, 16 is written as 10. The numbers are written with the same characters, but the value they represent depends upon the number system, or base, that is being used.

Figure 3-1 is a simple summary of the 16 different hexadecimal digits, with their decimal equivalents and the four binary bits that they represent. Remember that, for working with computers, hex numbers are really used as shorthand for groups of four bits.

In this book we will be representing many numbers. We will use decimal where practical and, when it's useful, we'll give the hex equivalent. Whenever we use hex, we'll indicate very clearly that hex notation is being used.

Numbering Bits

Occasionally we'll have to refer to particular bits that are used in the computer. We'll then use the same notation that IBM uses, which is to number

Hex Digit	Binary Bits	Decimal Equivalent
0	0000	0
1	0001	1
2	0010	2
3	0011	3
4	0100	4
5	0101	5
6	0110	6
7	0111	7
8	1000	8
9	1001	9
A	1010	10
B	1011	11
C	1100	12
D	1101	13
E	1110	14
F	1111	15

Figure 3-1. Hexadecimal number system

the bits from right to left starting with 0. This may seem to be a confusing way to refer to particular bits, but it is traditional and, more importantly, it is consistent with the usage in IBM manuals.

There are two fundamental sizes of data our computers work with: the 8-bit *byte,* and the 16-bit *word* (which is made up of two 8-bit bytes). When we refer to the bits in an 8-bit byte, they will be numbered 0 through 7, with the 0-bit being the rightmost, or low-order bit, and the 7-bit being the leftmost, or high-order bit. Similarly, the bits in a 16-bit word will be numbered 0 through 15.

To help make this bit notation clearer, Figure 3-2 shows a table of the bits in an 8-bit byte. The table shows the bit number, its location in a byte, and its numeric value.

If you are mathematically inclined, you'll see that the bit number is the power of 2 represented by that bit position; so, for example, bit number 3 has the value of 2 to the 3rd power, or 8.

Text as Numbers

Computers don't work just with numbers; they also work with letters of the alphabet, punctuation, and so forth—the kind of symbols that you are reading here. This kind of information in computers is called *text,* or *ASCII* text.

Bit Number	Location in a Byte	Numeric Value of the Bit
7	1.......	128
6	.1......	64
5	..1.....	32
4	...1....	16
3	....1...	8
2	.....1..	4
1	......1.	2
0	1	1

Figure 3-2. Bit notation

(ASCII is the acronym for American Standard Code for Information Interchange.) Since everything is a number to a computer, letters of the alphabet and other text characters are represented by code numbers, and ASCII is the standard code for representing text in computers. For example, the capital letter A has the numeric value 65 in the ASCII coding scheme, while a comma has the value 44.

We will refer to ASCII characters in one of two ways. When the character symbol is familiar to us all, we will just show it by itself, like the letter A, or in quotes, like the comma ",". At other times, we will refer to the numeric value of the symbol, either because we want to know the value of the ASCII character, or because the character is special and doesn't have a familiar appearance. For this purpose, we'll refer to ASCII characters using the same notation as the BASIC programming language. Here are two examples: The capital letter A is CHR$(65), while the lowercase letter a is CHR$(97). Note that the difference between A and a is 32. All lowercase letters of the alphabet have numeric values 32 higher than their uppercase equivalents. Want to prove what we just claimed? Figure 3-3 shows a simple BASIC program that demonstrates the ASCII values of the letters of the alphabet. You can try it on your own PCjr.

The Meaning of K

There is one more kind of notation we need to mention. In computer jargon you frequently encounter the letter *K*. K—which is short for kilo, the metric word for 1,000—is used with computers to represent a binary number whose exact value is 2 to the 10th power, or 1,024. Since 1,024, or K, is a round

```
10 ' ASCII value of alphabetic characters
20 '
30 FOR I = 65 TO 90
40    PRINT I; " is "; CHR$(I); ", ";
50    PRINT I; " plus 32 is "; CHR$(I + 32)
60 NEXT I
70 END
```

*Figure 3-3. A program to demonstrate the ASCII values
of letters of the alphabet*

number in binary and close to a round number in decimal, K has become a convenient shorthand symbol for representing large computer numbers.

More than anything else, K is used in reference to memory capacity. For example, the Junior comes with either 64K or 128K of memory, which means that it has 64 times 1,024 bytes (65,536) or 128 times 1,024 bytes (131,072). Our diskettes can each hold 320K (327,680). For simple mental figuring, you can think of K as being 1,000 (and sometimes people use K when they really mean thousands: "I sold my old car for 3K"). But when you need to be exact, remember that each K is 1,024.

Now that we are all speaking the same language, let's get back to our IBM Personal Computer Junior.

4

THE PCJR'S BRAIN: THE 8088

The Intel 8088 microprocessor
is the "thinking," working, active part
of our computer, so in this chapter
we'll take a closer look at it.

THE 8088's INSTRUCTIONS

Built into the 8088 is a very complicated set of instructions. This *instruction set* was designed for power, for flexibility, and especially for compactness. The size of each instruction varies from one byte to as many as six bytes. By design, the most basic and often used instructions are among the shortest. In most cases, each simple operation, such as adding or subtracting, has dozens of different forms. These variations on the instructions depend upon the size of the numbers being handled, on whether they are single bytes or 2-byte words, on where the numbers are (in memory or in quickly accessed, temporary storage areas called registers), and on how they are to be found (since there are quite a few ways to find things in memory).

Like most microprocessors, the 8088 has instructions to add, subtract, multiply, and divide. It also has special instructions to add or subtract the number 1 to or from another number—a very common operation in computer programs. It is tricks like these special instructions that help make the 8088's programs so compact. On the first computer I ever programmed, the IBM 1620, an instruction ten bytes long was needed to add 1 to a number; with the 8088, it can be done with an instruction only one byte long.

Similar tricks common to most microprocessors allow for very compact forms of instructions that transfer control of the computer from one part of a program to another, such as the JMP (jump) and CALL instructions.

WORKING WITH DATA

The 8088 microprocessor works with very few, simple forms of data. Everything that we do with the computer is founded on two simple building blocks: the 8-bit byte and the 16-bit word. The byte is the more fundamental unit, and when the 8088 addresses its memory, bytes are the basic unit addressed. When the 8088 works with words, it is simply taking two adjacent bytes and treating them as a single unit, which we call a word.

Bytes and words can be handled and interpreted in several different ways. However we look at it, a byte is made up of eight separate bits, so that a byte can hold a value that can be any of 2 to the 8th power, or 256, distinct possibilities. A word, with 16 bits, can hold any of 2 to the 16th power values, or 65,536 in all.

We can interpret these values in various ways. If we are working with text data, like the text of this book, each byte is used to store a single character of the text represented by its ASCII numeric code. For example, the letter A is stored as CHR$(65) (hex 41), while the blank-space character is stored as

CHR$(32) (hex 20). For text data we always use bytes—16-bit words are of no use when we're dealing with text data.

There is quite a bit more to know about text data, but much of it relates to how text data are stored on diskettes, so we'll put off more discussion until Chapter 10.

When we work with numbers, there is a host of ways to look at bytes and words. First let's just consider whole numbers. These are what BASIC calls *integer* values and identifies with the % symbol as, for example, in the variable names A%, THIS%, and THAT%.

When the 8088 works with a byte, it can treat that byte as an unsigned, positive number, which could have any value in the range 0 through 255 (hex FF, the largest byte value). We can also tell the 8088 to treat the same bytes as signed numbers, which can take on both positive and negative values. The range for bytes interpreted as signed numbers is from −128 through +127. (When we work with signed numbers there is an unequal number of values available for positive and negative numbers. For reasons too complex to go into here, the extra value is given to the negative range, so there is one negative number, −128, that doesn't have a corresponding positive number.)

When the 8088 works with 2-byte words, we have a wider range of values. A word interpreted as an unsigned, positive number can have a value ranging from 0 through 65,535. As a signed number, the value can range from −32,768 through +32,767.

We can make up whole integer numbers with three, four, or more bytes for a wider range of values. Unfortunately the 8088 doesn't work easily with numbers this large—this is what makes it a 16-bit computer. We can do arithmetic on these larger numbers, but it involves some special programming—the ability is not built into the 8088.

Of course, we don't do all of our work with whole numbers; we need fractional numbers as well. Computers deal with fractions through the use of what are called *floating-point numbers*. Floating-point numbers are made up of some numeric digits, and a number that indicates where the decimal point is for the number. The decimal point can "float" around, which allows the number to be very large or very small and still be accurate for as many digits as there are in the number. In BASIC, floating-point is called single or double precision, depending upon how many bytes are devoted to storing the number. A *single-precision* number is stored in four bytes and is accurate to about six decimal digits; a *double-precision* number is stored in eight bytes and is accurate to about 14 decimal digits.

Like integers that are three or four bytes long, floating-point numbers are not handled automatically by the 8088; so everything we do with floating-point numbers on the PCjr must be done with the help of lengthy subroutines. Because of this, Junior can work with integers much faster than it can work with

```
100 ' testing integers and floating-point numbers
110 '
120 PRINT "      Start with integers at ", TIME$
130 FOR I% = 1 TO 5000
140 NEXT I%
150 PRINT "       End with integers at ", TIME$
160 PRINT
170 '
180 PRINT "Start with single precision at ", TIME$
190 FOR J = 1 TO 5000
200 NEXT J
210 PRINT " End with single precision at ", TIME$
220 PRINT
230 END
```

*Figure 4-1. A program to show handling speeds for
integers and floating-point numbers*

floating-point numbers. If you are programming in BASIC, you will find that your programs run faster when you use integer variables.

To see some of the difference in speed between using integers and using floating-point numbers, try the program in Figure 4-1.

With interpreted BASIC (the ordinary BASIC that comes with the PCjr), you'll see some time difference, but it won't be dramatic—that's because BASIC's normal high overhead will mask a lot of the difference in speed. But with compiled BASIC, or any compiled program, the difference will be considerable. For example, when I compiled this program, the difference in speed between the two sections was about 20 to 1.

HOW FAST IS FAST?

The 8088 uses a *clock signal* to regulate and synchronize its operation. In the PCjr, the clock runs at 4.77 MHz, or slightly less than 5 million clock cycles each second. This is the same basic rate as the clock in the PC and XT, so Junior ticks along at the same speed they do. Each of the instructions that the 8088 can carry out takes some number of clock cycles, and from that we can calculate how much work the 8088 can do.

One of the fastest instructions in the 8088's repertoire is addition with the numbers already on hand (loaded into registers). This ADD instruction takes only three clock cycles, so the PCjr can do 1½ million additions of this type per second—an incredible amount of work for a little computer.

At the other end of the spectrum, some of the slowest instructions for the 8088, such as multiplying and dividing 16-bit numbers, take about 120 to 150 clock cycles. That's a rate of about 30 to 40 thousand instructions per second— much less, but still impressive. (The time varies according to how hard the numbers are to work with—remember, you and I can multiply a number by 100 much faster than we can multiply it by 37.6.) In between these extremes we'll find other instructions, such as one that moves data around and takes 22 clock cycles, or the equivalent of about a quarter of a million instructions per second.

How fast the 8088 runs on the average depends on the typical mixture of instructions it is given. On the basis of our figures and the fact that short, fast instructions are used much more than long, slow ones, we can say that our PCjr's 8088 microprocessor hums along performing about half a million instructions each second. If we had to think up these instructions one by one, we'd be hard-pressed to keep Junior busy. It is always possible to give any computer, even the very fastest, more work than it can handle. But in practical terms, at half a million instructions a second, the 8088 provides us with as much computing power as we're likely to need, or more.

While we are on the subject of speed, we ought to mention that there are some speed differences among the PCjr, the PC, and the XT, even though they all start out with the same basic brain and horsepower: an 8088 running at 4.77 MHz. Two factors account for these speed differences: disk and memory. Disk drives vary in speed, so heavy use of disk storage can make a significant difference in the total performance of the computer. The XT uses a very fast, Winchester-type, hard disk system, which operates five to ten times faster than the diskette drives used in the PC and PCjr. With a program that uses the disks a great deal, use of a hard disk can mean a significant difference in performance. While the diskette drive in the PCjr runs just as fast as the ones in the PC, the way in which the PCjr controls its diskette drive ties up the computing power of the 8088. Thus, Junior's disk drive slows down the overall performance of the computer (compared to a PC) somewhat, though not a great deal.

Memory is the other factor that sets the speed of the PCjr apart from its brothers. In all three computers, it takes four clock cycles for the 8088 to use the memory, but in the PCjr, the 8088 shares use of the memory with the display screen (as we'll learn more about later). For all practical purposes, this means that the PCjr needs six clock cycles for each use of the memory, instead of only four, because it has to wait while the display circuitry gets its share of memory use. The 8088 doesn't use its memory all the time, so these lost clock cycles don't cost as much as you might think. On the average, Junior runs perhaps 20 percent slower than the PC and XT— not much of a sacrifice in speed for a considerable savings in price.

There is much more to know about the 8088 than this, of course, but we have covered enough important and fundamental information to be able to move on to a discussion of how the 8088 communicates with us and with the other parts of the computer.

GETTING THE 8088's ATTENTION

Computers are the most wonderful and powerful tools that mankind has invented. Our Junior's 8088 microprocessor can do almost anything for us—but first we have to get its attention. If the computer's microprocessor doesn't know what needs to be done, it can't do anything useful.

A computer could just mind its own business, running some program in a very introspective way, but that wouldn't do us much good. To be able to respond to our needs, the computer must be able to find out what we want it to do. There are two general ways for the computer to do this: by *polling*, in which it looks for something to do, or by *interrupting*, in which it is told there is something to do. Interrupting will be our main concern in this section, but if you want to understand computers, you need to understand polling as well.

Polling

Let's suppose that we have just pressed a key, such as the Enter key, on our computer's keyboard. Naturally, we want the computer to respond to the keystroke. How does the computer know we have pressed a key? One way is for it to look at the keyboard electronically to see whether a key has been pressed. This is called polling; the computer goes looking for work, to see if there is anything to be done. Polling is a relatively simple and straightforward process, and it used to be the way all computers interacted with the world. To understand polling better, let's look at a couple of simple examples in BASIC that mimic what the computer does when it polls.

For the first example, let's suppose the computer has no other work to do—it is waiting for us to give it some information at the keyboard.

```
10 ' in line 30, the computer
20 ' will wait for keyboard input
30 INPUT A$
40 ' we've passed line 30, so
50 ' there was a keyboard response
```

What the computer actually does in polling is both much more primitive and much more detailed than this, but line 30 of this program shows the general idea: The computer looks to the keyboard for input and doesn't budge until the request for input is satisfied. So no other work gets done.

The more common method of polling is for the computer to stop what it's doing for a moment to test for input and then proceed. Our next BASIC example does just that:

```
 60 ' in line 90, the computer
 70 ' will read keyboard input
 80 ' but not wait
 90 X$ = INKEY$
100 ' next we'll see if
110 ' anything was there
120 IF LEN (X$) = 0 THEN 130 ELSE 160
130 ' we come here if there wasn't
140 ' any keyboard input
150 GOTO 180
160 ' we come here if there was
170 ' keyboard input
180 '
```

In line 90, we ask the computer to look at whatever key has been pressed (which might be no key at all). Then in line 120, it inspects what it got and acts on it, going to one part of the program—line 130—if there wasn't a keystroke, and to another part—line 160—if there was.

In crude and simple terms that is how polling works. It is useful but has two major drawbacks. First, the computer has to waste some of its working power just checking to see if anything is there. In our last example, the computer has to execute lines 90 and 120 as often as we want it to poll for input. If it polls frequently, a lot of overhead will be added to the operation. The second disadvantage of polling is that the computer can only respond to our input when it polls us; if our program does not tell the computer to poll often enough—or neglects to tell it to poll at all—then we are left waiting at the keyboard. *Interrupts* solve both of these problems.

Interrupting

There is a wonderful, corny old joke about a man who had a mule that was so stubborn the man hit it all the time. A friend told him, "Don't hit that mule—you should treat it gently. Let me show you how." Then the friend took a big stick and hit the mule over the head with it. The man said, "But you told me to treat it gently." The friend replied, "Sure—but first you have to get its attention."

The idea behind an interrupt is very simple: The computer goes merrily about its business until something hits it over the head with a stick, at which time it drops what it is doing, and devotes its attention to the interruption. Here is how a BASIC program can respond to keyboard interrupts:

```
200 ' in the next two lines, we set up an
210 ' interrupt for function key#1
220 ON KEY (1) GOSUB 280
230 KEY (1) ON
240 ' now the computer can go about its business
250 PRINT "*";
260 GOTO 250
270 ' our function key#1 subroutine
280 PRINT
290 PRINT "Function key#1 was just pressed."
300 RETURN
```

This sample program—which you might want to key in and run on your Junior—sets up and activates an interrupt in lines 220 and 230 and then goes about its normal business of printing asterisks endlessly (not a very important program, to be sure). When we activate function key number 1 by pressing the Fn key followed by the 1 key, our asterisk program is interrupted and the computer proceeds to our interrupt handler (lines 280 through 300).

An *interrupt handler* can do anything it needs to do; ours just reports that the key was pressed. Normally an interrupt handler does its work quickly and then returns control of the computer to whatever task was being performed. This is exactly what our program does with the RETURN statement in line 300. An interrupt handler does not have to return control. It may, for one reason or another, never go back to what was being done. Normally, though, the interrupt is serviced and then life carries on as usual.

While polling is an important and useful mechanism for certain kinds of computer work, interrupting is the best general way for the computer to deal with the demands of the outside world. When the computer's attention is needed, it responds immediately. When there is no outside work to be done— which is just about all the time—the computer can go about its business, without wasting a fraction of a second of its time.

The concept of the interrupt was an important milestone in the development of computers, and all computers now have interrupts worked into the fundamentals of their design. Interrupts are one of the most important factors in enabling a computer to operate successfully.

THE 8088 INTERRUPTS

Of course, the 8088 microprocessor doesn't work exactly like the BASIC programming language, but the working principles of its interrupts are the same as those demonstrated in the previous program.

Interrupts are built into our 8088 microprocessor in such a way as to allow a good deal of flexibility. Each different sort of interrupt is given an interrupt number. In the lowest part of the computer's memory there is a table of the locations of the programs that handle each interrupt; the entries in the table are equivalent to the GOSUB 280 part of our sample program. When an interrupt occurs in the computer, the location of the corresponding interrupt-handler program is found in this table and the computer passes control to the interrupt handler. In technical jargon, the entries in this table are called *interrupt vectors*, and the table itself is called the *interrupt vector table*. If you run into those terms, you'll now know what they mean.

There are times when the computer is doing something so critical that it should not be interrupted. To prevent interruptions, there is one special instruction that temporarily suspends interrupts and another that turns them back on. These instructions are known as *CLI*, or *clear interrupt flag*, and *STI*, or *set interrupt flag*. Normally, only a handful of computer instructions, taking a tiny fraction of a second, are executed between the time CLI turns off the interrupts and STI turns them back on. If an interrupt appears while CLI is in effect, the interrupt is intercepted and stored by the 8259A chip (the PIC, programmable interrupt controller, discussed briefly in Chapter 2) until an STI instruction turns the interrupts back on.

Occasionally, your PCjr may just die on you, suddenly becoming completely unresponsive to any keyboard actions. One possible cause is a program that has suspended interrupts with a CLI without providing a matching STI. This sort of thing isn't supposed to happen, but then programs aren't supposed to have bugs in them either.

There is one special interrupt that is not suspended even by CLI: the *NMI*, or *non-maskable interrupt*. The NMI is a sort of fire alarm that can be used to have the computer take some last-minute, desperate steps before trouble sets in. The IBM personal computers are set up to get a non-maskable interrupt when the power is failing, and our Junior also uses them for keyboard interrupts, as we'll see later.

While interrupts were invented to solve the problem of finding an efficient way for the computer to respond to outside events, designers quickly realized that interrupts were powerful enough to be used in many other ways. As a result, there are many categories of interrupts. To the computer, they are all equal and are all handled the same way. But looking at the source and use of the interrupts, we can see that they fall into distinct categories.

Intel's Interrupts

First, there are the interrupts that Intel, the makers of the 8088, created and defined. These interrupts apply to any 8088 microprocessor, no matter what computer it is used in. There are five of these interrupts, numbered 0 through 4. Only one of these, the NMI (number 2), is activated by an external signal coming to the 8088 microprocessor. The computer's designer, in our case, IBM, can decide what will create this NMI signal, but IBM can't change the way that the 8088 handles an NMI.

The other four interrupts built into the 8088 by Intel are all what I would call logical interrupts. They are all created by special situations inside the computer that relate to what is happening with the program being run. Two of these four have to do with arithmetic:

■ *Interrupt 0* is generated automatically when the computer is given a command to do division arithmetic with a divisor that is zero (which is considered mathematically impossible).

■ *Interrupt 4* signals "overflow" when the result of an arithmetic operation is too big to fit into the space allotted to it.

The other two built-in interrupts are used to help in tracing and debugging programs:

■ *Interrupt 1* is used to step through a program one instruction at a time.

■ *Interrupt 3* is used to set breakpoints to stop execution at specific points in the program.

Those of you who work with the DEBUG programming tool that is a part of DOS can use interrupts 1 and 3 indirectly. The TRACE command of DEBUG uses the single-step interrupt and the GO command uses the breakpoint interrupt.

IBM's Interrupts

Aside from the five Intel interrupts, the designers of a computer can use other interrupts for any purpose they wish. In the IBM personal computers, including the PCjr, the additional interrupts fall into several groups.

Hardware Interrupts

Eight interrupts, 8 through 15 (hex 8 through F), are reserved for these interrupts, all of which are under the supervision of the 8259A PIC chip. The hardware interrupts are all designed and wired into either the 8088 microprocessor or into some of the circuitry on the PCjr's system board; the interrupt numbers that they use are fixed when the computer is designed.

■ *Interrupt 8* is used to keep the computer informed about the time of day. The computer's clock chip generates an interrupt 8 every time the clock ticks, or about 18.2 times each second. The interrupt handler for this interrupt keeps track of the number of times the clock ticks. Other programs, which are a part of the DOS operating system, can then calculate the time of day from the count of ticks.

■ *Interrupt 9* is generated whenever we press or release a key on the computer's keyboard. The interrupt handler for the keyboard interprets the meaning of each press and release of each key by doing such things as keeping track of whether a shift key is being held down as another key is pressed. When we type away at our Junior, it is being interrupted twice for each key we hit. That seems like a tremendous number of interruptions, but the 8088 is able to handle them so quickly that responding to our typing takes very little of the computer's time.

■ *Interrupt 10* (hex A) is left open.

■ *Interrupts 11 and 12* (hex B and C) are reserved for communications use.

■ *Interrupt 13* (hex D) is for the XT's fixed disk system and is not used by the PCjr.

■ *Interrupt 14* (hex E) handles interrupts from the diskette drives in the PC and XT; the PCjr handles its diskette drive in a more direct way, and so does not use interrupt 14.

■ *Interrupt 15* (hex F) is reserved for the printer.

Software Interrupts

Now we come to a new kind of interrupt, which I call the software interrupts. With an interrupt mechanism handling external events from inside the computer, clever programmers realized that the same mechanism could be a real help in running programs more efficiently.

Programs frequently call on the services of other programs, usually known as *subroutines*. To use a subroutine, a program must be able to pass control to it. Before the use of interrupts, a program would have needed to know the location of the subroutine. It is safer and more flexible, though, for a program to be able to invoke a subroutine without specifying its location, since the program doesn't have to worry about knowing the right location. Interrupts make this possible. If a program needs a service performed, that service can be invoked by an interrupt-handler subroutine. All the program needs to know is the appropriate interrupt number.

41

Unlike the built-in hardware interrupts, software interrupts can be created by any program at any time, and they can use any interrupt numbers, even mimicking the fixed numbering of the hardware interrupts. To make all this possible, the 8088 has an interrupt-generating instruction called INT (for interrupt). Programmers can use this instruction followed by an interrupt number of their choice, as in INT 10. Once the INT instruction takes effect, this software interrupt works just like any other. Naturally there are conventions about which software interrupt numbers are used for which purpose, but the conventions are not cast in bronze.

As part of their design, IBM personal computers have a number of software interrupts reserved for some special purposes. The ROM-BIOS control programs include a host of useful service subroutines, all invoked through interrupts. Most of these interrupts are located in the interrupt vector table in a block from 16 (hex 10) through 26 (hex 1A), though one of them, interrupt 5, which performs the print-screen operation, is nestled right next to the first five interrupts set by Intel. Interrupts 16 through 26 are known as the *BIOS entry points*, since they are the means by which the ROM-BIOS programs are activated.

After the BIOS entry points come two special and interesting interrupts: the user-interface interrupts. They are based on the clever idea of providing interrupts for two important events that our programs might need to know about: the pressing of the Break key on the keyboard (Interrupt 27, hex 1B), and the ticking of the clock 18.2 times a second (Interrupt 28, hex 1C). (Interrupt 28 occurs in connection with the interrupt 8 that we have already discussed.) When either of these things happens, the BIOS routines generate one of these two interrupts. Normally, the interrupts then activate a *dummy interrupt handler,* which does nothing. It takes sophisticated programming skills to make use of either of these events, but we can do it by replacing the addresses of the dummies in the interrupt vector table with the addresses of our own interrupt handlers.

The interrupt vector table contains the vector addresses of interrupt-handling programs; but since it already exists anyway, it can also be used as a place to keep other important addresses, even if they are not the addresses of interrupt-handling programs. Interrupts 29 through 31 (hex 1D through 1F) are used to hold three such addresses, meaning that numbers 29 through 31 cannot be used as actual interrupts, since their corresponding places in the vector table have been used for other purposes.

These three entries form another unusual and interesting category known as the *BIOS parameters*. The BIOS parameters are the *video initialization table*, which gives some technical parameters used to start up the PCjr's display controller; the *disk base*, which gives various parameters controlling the diskette drive; and the *table of video graphics characters*, which don't exist, unless we provide them. We'll look into the details of these tables later.

All the interrupts (0 through 31) that we've covered so far are quite fundamental to the operation of the PCjr. Beyond them, there is a host of other interrupts that service the special needs of DOS and BASIC. We'll cover some of them later in the book. In general terms, DOS uses interrupts 32 through 63 (hex 20 through 3F), and BASIC uses interrupts 128 through 240 (hex 80 through FO). Other interrupts are also available for other uses, including use by our own programs.

PORTS—WINDOWS TO THE OUTSIDE WORLD

Once you get the attention of a mule by hitting it over the head, you then have to talk to it—otherwise it won't know what you want it to do. So it is with our 8088 microprocessor. The 8088 communicates with the world around it in two ways: One way is by reading or writing information in its memory (more about this later); the other is by using *ports*.

Ports provide a general way for the microprocessor to talk to the other parts of the computer's circuitry. Each port has a port number that identifies it. The 8088 can listen and talk to its ports, and data can be passed through the circuitry to and from the ports a byte or a word (two bytes) at a time. The 8088 itself doesn't know anything about what is on the other side of the portholes—it just talks to them by port number. There are 65,536 different port numbers, and most of them are not in use. The designers of the computer decide what purposes the various port numbers will serve and the programs that run on our PCjrs know which ports to use for which purposes. Figure 4-2 shows the ports used by Junior.

Component	Port Numbers (In Hex)
Modem attachment	3F8 - 3FF
Video controller chip (the 6845)	3D0 - 3DF
RS-232 serial adapter	2F8 - 2FF
Joysticks	200 - 207
Diskette drive adapter	F0 - FF
TI sound generator	C0 - C7

Figure 4-2. Major ports used by the PCjr

```
100 ' here we'll take a quick look at the port
110 ' that controls the speaker on the PCjr
120 '
130 ' save the value stored in the speaker port
140 X = INP (97)
150 PRINT "The current value ";
160 PRINT "of the speaker port is ", X
170 '
180 ' turn on the speaker by setting
190 ' two bits in the port value
200 OUT 97,(X \ 4) * 4 + 3
210 PRINT "Press any key to stop the sound."
220 '
230 ' kill time, waiting for a keystroke
240 IF LEN (INKEY$) = 0 THEN 240
250 '
260 ' when we press a key,
270 ' the port is reset to its old value
280 OUT 97, X
290 PRINT "The test is done."
300 END
```

*Figure 4-3. A program to turn on the speaker and
demonstrate the use of ports*

The way the whole thing works is roughly like this: When the 8088 needs
some information, it simply shouts electronically over circuits to the appropriate port, "Port 97, give me some data." The various parts of the computer are
listening at their port holes, and if they hear their number called, they respond.
The 8088 can send data out to the port with the machine-language OUT
instruction, and it can request that the port send data with the IN instruction.

Ports are used for all sorts of things, generally falling into two categories.
One is for control information—such as turning the PCjr's speaker on and off
(we'll experiment with that in a second). The other is to pass data around; for
example, any data moving to or from a cassette recorder passes through port 98
(hex 62) on its way to or from the 8088.

We can experiment with ports very easily in BASIC, because BASIC gives
us commands that perform the IN and OUT machine-language instructions:
INP and OUT. For the example in Figure 4-3, we need to know that Junior's
built-in speaker is partly controlled by two of the bits assigned to port 97 (hex
61). We can find out the current setting of this port using the BASIC INP
function and the number for that port: INP (97). Likewise, we can turn on the

speaker by setting the two low-order bits of the port on with the OUT statement. The program in Figure 4-3 shows how it is done; you might want to key it into your PCjr to see what happens.

Line 140 saves the current value of the speaker port as the variable X, and line 160 reports the value (probably 12) to us. In line 200 we do some calculating to make certain that the two low-order bits are turned on, and then we send that value back OUT to the port. The speaker immediately begins to sound, and it keeps sounding until we press a key at the keyboard, causing the computer to reset the port, in line 280, with the original value that we saved in the variable X.

Running this program will quickly demonstrate both how ports work and a little of how the PCjr's speaker works.

Ordinarily, we don't have any practical use for the ports. They are almost exclusively the territory of Junior's most intimate control programs, the ROM-BIOS. Even if we were doing some very sophisticated programming, it is unlikely that we would have any direct use for the ports. Although I am sure that there are programmers who do use the ports directly, for us the use of ports is mostly a matter of intellectual curiosity.

5

A LOOK AT MEMORY AND REGISTERS

The computer needs somewhere to
keep the programs and data that
it is working with; this "somewhere"
is the computer's memory.

MITS

To a computer's processor, like our PCjr's 8088, there is a profound difference between programs and data. To the memory, there is no difference at all—they are both something to keep track of, that's all.

THE COMPUTER's PLACE OF WORK

Memory is the computer's essential working place. The word "memory" is very familiar to us, so we might be tempted to think of the computer's memory as something like our own. But it is not. Our memory is where we keep information in our brains, more or less permanently; the part of a computer most analogous to our memory is its disk storage or program cartridges.

The computer's memory is quite different from ours. In a computer, the memory is a work space where the computer keeps the information it needs at the moment. Computer memory can be compared to a desk or workbench. Suppose we bought a kit to make a model airplane. When we wanted to put the kit together, we would open the box and spread the contents out on our workbench. In our analogy, this would be equivalent to the computer loading information into its memory.

What would we find in our model airplane kit? What would the computer load into memory? We would find an instruction booklet; our Junior would load program instructions. We would also find the airplane parts; our Junior would load the program's data. To build the model airplane, we would follow the instructions and put the parts together; our computer would follow the program instructions, operating on the data. As we built the model, we would use some of the free room on the workbench to hold our work in progress; the computer would use some of its memory to store the intermediate results of its calculations.

This workbench analogy is very close to the way a computer uses its memory—the memory is a temporary working space, used to hold programs, data, and any additional information that is needed while the work is being done. The use of memory is not permanent; it is temporary. When we have finished building our model airplane, we would clear our bench for some other task; when our PCjr is finished with one program, the memory is free for use with another program.

Not every bit of the memory is up for grabs, though. Just as some part of a workbench might be permanently taken up by a vise or some other tool, so some small parts of our computer's memory are dedicated to special uses, such as the interrupt vector table discussed in the last chapter. Another part is used by the stack, which we'll discuss later. Apart from these relatively small parts of the computer's memory, though, the majority of the memory space is free for general use.

THE COMPUTER's VIEW OF MEMORY

The computer's memory consists of a large number of places where values—numbers—can be stored. A value can be put into any of the places, and later it can be read out of the place where it was put. Think, if you wish, of the computer's memory as a big piece of paper, ruled off into small squares. We can write a number in any of these squares, and later we can read the number that has been written there. When we read the number in the square, it still stays written there, so we can read it again as many times as we want. When we write a new number in one of the squares, however, we first have to erase any old number that was already there. The new number would completely replace the old number, which would then be gone forever. This is exactly how a computer's memory works.

NAVIGATING AROUND THE MEMORY

How would we locate the little squares on our piece of paper? For the computer's memory, each place, each location, is given a numeric *address*. The memory locations are numbered, one right after another—location one, two, three, and so forth—for as many memory locations as we can have.

When the computer needs to read or write values in these locations, it specifies the numeric address that it wants to work with. Part of the task of preparing a computer program is planning the use of these memory locations, and keeping track of them.

In most computers, including our PCjr, each memory location is the size of one byte; this means that each location can hold any of 256 different values. When we need larger and more complex values, our PCjr's 8088 microprocessor combines several bytes and uses them together; for example, for a 16-bit word, two bytes are used together. Not all computers address each byte individually; some computers, particularly old-fashioned ones, have large words as their basic unit of memory. These words can be as large as 64 bits, and the words have to be broken down to get at the bytes inside them. Our PCjr doesn't have this clumsy problem, since it addresses each byte individually.

Since each byte in memory has its own numeric address, the 8088 can use its arithmetic skills to calculate its way into the correct memory locations. This ability to use arithmetic both to work with data and to calculate memory locations is standard in computers.

You'll recall that our PCjr's 16-bit 8088 microprocessor can easily work with numbers from 0 up to, but no larger than, 65,535. This means that it is easy for the 8088 to address 65,536, or 64K, bytes or memory locations, but that some trick would have to be found to address more. Unfortunately, 65,536 bytes is not enough memory to do the kinds of things the IBM personal computers need to do. Some solution had to be found.

EXPANDING MEMORY WITH SEGMENTED ADDRESSES

Intel, the designers of the 8088 microprocessor, found a trick solution in something known as a *segmented address*. After a little head scratching, the people at Intel realized that, while the computer needed access to more than 64K memory locations, programs were rarely working with more than 64K bytes of data at any given time. Most programs could happily do their address arithmetic within the confines of 16 bits, addressing only 64K of data, as long as a way could be found to place those 64K data bytes inside a larger memory space. This larger space would then be able to accommodate the necessary systems programs, our own programs, the computer's workbench, and our 64K bytes of data.

The size of the memory space is, in effect, determined by the highest number that the computer's microprocessor can handle, so Intel needed to find a way to enable the 8088 to work with numbers larger than 65,535. Here's how the trick was done. First, Intel gave the 8088 an addressing scheme 20 bits wide, which expanded the full range of memory locations that the 8088 can work with from 2 to the 16th power, or 65,536, to 2 to the 20th power, or roughly 1 million bytes (1,048,576 to be exact). Then it had the 8088 use a 2-word addressing technique to create 20-bit addresses using only 16-bit numbers.

How do you get a 20-bit number out of two 16-bit words, or numbers? Simple. You take two 16-bit numbers and shift one of them over by four bits, in effect multiplying that number by 2 to the 4th power, or 16. Then you add the shifted number to the other, unshifted number, and you have a complete 20-bit number.

Let's write out an example, expressing our numbers in hexadecimal. You'll remember that each hex digit is shorthand for four bits, so it takes four hex digits to write a 16-bit number. Let's arbitrarily take two hex numbers, say 1234 and 4321; each is a 16-bit number with which the 8088 has no trouble doing arithmetic. Now, let's take the first number, 1234, and shift it over four bits (one hex digit), or multiply it by 16. To do this, we just add a hex 0 on to the end to get 12340. (What we have just done is similar to multiplying a decimal number by the base number 10; for example, to multiply 42 by 10 we can just shift 42 over one decimal digit and add a decimal 0 on to its end, resulting in 420. In the example above, instead of representing a power of 10, each digit represents a power of 16.)

Now, 12340 is a 20-bit number, but one that has a zero on its end, so shifting 16-bit numbers over doesn't generate all possible 20-bit values. Our shifted, or multiplied, number can only take on a value that is an exact multiple of 16. To be able to address a byte in any 20-bit address space, we have to be able to generate all possible 20-bit numbers. So we complete this process by taking our second number, 4321, and adding it to the shifted first number:

```
    12340
  +  4321
    16661
```

Now we have a way to generate a 20-bit number that can take on any value. It can be used to address a 20-bit address space, that is, to locate any byte out of over a million bytes.

This is the technique that Junior's 8088 microprocessor uses to create its addresses. Two 16-bit numbers are combined in this way to make up a 20-bit address.

The two parts of these 20-bit addresses are referred to as the *segment* part (the number that is shifted over) and the *offset* part (the number that is added in). The segment part refers to any location in the 1,024K byte memory space that is a multiple of 16. (These locations are known as paragraph boundaries and each unit of 16 memory locations is known as a *paragraph.*) The offset part refers to any location that is up to 64K bytes away from the segment location. The segment part thus addresses a base location for the offset part's 64K working area. Together, the two parts make up a complete segmented address.

The offset part of an address is also sometimes called the *relative* part, or the *relative offset,* since it indicates a memory location relative to the starting point given by the segment part.

When we need to write the segmented addresses out on paper, there are two ways we can do it. One way is to write out the finished 20-bit address with five hex digits, such as the 16661 in our example. When you read about the PCjr's addresses, you will sometimes see them written this way. The other way, which is more common, is to write the address in its two separate parts, separated by a colon, such as 1234:4321. When you read technical information on the 8088, or when you deal with assembly-language programming, you will often encounter addresses written in this form.

There is one disadvantage, or complication, that you should know about in using the segmented notation (the two numbers with a colon). The exact same address can be written several ways. For example, 0012:0034 and 0015:0004 are the *same* address, even though they are written differently.

51

HOW A COMPUTER USES
SEGMENTED ADDRESSES

There is a customary way for programs to work with segmented addresses. First you need to know that computer instructions can specify memory locations either by providing the memory address directly in the instruction (called *immediate addressing*), or by indicating that the address is located in one of the computer's working *registers*. (We'll discuss registers shortly.) The offset part of a segmented address can be given either immediately or through a register, but the segment part is always taken from a special-purpose *segment register*, so a program does not have to worry about providing the segment part itself.

There are separate segment registers for four distinct uses. First, there is a *program segment register*, called *CS* (short for code segment), which is used to locate the program that the computer is running. Then there is a *data segment register*, called *DS*, used to locate data in memory. For the stack—which we'll discuss shortly—there's a *stack segment register*, called *SS*. Finally, there's an *extra segment register*, called *ES*, which can be used in a pinch as a spare segment pointer. All four segment registers together provide the master supervision of how memory is used.

The way this normally works is that the computer's supervisory programs (the DOS operating system in the PCjr) decide where in memory a program and its data should be located and set the segment registers to point to that part, or segment, of memory. When a program is being run, it is not concerned with where the segment registers have put it. Instead, the program only has to work with the offset part of its addresses; combined with the part of the address in the segment registers, the program's offset addresses will find their way to the right locations in memory.

Since ordinary programs only have to worry about 16-bit offset addresses, they can do all of their address work with the 8088's 16-bit arithmetic and never run into difficulty. This does mean, though, that our programs are limited to using only 64K of data. If a program needs to work with more data than this, then the program must use more sophisticated programming techniques, so that the segment registers are manipulated by the program itself, instead of by DOS.

There are two interesting sidelights to this. When we are using BASIC on the PCjr, the actual program that is running is the BASIC interpreter. What you or I think of as our BASIC programs are actually data with which the BASIC interpreter works. Because of this, we are limited to a total of 64K for our program and data combined. Even if we have more memory, BASIC can't use more than 64K for our programs and their data, because to BASIC they are both data, and data are normally limited to 64K.

Except for the special case of interpreted BASIC (and other interpreted languages such as LOGO), a program can have a full 64K of data, no matter what the size of the program (provided that the computer has enough memory for it all). The program's code uses the CS register for itself and the DS register for its data. This means that a program can have up to 64K of data and also 64K of program—if there is enough memory to accommodate them. On our PCjr, we have only 64K or 128K total; after some overhead is used, there isn't enough memory for both 64K of data and 64K of program in a PCjr, but the address scheme does allow for it. On a PC or XT—our PCjr's bigger brothers—there could be enough memory for all that information.

For all practical purposes, data are limited to 64K. On the other hand, the size of a program may or may not be limited to 64K, depending upon what rules the program follows.

How can programs use more than 64K of memory? It depends on whether or not the program allows itself to change the segment registers. If the code segment register is left alone, the maximum size of a program is the 64K limit of an offset address. If the code segment register can be changed while the program is running, however, a program can break out of the 64K limit. Whether or not the segment register can be changed depends upon which programming language is being used (and can vary from one version of a language to another). For example, IBM Pascal, provided by Microsoft®, can break out of the 64K program limit; Microsoft BASIC Compiler cannot.

Very few programs are big enough to come even close to the 64K limit, and it is unlikely that you or I would ever write a program that huge. In any event, for the PCjr, running programs bigger than 64K is rarely practical (although it can be done, on a 128K Junior).

MAPPING THE PCJR'S MEMORY

Now that we know something about the PCjr's memory and how to address it, we ought to see how it is organized. Since the PCjr is part of the IBM personal computer family, it uses the memory space of the 8088 pretty much the same way as the rest of the family. But there are some interesting new twists added for the PCjr.

The 8088 has an address space of 1,024K, or over 1 million bytes. This is the number of addresses that the 8088 can use, but it isn't the amount of memory that any of our IBM personal computers actually has. The real working memory can be located in any part of this space. In effect, the 8088 provides a plot of bare land, 1 million bytes big, where the architects of any computer can build. How they use this land, and how much space their computers take up, depends upon the decisions that the architects make.

For the IBM personal computers, this 1,024K space is used in several parts, and there are four distinctly different categories of memory, as we'll explain.

Figure 5-1 shows a general map of the memory used by the IBM personal computers; you can refer to it to put all of the remarks in this section into the context of the whole memory.

To talk about the memory used by the PCjr, we need to be able to refer to specific parts. We'll use the segment part of a 20-bit address, expressed in hexadecimal. Talking this way, the very beginning of memory starts at segment paragraph address 0000; the end of memory is at FFFF. The first 64K of memory goes from 0000 up to but not including 1000 and the second 64K goes from 1000 to 2000, all expressed in hex.

RAM

Let's begin at the beginning. Each of the IBM personal computers, including the PCjr, puts its ordinary working memory (RAM) in the lowest memory locations, starting with 0000. RAM, or random access memory, is the part of memory people are talking about when they refer to how much memory a

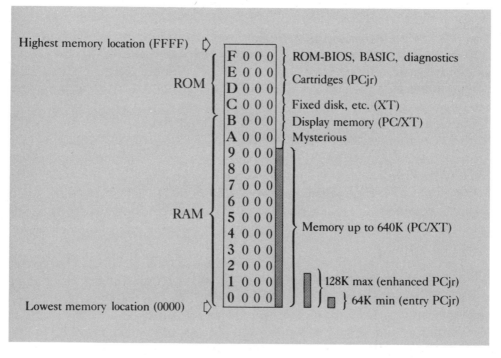

Figure 5-1. General memory map

computer has. While our IBM personal computers have lots of other memory, this is the main working memory, the workbench where programs and data reside. If you have a 128K Junior, it has RAM from 0000 to 2000.

More than 128K is set aside in the 1,024K address space for this working RAM—in fact, a full 640K, from 0000 to A000, is dedicated to it. The PCjr can't use more than 128K, but the other IBM models can accommodate the full 640K if it is needed.

For the next use of memory, let's skip to the end of the address space, and see what is done with the highest memory locations.

ROM

One of the greatest virtues of the IBM personal computers is that they come equipped with some very powerful built-in programs, stored in a form of memory known as ROM, or read only memory. ROM cannot be erased or lost—it is always there, faithfully, whenever the computer is running. The highest memory space, the 64K block of memory from F000 through FFFF, is used for these ROM programs so that they will be out of the way, leaving as much of the rest of the memory space as free as possible.

There are two types of ROM programs. The first is the ROM-BIOS, or Basic Input/Output System. The ROM-BIOS is responsible for the most intimate supervision and control of the computer. For example, the ROM-BIOS provides the actual controlling programs for the display screen, the keyboard, and nearly every other part of the computer. The ROM-BIOS is divided into three parts. There is 8K of BIOS located from paragraph FE00 through to FFFF; all models of IBM personal computer have BIOS here (although the actual programming may differ from model to model). The PCjr also has two other BIOS areas; it needs more BIOS simply because it substitutes hard-working BIOS programs for the more expensive smart hardware of the PC and XT. The PCjr's second BIOS area is 8K of programs located at F000. The third area is 16K located from F200 up to F600; this area contains diagnostic programs, which we could consider a special kind of BIOS.

The second type of ROM program provides an application rather than a control program. The PCjr comes with two of these applications: One major one is the core of BASIC, the part that is called ROM-BASIC; the other minor one is the *Keyboard Adventure program*. The ROM-BASIC program is common to all the IBM personal computers; it can stand by itself, or it can be used with disk and cartridge supplements, which add richer features to the BASIC language.

The ROM-BASIC starts at memory location F600, and occupies 32K. The Keyboard Adventure program is kept together with the diagnostic programs.

Actually, the entire memory from C000 to the top is reserved for various kinds of ROM use. A small part of the 64K block from C000 to D000 was used when the Winchester-type, fixed hard-disk system was added to the PC to make the XT. This new disk required its own small amount of ROM-BIOS support, and these BIOS programs were placed right in the middle of the C000 block, from C800 to CC00. Future additions to the BIOS are very likely to appear in the same area.

ROM Cartridges

There are two 64K blocks of memory between the ordinary ROM block at F000, and the ROM additions block at C000: the D000 block and the E000 block. Our PCjr uses these two blocks of memory for the plug-in ROM cartridges. When any of these cartridges is used, the ROM that is physically located in the cartridge is logically placed somewhere within these two memory blocks; just where is controlled by the cartridge. The cartridges contain as much or as little memory as they need for their purposes, up to a limit of 64K each. Since the original PC and XT do not use cartridges, this part of the memory address space remains empty for them.

So far, we have seen three of the four categories of memory use: permanent ROM support programs at the top, removable ROM cartridges just below ROM, and working RAM at the bottom. There is one more kind of memory used in the PC and XT, but only indirectly used in our PCjr.

Memory-Mapped Display

The IBM personal computers use memory to control what is on the display screen. This technique is called *memory-mapped display,* meaning that any display-related change to the memory causes an immediate change to the display screen. This is a very fast and very efficient way to operate a display screen.

All of the models of IBM personal computer use memory-mapped displays, but the PCjr does it a bit differently from the PC and the XT. In the other models, the display adapters contain their own memory locations, which are specially built for fast operation. The memory in these display adapters has two paths, which means that both the 8088 microprocessor and the display screen can talk to the memory at the same time with a minimum of interference. Parts of the B000 block of memory are set aside for the use of the display memory, and the remainder is reserved, likely for future enhancements to the display formats. The monochrome adapter (which has no equivalent in our PCjr) uses 4K of memory located at B000, and the original color/graphics adapter (which is equivalent to the display adapter built into our PCjr) uses 16K located at B800.

Our PCjr uses some memory for its display just like the color/graphics adapter. But, instead of using a more elaborate, two-path memory, the PCjr borrows some of the top part of its RAM to use for the display. It thus does not use the B000 block of memory locations for its display. Since many programs for the other IBM personal computers work with these memory locations, however, the PCjr contains special hardware known as a *video gate array,* or *VGA,* to divert any reference to the B000 display memory down to the actual RAM locations it is using. This helps make it possible for programs developed on either of the other models to be used on the PCjr, and vice versa.

There are two parts of the computer's memory map that we haven't yet covered, and they are unknown areas at this time. We mentioned that two parts of the B000 block are used in the PC and XT for display memory. The rest of the B000 block is also reserved, presumably for further enhancements to the display formats. Likewise, the entire 64K block at A000 is reserved for some future use. It might be intended for display use, like the B000 block, or for another purpose.

THE ESSENTIAL REGISTERS

One of the keys to the efficient operation of our PCjr's 8088 microprocessor is its use of some very fast temporary memory locations called registers, so we will now take a look at these registers and what they are used for.

There are two main uses for the 8088's registers: One is for *addressing* and the other is as a *scratch pad.* Let's look at the scratch pad first.

The Working Registers

When a computer works with data held in its memory, it takes a certain amount of time to use that memory. The reason is simple. The memory is located outside the microprocessor and isn't totally under its control. To use memory, the 8088 must send a request out into the world of its external circuitry and then wait for the result—the wait isn't long as you or I measure time, but it's noticeable by the 8088's standards. To handle this delay, the 8088 is given some very private memory of its own, which it can access at lightning speed. This private, scratch-pad memory is in the form of four registers.

While the computer's memory is accessed by numeric addresses, the four 16-bit, scratch-pad registers are referred to by letter names: *AX, BX, CX,* and *DX.* Each of them can be used freely by the 8088's programs to hold any temporary working numbers that are needed. If a number is to be used repeatedly, it can be kept in a register as long as the program needs it, so that the 8088 can get to it very quickly.

The AX, BX, CX, and DX registers each hold 16 bits, but sometimes we only need enough space to hold an 8-bit byte. To make more efficient use of the register space, each register can be split into two 8-bit registers. For example, AX can be split into AH and AL, corresponding to the high- and low-order bytes of the 16-bit word that can be stored in AX. Each of the other three registers can be similarly split. The full X register is exactly made up of the H and L parts; so if we change the AX register, we also change the AH and AL values, and vice versa.

The four (or eight) registers can be used for any general purpose. Some- times, though, a computer instruction needs to use a dedicated register for one reason or another. So, in addition to their general use, the registers each have some special uses as well. For example, often programs need to count how many times some operation is to be repeated. When this is done, the CX register is used automatically. There are similar special uses for each of the other registers.

In Chapter 7, when we have finished enough of our homework, we will pore over some assembly-language programming; you will then have a chance to see in detail the use of some of these registers, as well as the relationship between the whole X registers and their halves.

The Address Registers

As we have already mentioned, the other main use for registers is address- ing. Nine registers are dedicated to this task. Like the scratch-pad registers, they are referred to by letters.

First, there are the four segment address registers that are used to locate the 20-bit segmented addresses. Three of the four are dedicated to addressing three particular uses of memory.

■ *The code segment (CS) register* is used to locate the program that is being executed.

■ *The data segment (DS) register* is used to locate the data the program is working on. (The *data segment* is the area of memory where the data are located.)

■ *The stack segment (SS) register* is used to locate the temporary workplace called the stack that keeps track of tasks in progress.

■ *The extra segment (ES) register* is used to supplement the others, mostly the DS register. It also has some dedicated uses, just as the general-purpose, scratch-pad registers do. Whenever our programs need to get to some data that aren't covered by the DS, CS, or SS registers, they can use the ES register.

The four segment registers are used to locate a general working portion of memory, but you will recall that an offset address must be used with the segment part to complete the address. There are five registers for this purpose.

■ *The instruction pointer (IP)*, also called the *program counter (PC)*, is used with the CS register to track the exact current location in the program that is being executed. Either name refers to the same thing: the offset part of the current program address.

■ *The stack pointer (SP)* and the *base pointer (BP)* are two offset address registers that work with the SS (stack) register. We'll learn about these registers in the next section, and see how they are used.

■ *The source index (SI)* and the *destination index (DI)*, the two remaining offset address registers, are used when data have to be slung around in two locations. A typical use for these registers would be when moving a large number of bytes from one place to another within the data segment. When these registers are used, they are usually incremented automatically, so we don't have to add 1 to them each time we want to move on to the next byte.

The Flag Register

To complete our coverage of the registers, you should know about one "sort-of" register. The 8088 has a variety of bits, called *flags*, that control various things in the computer. For example, one flag bit controls whether interrupts are suspended or are active. The *flag register* enables the computer to work with all the flag bits collectively. The flag register cannot be manipulated like the other registers, but it is still referred to as a register. Later on, you'll find us referring to the carry flag, the zero flag, and other flags. They are all parts of the flag register.

KEEPING TRACK WITH THE STACK

One of the most important and useful elements in computer design is the *stack*. To understand stacks, it helps to understand the problem that makes stacks so essential.

When we discussed interrupts in Chapter 4, we mentioned that, when an interrupt occurs, the computer sets aside the task it is doing and works on the interrupt. How can the computer keep track of what it was doing, so that it can return to it when the interrupt is over?

For example, when a program calls a subroutine, what does it do with the work in progress while the subroutine is being executed? If the subroutine calls another subroutine, which happens a lot, how does the computer keep track of who called whom, so that it can find its way back to the very first program?

The solution to all these problems, and others that are closely related, lies in the use of a stack.

A stack is a part of the computer's memory that is set aside for use in a special way. Any part of memory can be used as a stack; what is special is not the section of memory, but the way that it is used.

A stack gets its name from its (conceptual) resemblance to the spring-loaded plate holders that are often used in cafeterias. In a cafeteria, clean plates are put on the top of the stack of plates, and the stack is pushed down. When we need a plate, we take it off the stack, and the spring pops the rest of the plates up. The special thing about this kind of stack is that the plates are used in reverse order. The last plate to be put onto the stack is the first one to be taken off—a stack doesn't work like a queue of people waiting in line, where it's first come, first served. Instead, with this kind of stack, the last one in is the first one out (technically called *LIFO*).

When work in a computer is put on hold, the computer must keep track of what is happening so that it can return to the most recent task first. After all, if I am a subroutine, when I have finished my work, I need to return control of the computer to the program that called me, and not to some previous program. For this to happen, the computer's holding file needs to work on a LIFO basis, and it must act like the plate holder in a cafeteria.

To accomplish this, a special mechanism was designed into micro-processors like our 8088 that makes it possible for them to have a working stack. A section of memory is set aside to be used as a stack and a record is kept of where the "top" of the stack is. Since the 8088 uses segmented addresses, naturally there is a segment register set aside just to control the location of the stack; this is the SS, or stack segment register. To keep track of the top of the stack, there is an offset register called the SP, or stack pointer register.

In a stack of plates, all the plates physically move when plates are added or taken off. In our computer's stack, the contents of the stack don't move when other information is *pushed* onto the stack or *popped* off. Instead, the stack stays put, and it is the location of the top of the stack that moves. The SP register indicates where the top of the stack is, and its value changes when information is pushed onto or popped off the stack. In Figure 5-2, *a, b,* and *c,* show how this works.

In Figure 5-2*a,* we see a stack before we start using it. If we need to save some information, we use the PUSH instruction. The information is stored at the top location, indicated by the SP register, and the SP value is changed to show the new top of the stack. Figure 5-2*b* shows how the stack looks after we have pushed some information onto it. When we need the information back, we use a POP instruction. The data are copied from the stack to wherever we

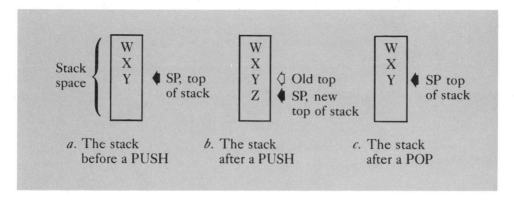

Figure 5-2. The status of the stack

need them, and the SP register's value is changed to indicate that the top of the stack has moved back, as Figure 5-2*c* shows.

There is one interesting trick that makes it easier to use stacks: Stacks run backward. Backward? What does that mean? It means that the top of the stack is at a lower memory location than the bottom of the stack. When more information is pushed onto the stack, it goes into locations with smaller addresses, and the value of the SP register is decreased, not increased. Functionally, this makes no difference to the stack itself, since a stack can run backward just as easily as it could run forward. But there is one big advantage in a backward stack.

We never need to look past the top of a stack, since there isn't anything there to look at. But sometimes we need to look lower down, at prior contents of the stack. We'll see why we might want to do this shortly. If the stack ran forward, so that old contents were at a lower location than the SP register indicated, we would have to use a negative displacement to find locations earlier in the stack. But with the stack running backward, we can use a positive displacement to find our way to earlier points on the stack. Figure 5-3 shows how this works.

Why would we want to look at earlier information on the stack? One of the most important reasons has to do with programs calling subroutines.

When a program calls a subroutine, it usually has *parameters* to pass to the routine; the parameters indicate part of what is to be done. For example, the SIN function in BASIC calculates the trigonometric sine of a number—but we have to give the SIN function a number to calculate from, and this number is a parameter of the SIN subroutine. These parameters have to be stored somewhere, and for many technical reasons the stack is a natural place to put them.

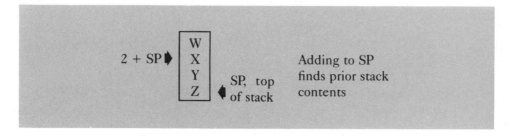

Figure 5-3. Finding prior contents of the stack

Once the parameters have been pushed onto the stack, the SP register will be pointing beyond them to a lower address. Then, any subroutine that needs these parameters can add a displacement value to the SP register and get to these parameters easily.

There is one little hitch to this business of using a displacement from the SP register to find your parameters: Programs routinely do lots of pushing and popping with the stack. With each PUSH or POP instruction, the SP register changes; this makes the displacement between the current value of the SP register and any parameters a moving target.

There is, however, a very simple solution to this problem: The BP, or base pointer register is used to freeze a location on the stack. This is the way it works. Suppose we are a subroutine, and we are called to work with some parameters. When we begin operation, the SP register is located near our parameters, and we know exactly where they are. So one of the first things we do is copy the value of the SP register into the BP register. From that point on, we can push and pop the stack as much as we want, and we still have a secure record of that fixed point on the stack that is near our parameters.

Altogether, then, three registers are used to support the stack. One is the SS, or stack segment register, which is used to locate the stack in memory. The other two are both offset registers used with the SS register: The SP, or stack pointer register, controls and supervises the stack, and the BP, or base pointer register, takes a "snapshot" of the current value of the top of the stack so that later on we will know exactly where in the stack certain information is located.

Is there only one stack? Usually. However, there can be as many stacks in use at one time as our programs might need. A new, separate stack can be created simply by setting aside some memory and changing the SS register to point to it. Having several stacks standing around, though, can become both messy and wasteful, so the standard practice is that only one stack exists at a time.

When DOS or ROM-BASIC is in charge of the computer, it will create and use its own stack. When we tell DOS to run a program for us, DOS sets up the program and creates a good-sized stack for it. From that point on, everything uses the same stack. The program uses it, and when the program calls on the services of DOS or the service routines built into the ROM-BIOS, the same stack is used. DOS and the ROM-BIOS can share the program's stack with no difficulty at all.

6
ELEMENTARY EDUCATION: THE ROM-BIOS

One of the many analogies between
computers and people is that both
require an education to realize their
potential and become productive
elements of society. In computers,
education takes the form of programs.

The computer's most elementary education is embodied in its ROM-BIOS programs, its Basic Input/Output System.

In the IBM personal computers, including our Junior, the ROM-BIOS is permanently installed in ROM (read only memory), which provides an enormous advantage in that it is always ready to be used and cannot be erased or otherwise lost. If the BIOS were not built into ROM, it would have to be loaded into memory from, say, a diskette. Not only would this be a nuisance, but there is also some danger that the wrong BIOS program might be loaded, or that we might forget to load it, or that we might lose our only copy of the program. Life is made simpler, for us and our PCjr, by having the BIOS built into ROM.

There is a potential disadvantage, though. Computer programs are notorious for having bugs, or errors, in them. What if the ROM in our PCjr turned out to have a major bug in it? We'd be up a creek, wouldn't we? Not quite.

First, the ROM-BIOS is physically embodied in removable, plug-in memory chips. If there were an error in the ROM-BIOS important enough to require changing it, then these chips could be replaced. The process would require some handyman skills, but it would be relatively simple. In fact, when a fixed disk system is added to a PC, the ROM-BIOS chip is replaced, not because there is an error in the old chip, but because the programs must be changed to accommodate the fixed disk.

Second, we have little reason to worry about errors in the ROM-BIOS. Because these programs are so critical, and because it would be so expensive for IBM to recall thousands of PCjrs to correct any problems, the programs are checked and tested very carefully before release. Needless to say, the very first release of these programs is the version that is most likely to contain errors. However, as an indication of exactly how careful IBM is, when the PC was first introduced, the errors in the first ROM-BIOS version were so insignificant that no immediate change was needed. The ROM-BIOS in our PCjr is very close to the ROM-BIOS used in the PC and XT—the only differences relate to Junior's new features—so most of our ROM-BIOS has already been tested on hundreds of thousands of computers. We don't have much to worry about in this regard.

There is a lot of programming in the ROM-BIOS—thousands and thousands of lines of assembly-language code. It contains a wealth of goodies divided into four logical categories, which we will call diagnostics, start-up, services, and support.

DIAGNOSTIC PROGRAMS

A full set of *diagnostic routines* can be time-consuming to run and involves testing the keyboard, the diskette drive, and so forth. It would be unreasonable to do all the diagnostic routines every time we use the computer, so they are divided into two groups: a complete, interactive set of diagnostics that is incorporated into a separate part of the ROM, and the simple, quick, but essential diagnostics that are performed by the ordinary ROM-BIOS.

There are actually two sets of ordinary diagnostics in the ROM-BIOS: one set that is used for testing during the PCjr's manufacture, and another set that is performed when we turn it on. It is this second set that is particularly important to us. We don't want to discover right in the middle of a program that some part of the computer is malfunctioning; we would prefer to learn about it before we start work. So when we turn on our PCjr, a set of diagnostic programs called *power-on self test*, or *POST*, is executed to check the computer out.

START-UP PROGRAMS

Start-up, or *bootstrap*, programs get Junior going. They are executed automatically after the POST diagnostics and they are also executed when we restart our PCjr by pressing the Ctrl-Alt-Del key combination. The start-up program has to figure out what program should be placed in charge of the computer by following a hierarchy of things to check.

The highest priority is given to the diskette drive: If the PCjr has the diskette-drive adapter installed, the start-up program tries to read a *bootstrap*, or *boot, record* (which is a diskette start-up program) from a diskette (we'll explain this later). If there is no diskette-drive adapter, or if no information can be read because we have not put a diskette into the drive, the ROM-BIOS start-up program executes a special interrupt, interrupt 24 (hex 18), to pass control to the built-in ROM-BASIC.

So far, the PCjr operates exactly like the other members of the family; but now, the PCjr goes one step further. A cartridge program plugged into the PCjr can override interrupt 24, so that the start-up program passes control not to the ROM-BASIC, but to part of the cartridge program. The BASIC language cartridge uses this to override the ROM-BASIC. This is one of the ways that a cartridge program can take control of the computer; we'll see about the other way when we discuss cartridges.

SERVICE PROGRAMS

The greatest part of the ROM-BIOS is devoted to providing our programs with a large set of *services* that are ready for use at their command. Each peripheral—the screen, the keyboard, the diskette drive, the cassette drive, the printer, the communications line, the light pen, and the joysticks—is provided with whatever functions and operations it needs to make it easy to use. For example, the display screen is provided with service routines that will write information on it, change its mode from text to graphics, and so forth.

To organize these service routines, each peripheral is given its own interrupt code, and under each interrupt there are as many service codes as there are separate services to be performed. In addition, the ROM-BIOS service routines follow a consistent set of conventions and working rules.

Working Rules

The rules are designed to make the service routines easier and more reliable to use and to reduce the amount of programming that is needed to use them.

All of the ROM-BIOS services are invoked by their interrupts and must be accessed through assembly language. We can't get to these services directly if we are programming in BASIC or any of the other popular programming languages, and this is as it should be. The ROM-BIOS services are intended, first and foremost, to be used by the computer's main control programs, such as the BASIC interpreter itself and DOS. Second, but still very important, the ROM-BIOS services are to be used by sophisticated application programs, including word processors, such as Microsoft® Word, and spreadsheet programs, such as Multiplan™.

The programs you and I write in BASIC usually get along very nicely with the service routines provided by the BASIC interpreter program, or by whatever other programming language we might be using. These service routines build on those of the ROM-BIOS. If we need more flexibility than the language services provide, we can use assembly-language interface routines to use the ROM-BIOS services in ways that are beyond the scope of our high-level language. Programmers often use this approach when they want the advantages of high-level languages, but also need special tricks that these languages may not provide. My own Norton Utility™ programs are an example of this. I have been able to write 99.9 percent of them in the Pascal and C languages; only to make a quick connection to the ROM-BIOS do I use assembly language. If any of your programs need the ROM-BIOS services, you will probably want to use the same technique; we'll get into most of the necessary details in Chapter 20.

As we've said, each of the ROM-BIOS services is invoked through an interrupt. There are two very important reasons for this. First, an interrupt provides the surest way to get to a standard subroutine. Any subroutine could be invoked by the machine-language CALL instruction, but a CALL needs to know the location of the program it is calling. We could look up the location of the ROM-BIOS services in the *Technical Reference* manual, but then our programs would be dependent upon the PCjr version of the ROM-BIOS. On the

PC or XT, or a revised PCjr, the same routines might be located in slightly different places. It would be foolish to write programs that depended on specific locations.

Using interrupts to invoke the ROM-BIOS services solves this problem by making the calling program completely uninterested in where the interrupt service routine is. As long as the meaning of each interrupt number is understood—for example, that interrupt 5 performs the print-screen operation—and as long as the interrupt vector table has been set up properly, then any program can use any ROM-BIOS interrupt service freely and reliably.

The second important reason why interrupts are used to invoke the ROM-BIOS services is so that the interrupts can be overridden. It may become important to change a service: Perhaps an improved way to do the same operation is found, or perhaps we want to add something special. By using interrupts, we can always replace one interrupt-handling program with another.

How can this be done? Well, we can't actually replace the programs in the ROM-BIOS; after all, ROM is read only memory, so we can't write changes into it. But we can put an equivalent service program in another part of memory (RAM), and then change the interrupt vector table to point to the new program. If an interrupt vector points to our new program rather than into the ROM-BIOS, then that interrupt will automatically be rerouted to our program.

So, all the ROM-BIOS service routines begin with interrupts. As we mentioned, each basic service area (diskette operations, display screen operations, and so forth) has its own individual interrupt. Within each area, separate subservices are given service numbers, starting with service number 0.

For all the services, the service number is placed in the AH register. If the operation being invoked returns a status code indicating what happened, or how things might have gone wrong, AH is usually, though not always, used. (The services are not rigorously consistent in this regard—by nature they have to vary from one to another.)

The 8088's status flags are also used as a quick and efficient way for the ROM-BIOS services to return a success/failure signal. Most commonly the carry flag, CF, is used; if carry is set (CF = 1) then an error has occurred. The zero flag, ZF, is also used for some signals passed back to the calling routine.

Whenever the services need to pass values in or out, they use the AX, BX, CX and DX registers. For example, when the computer reads from the keyboard, it passes the results back to the AX register; when it writes to the printer, it uses AX to indicate the character to be printed and DX to indicate which printer (since there can be more than one).

It is customary for the printer service to use AX and DX, and leave BX and CX alone as much as possible. The register most likely to be left unchanged is BX, and the next most likely is CX. This is of no consequence if we are using these services in connection with high-level language programming; but if we are programming in assembly language, we can take advantage of it and use BX and CX more freely.

For the most part, the ROM-BIOS services do not use or manipulate any of the segment registers. But a few of them need a full 20-bit segmented address, and the extra segment register, ES, is used to provide the segment part of the 20-bit address for them.

Programs generally need a stack to work with; the ROM-BIOS service routines do as well. Part of the philosophy of the ROM-BIOS is to leave the registers undisturbed, except for those that are being used to pass status codes back and forth. However, ROM-BIOS programs need registers for working storage just like most other programs. So, to preserve the values in registers they want to work with, the ROM-BIOS services push the values onto the stack, and later pop them off back into the registers. The result is that when the service routine has finished its work, the registers look as though they have not been disturbed.

The ROM-BIOS does not create its own stack for saving register values: It relies on our existing stack. So how much stack do we need? I am not aware of any official, published figure (this sort of thing is usually overlooked), but the needs of the service routines are quite modest. After inspecting some of the ROM-BIOS code, I judge that 32 bytes should be plenty, and 64 would provide a very generous cushion. This is well within the amounts of stack that are usually available.

This is about as much as can be said in general about the ROM-BIOS service routines. We will be discussing them in more detail, case by case, in the later chapters. When you need more thorough information, though, you should turn to the ultimate source of information about the ROM-BIOS routines, the *Technical Reference* manual.

SUPPORT PROGRAMS

The last of the four categories of ROM-BIOS programs is *support routines*. These are the routines that help make the PCjr run, but which aren't service routines like those we have just discussed. The clearest example of a support routine is the keyboard interrupt program. Whenever we pound away on Junior's keyboard, the computer has to pay attention to what we have typed, whether or not any program is expecting to receive input from the keyboard. The keyboard support routine is given the task of noticing which keys have been pressed and released, and then translating key actions into meaningful characters. Translation is necessary, since the meaning of many keys is dependent on whether a shift key is also pressed. Besides translating key actions into their resulting characters, the keyboard support routine also buffers, or stores, a small number of keyboard characters, in case our programs can't read and use each character before another is keyed in.

There are some interesting things to explore in the ROM-BIOS, as well as in other parts of the ROM. In the next chapter, we are going to learn how to use the DEBUG tool, which is a part of DOS, to snoop around. In the process, we will also learn some assembly language.

7
USING WHAT WE KNOW TO GO EXPLORING

Want to see a little of what actual
machine language and assembly language
are like on the 8088? This will give
us a chance to dive in head-first and
see what the waters are really like.

In this chapter, we are going to take a small section of the ROM-BIOS programs that are built into Junior, and pore over it, instruction by instruction. While we explore the ROM-BIOS, we'll get some practice using segmented addresses and see interrupts and registers in action.

How can we do all this? First, we have access to a listing of the ROM-BIOS programs, complete with the programmer's comments, in IBM's *Technical Reference* manual for the PCjr. You can, and we could, use that listing to study some ready-made assembly code. But there is another way to look at machine-language code that can be used even with programs for which we don't have listings; we can use the *DEBUG* program. We'll use that method, since it will show you how you can go exploring inside any program.

DEBUG

We are going to use one of the most powerful and complex parts of the DOS operating system, the DEBUG utility program. DEBUG is intended as a working tool for advanced programmers. It enables us to explore memory, disks, programs, and data.

One of the many wonderful tricks that DEBUG can do is look at the machine-language form of any program and translate it into assembly code. This means that DEBUG can take an unintelligible hex code, such as B85000, and tell us that it is an instruction to move the number 80 into the AX register. This translation process is called *disassembling*, since it reverses the process followed by an assembler when it translates assembly language into machine language.

There is one disadvantage to studying a disassembly listing instead of an original assembly listing: The assembly listing should have its author's helpful comments; a disassembly listing can only reconstruct the executable program lines. In other words, a disassembly listing shows us what is being done, but it doesn't show us why; that remains a puzzle for us to solve.

The unique advantage of disassembling, though, is that you can disassemble anything and study it. So if you learn to decipher disassemblies, you potentially have access to the inner workings of any program. Very few programs come with annotated assembly listings (the ROM-BIOS is one of the rare examples), so we have few opportunities to look over a programmer's shoulder and read the original notes and comments in a program. The ROM-BIOS routines that we will look at in this chapter do come with a listing, which appears in the *Technical Reference* manual, and we'll actually make use of that listing to help us understand what's going on. However, for this exercise, we'll work mostly with the disassembly produced by DEBUG. That will give us an education in how to snoop around inside programs.

THE PRINT-SCREEN ROUTINE

Our object lesson will be the ROM-BIOS program that performs the print-screen service when we press the PrtSc key combination—the Fn key, followed by P. Before we dig into it, some background information would be useful—in fact, this information will give you many clues to understanding how Junior is organized and how its ROM-BIOS works.

Part of the ROM-BIOS has the job of looking after the keyboard. These programs detect when we press and release keys, and they keep track of anything special, such as combinations of shift keys and other keys. The keyboard routines are also charged with the responsibility of detecting anything really special in keyboard actions. Two examples are the Ctrl-Alt-Del combination, which "reboots" the computer, and the Fn-P combination, which generates the PrtSc key-code. When the keyboard routines detect the Fn-P key combination, they activate the print-screen service.

Wisely, the print-screen service was not made a part of the keyboard routines. Instead, it is a completely separate routine activated by interrupt number 5. This makes it possible for any program to request a print-screen operation simply by generating interrupt 5.

What we'll be looking at in the print-screen routine has lots of goodies in it. It is an interrupt handler, so we get to see something of how interrupt handlers must work. It works with the display screen, since it must read the screen contents. It works with the printer, since it must write the information there. And it has to look for any trouble that comes up along the way. For a modestly sized program, the print-screen routine gives us lots of examples to look at. It's a good way for us to get our feet wet in machine language.

With that word of explanation out of the way, we're ready to begin. We'll use the listing in the PCjr *Technical Reference* manual to give us some guidance, but we'll actually be working with a disassembly listing produced by DEBUG. Figure 7-1 shows the whole DEBUG process. We will be going over it line-by-line in the text, but you can use Figure 7-1 to see the complete picture. If you want you can follow along in the *Technical Reference* manual.

PRINTING A COPY
OF THE DISASSEMBLY

If you are going to do this disassembly on your own PCjr, you should know that DEBUG spits out all of its information to the display screen. You can get a printed copy of the display by activating the echo feature, which you do by

```
DEBUG
-U F000:FF54 L 77
F000:FF54 FB            STI
F000:FF55 1E            PUSH        DS
F000:FF56 50            PUSH        AX
F000:FF57 53            PUSH        BX
F000:FF58 51            PUSH        CX
F000:FF59 52            PUSH        DX
F000:FF5A B85000        MOV         AX,0050
F000:FF5D 8ED8          MOV         DS,AX
F000:FF5F 803E000001    CMP         BYTE PTR [0000],01
F000:FF64 745F          JZ          FFC5
F000:FF66 C606000001    MOV         BYTE PTR [0000],01
F000:FF6B B40F          MOV         AH,0F
F000:FF6D CD10          INT         10
F000:FF6F 8ACC          MOV         CL,AH
F000:FF71 B519          MOV         CH,19
F000:FF73 E8E9FA        CALL        FA5F
F000:FF76 51            PUSH        CX
F000:FF77 B403          MOV         AH,03
F000:FF79 CD10          INT         10
F000:FF7B 59            POP         CX
F000:FF7C 52            PUSH        DX
F000:FF7D 33D2          XOR         DX,DX
F000:FF7F B402          MOV         AH,02
F000:FF81 CD10          INT         10
F000:FF83 B408          MOV         AH,08
F000:FF85 CD10          INT         10
F000:FF87 0AC0          OR          AL,AL
F000:FF89 7502          JNZ         FF8D
F000:FF8B B020          MOV         AL,20
F000:FF8D 52            PUSH        DX
F000:FF8E 33D2          XOR         DX,DX
F000:FF90 32E4          XOR         AH,AH
F000:FF92 CD17          INT         17
F000:FF94 5A            POP         DX
F000:FF95 F6C429        TEST        AH,29
F000:FF98 7521          JNZ         FFBB
F000:FF9A FEC2          INC         DL
F000:FF9C 3ACA          CMP         CL,DL
F000:FF9E 75DF          JNZ         FF7F
F000:FFA0 32D2          XOR         DL,DL
F000:FFA2 8AE2          MOV         AH,DL
F000:FFA4 52            PUSH        DX
```

(continued)

Figure 7-1. The print-screen routine disassembly listing

```
F000:FFA5 E8B7FA        CALL        FA5F
F000:FFA8 5A            POP         DX
F000:FFA9 FEC6          INC         DH
F000:FFAB 3AEE          CMP         CH,DH
F000:FFAD 75D0          JNZ         FF7F
F000:FFAF 5A            POP         DX
F000:FFB0 B402          MOV         AH,02
F000:FFB2 CD10          INT         10
F000:FFB4 C606000000    MOV         BYTE PTR [0000],00
F000:FFB9 EB0A          JMP         FFC5
F000:FFBB 5A            POP         DX
F000:FFBC B402          MOV         AH,02
F000:FFBE CD10          INT         10
F000:FFC0 C6060000FF    MOV         BYTE PTR [0000],FF
F000:FFC5 5A            POP         DX
F000:FFC6 59            POP         CX
F000:FFC7 5B            POP         BX
F000:FFC8 58            POP         AX
F000:FFC9 1F            POP         DS
F000:FFCA CF            IRET
-Q
```

Figure 7-1. The print-screen routine disassembly listing
(continued)

pressing the Fn-E key combination. You can also capture the results of
DEBUG by using DOS's redirection feature (see your DOS manual for details).
The listing you see in Figure 7-1 was captured this way.

WHAT TO EXPECT
FROM A DISASSEMBLY

Before we go any further, let's quickly outline what we'll see in the
disassembly that DEBUG will give us. Each line of the listing corresponds to
one machine-language instruction, and each line tells us several different
things. The part farthest to the left, which shows numbers like F000:FF54,
gives the actual address location of the instruction in segmented-address
format. The F000: part, remember, is the segment, and the FF54 part is the
offset. The next thing that appears is the actual machine-language coding in
hexadecimal—for example, FB. Since instructions vary in length, we'll see

varying amounts of hex data here. The first instruction that will appear, FB, takes only one byte; eight lines down, another instruction, 803E000001, is five bytes long.

After the hex form of the instruction, we see the disassembled, symbolic form of the instruction; this is the part that can be read and understood by those who are familiar with 8088 assembly language. Each instruction starts with its name, which is the operation to be performed, such as STI (set interrupt flag), PUSH, and MOV (short for move). These names represent the machine-language instructions, commonly called *opcodes* (for operation codes), that actually perform the operations.

Some instructions, like STI, stand by themselves, but most need one or more parameters, or *operands*. For example, in the instruction PUSH DS, the DS register is the operand. Many instructions take two operands; MOV, which moves (actually copies) data from one place to another, is one of these. According to assembly-language convention, an action takes place from right to left, so that MOV AX,BX moves, or rather copies, the contents of the BX register into the AX register, and not the other way around. Likewise, ADD AX,BX would add the contents of BX into AX, leaving the sum there, in AX, rather than the other way around.

With this brief introduction to reading assembly listings, we can now dive in and see what is going on. If you are new at this, don't be put off—just following along, even if you don't understand a lot of the material, will teach you a great deal about 8088 machine language and about how assembly language is written.

We begin the process by loading DOS into the PCjr. When DOS gives us its A> prompt, we start up DEBUG by typing the command:

```
A>
```

DEBUG will tell us when it is ready for a command by giving us its very terse prompt, a hyphen:

```
-
```

We then give it a disassemble command:

```
-U F000:FF54 L 77
```

Unless you are already familiar with DEBUG, this command will be quite cryptic to you. Let's go over it piece by piece. The letter U is the command to *U*nassemble (D for disassemble couldn't be used because DEBUG uses D for something else). The F000:FF54 part tells DEBUG the segmented address in memory where we want it to begin disassembling. We found out where this address was by looking in the *Technical Reference* manual, but we could also have gotten it, with a little detective work, by looking at the interrupt vector table for the address of interrupt 5. The last part of this command, L 77, tells DEBUG how much we want disassembled. Again, the *Technical Reference* manual provided us with this information, but if we had not had its help, we could have just disassembled an arbitrary amount and then snooped around until we found all we needed.

Everything else in Figure 7-1, except for the very last line, is the output of this disassemble command. When DEBUG is through disassembling, it gives us its hyphen prompt:

    -

and we respond with the Q command:

    -Q

telling DEBUG to quit and pass control back to DOS.

With that out of the way, let's plunge into the assembly code for the print-screen routine. Don't worry if you don't understand everything—we're going into the deep end of the pool here.

STEP-BY-STEP THROUGH
THE PRINT-SCREEN

The first disassembly instruction is:

    F000:FF54 FB   STI

which is the instruction to activate the interrupts. You'll recall that some programs, especially interrupt handlers, sometimes have to suspend interrupts temporarily. To make sure that interrupts don't interfere with each other, each interrupt that takes place automatically disables any further interrupts, so that the interrupt-handling routine can get to work without being harassed by another interrupt. Since our program here is the interrupt handler for interrupt number 5 (the print-screen interrupt), further interrupts have been suspended. The print-screen routine doesn't need to do anything that can't be interrupted, however, so the very first thing it does is turn the other interrupts back on. Even if there were some work that needed to be done with interrupts disabled, this STI would still be among the first few instructions.

The next thing to do is save any register values that ought to be preserved. The stack is used for saving old register values, so we use the PUSH command to put them onto the stack. The PUSH instruction takes whatever we specify (in this case, the contents of a register), copies its value onto the stack, and then moves the SP (stack pointer) register along, ready for the next item to be pushed. Here are the contents of five registers being pushed onto the stack:

```
F000:FF55 1E          PUSH          DS
F000:FF56 50          PUSH          AX
F000:FF57 53          PUSH          BX
F000:FF58 51          PUSH          CX
F000:FF59 52          PUSH          DX
```

All programs follow certain rules about which registers can be used freely and which ones must be safeguarded, either by being left alone or by being preserved on (and later restored from) the stack. We don't know the complete rules used in the ROM-BIOS programs, but we shouldn't be surprised to see this program saving the contents of a bunch of registers. In this case, the values in the four general-purpose registers, AX through DX, and in the DS (data segment) register are being saved. This is interesting and suggests that the program will monkey around with the DS register; we'll watch for it.

Moving on, we find two instructions that set up a new DS register value:

```
F000:FF5A B85000      MOV           AX,0050
F000:FF5D 8ED8        MOV           DS,AX
```

The hex number 50 (80 in decimal) is moved to the AX register and then passed on to the DS register. A number must be put into the DS register in this indirect way because there is no instruction to move a constant into the segment registers. (It is not a common operation.) So these two instructions are used to do what we really want, which would (if it were possible) be an instruction such as MOV DS,0050.

Why is the program putting hex 50 into the DS register? Knowing how the 8088 works, we can partly answer that question right away: This program will be working with some data located in the vicinity of segment paragraph hex 50 or absolute memory location hex 500 in low memory.

Studying the *Technical Reference* manual reveals that the ROM-BIOS uses some space at segment paragraph hex 40 for most of its working storage. But, for no reason that I know of, the print-screen routine happens to use one byte located at segment paragraph hex 50 for its working storage. So, the basic answer to why hex 50 is being loaded into the DS register is that this program locates its data there. If you ask, "Why there?" the answer is that the designers of the IBM personal computers chose that location.

What is the print-screen routine using this data area for? If we needed to, we could study the program in detail and probably figure it out; that's the sort of thing you do if you are disassembling a program without a listing to guide you. But fortunately we aren't flying blind—we have the comments in the *Technical Reference* manual to tell us that this print-screen program uses one byte located at segment paragraph hex 50 to signal the status of screen printing. If the byte is 0, nothing is going on; if it is set to 1, a print-screen routine is already in progress; if the byte's value is 255 (hex FF), there has been an error of some kind.

So what has the program done so far? It has turned interrupts back on, saved the values from five registers in the stack so that it can safely modify the registers, and set up the DS register to point to where its data are.

Now the routine is ready to proceed to the next step, which is to check whether it is in the middle of a previous print-screen routine. If so, the program assumes that a nudgy person is sitting at the keyboard and has pressed Fn-P, or PrtSc, twice. In that case, the program ignores the new request. How does it do this? It compares (CMP) the hex 50 data byte value to 1:

```
F000:FF5F 803E000001     CMP          BYTE PTR [0000],01
```

(The part that reads BYTE PTR [0000] is just assembler technical talk that says we are comparing one byte located at an offset of 0.)

After comparing that byte with the value 1, the computer jumps to another part of the program if the comparison is equal (JZ means jump if equal or zero):

```
F000:FF64 745F           JZ           FFC5
```

All that this disassembly tells us is that the jump is to location FFC5. Later, we'll learn that this is the location of the finishing steps of this program. So these two instructions logically translate into, "If the control byte is 1 (meaning that printing is already in progress) then jump to the exit steps."

If printing was not already in progress, the program needs to indicate that it is now. So the next instruction is to move a 1 into the hex 50 data byte:

```
F000:FF66 C606000001     MOV          BYTE PTR [0000],01
```

Now the program is going to read everything off the screen and copy it to the printer. To read the screen, it needs to know what the size of the screen is, since our PCjr could show either 40 or 80 columns of information, depending on its screen format. So the next step is to call one of the screen services to get the screen mode. Video service 15 (hex F) requests the screen mode and interrupt 16 (hex 10) activates the video services, so service number hex F is requested like this:

```
F000:FF6B B40F           MOV          AH,0F
```

and interrupt hex 10 is generated like this:

```
F000:FF6D CD10           INT          10
```

This puts the number of screen columns (40 or 80) into the AH register. (H and L, remember are the high and low halves of each full X register.) The value in AH is then moved to the CL register:

```
F000:FF6F 8ACC          MOV           CL,AH
```

and the number of rows on the screen, which is always 25 (hex 19) rows, is moved into the CH register:

```
F000:FF71 B519          MOV           CH,19
```

There is still some more preparation to do. This program has a subroutine that is used at the end of each line to give the printer the proper end-of-line signals, which are a carriage-return signal followed by a line-feed signal. (Those two together are the standard end-of-line signals.) I happened to learn what that subroutine does by looking it up in the *Technical Reference* manual; but, if we had to, we could discover what it does by using the U command to disassemble it. The next instruction in our print-screen disassembly calls that subroutine:

```
F000:FF73 E8E9FA        CALL          FA5F
```

Next, there is still more preparation. While the computer is reading the information off the screen, it is moving the cursor around. It needs to save the current cursor position, so that it can be restored when the program is done. This is the sort of attention to detail that separates good programs from bad. The program does it this way: First, it saves the row and column numbers that were stored in the CL and CH halves of the CX register, because even though you do not see it yet, CX will be disturbed by the service that reports the cursor's position:

```
F000:FF76 51            PUSH          CX
```

After saving CX on the stack, it prepares to request video service number 3, which reports the cursor position:

```
F000:FF77 B403          MOV           AH,03
```

and generates a video interrupt hex 10:

```
F000:FF79 CD10          INT           10
```

It then recovers the CX value from the stack:

```
F000:FF7B 59            POP           CX
```

and pushes the cursor position, which was placed into the DX register by the video service, onto the stack to save it:

```
F000:FF7C 52              PUSH         DX
```

Now there is only one more small bit of preparation left. The computer is going to loop through the entire screen, every column in every row, reading all the information written there. Naturally, it has to start at the top, so the program moves the cursor there. The top of the screen is row 0, column 0; so the DX register is set to 0, using the old programmer's trick for zeroing a register by exclusive-ORing it to itself:

```
F000:FF7D 33D2            XOR          DX,DX
```

This instruction is the same as moving 0 into DX, but is a more compact way of doing it.

Now, at last, everything is ready for the main part of the work. The computer will be looping through the entire screen, moving the cursor to the next position, reading what is stored at that position, sending it to the printer, and then moving the cursor on to the next position, until it has covered the entire screen.

So, the program begins its main working loop. How do we know that the next step is the start of a loop? We would not know from what we have seen so far, although we would discover it later when the program jumps back to this point. Again, looking at the remarks in the PCjr *Technical Reference* manual helps us realize that this is the beginning of the loop.

The first working action is to move the cursor to its next location. The first time the computer comes to this instruction, that location would be row 0 and column 0, which has already been set; later, when the loop is repeated, the cursor position will be the next position on the screen. To move the cursor, the program prepares to request video service number 2:

```
F000:FF7F B402            MOV          AH,02
```

and generates the video interrupt hex 10:

```
F000:FF81 CD10            INT          10
```

Next, another video service is called upon. This one, service number 8, asks that a character be read off the screen. Service number 8 is moved into the AH register:

```
F000:FF83 B408            MOV          AH,08
```

and another video interrupt is generated:

```
F000:FF85 CD10            INT          10
```

Again, even though you do not see it happen, this service loads the character from the screen into register AL, which is where the program will look for it.

Now, the screen might have any kind of information on it. If nothing is in the present cursor position, the fact will be reported as a hex 0 character. In that case, we want the printer to print a blank space corresponding to the space on the screen. But the printer won't print a hex 0 character as a space, so the next thing our program does is check for a hex 0, and changes it to a blank space (which is coded in ASCII as hex 20). First it tests the character loaded into the AL register with an OR (which amounts to a kind of true/false test to see if the character equals 0):

```
F000:FF87 0AC0          OR          AL,AL
```

Then, if the character is not hex 0, the program jumps over the next instruction (JNZ means jump if not zero):

```
F000:FF89 7502          JNZ         FF8D
```

If the character *is* hex 0, the next instruction moves a hex 20, a blank space, into register AL:

```
F000:FF8B B020          MOV         AL,20
```

Next, the computer needs to send the screen character out to the printer. This involves a little setup work. As before, the cursor row and column position in the DX register is saved on the stack, since the DX register will be used while printing:

```
F000:FF8D 52            PUSH        DX
```

Then, the program indicates that we want the regular printer by setting the DX register to 0:

```
F000:FF8E 33D2          XOR         DX,DX
```

Next, printer service number 0, the service to print one character, is requested by setting the AH register to 0:

```
F000:FF90 32E4          XOR         AH,AH
```

and the printer service is activated with an interrupt 23 (hex 17), which is similar to the video interrupt, but another interrupt number:

```
F000:FF92 CD17          INT         17
```

After the character is printed, the cursor row and column position, which was saved on the stack, is moved back into register DX:

```
F000:FF94 5A              POP          DX
```

At this point, though, the program doesn't really know whether all went well with the printer. Since the printer services return an error code to the AH register, the returned code is tested against a *mask*, which blanks out everything except the bits of the return code that the program is interested in. The right mask for this test—although you and I don't have any way of knowing it at this point—happens to be hex 29.

```
F000:FF95 F6C429          TEST         AH,29
```

If all the bits the program can see are zero, then all has gone well and the character has been printed. If they are not all zero, the computer jumps (JNZ or jump if not zero) to another part of the program, which turns out to be an error-handling routine:

```
F000:FF98 7521            JNZ          FFBB
```

However, if there is no error, the program proceeds to the next position on the screen. The screen column number in the DL register is incremented by one:

```
F000:FF9A FEC2            INC          DL
```

and the incremented value is compared to the maximum number of columns in the row (the value we are holding in the CL register):

```
F000:FF9C 3ACA            CMP          CL,DL
```

If we haven't come to the end of this row, the program jumps back to the beginning of its working loop:

```
F000:FF9E 75DF            JNZ          FF7F
```

This jump-if-not-zero jumps to location FF7F. You will see, if you look back, that this is the location of the top of the loop.

On the other hand, if we have come to the last column of a row, the computer needs to skip down to the beginning of the next row. First, the column number in the DL register is reset to 0:

```
F000:FFA0 32D2            XOR          DL,DL
```

and AH is also set to 0 (I'm not sure why, but we'll ignore it for now):

```
F000:FFA2 8AE2            MOV          AH,DL
```

In addition, since we've come to the end of a line, the computer needs to send an end-of-line signal to the printer. The cursor position in the DX register is temporarily saved on the stack:

```
F000:FFA4 52              PUSH       DX
```

and the program calls the subroutine that, as we already mentioned, is used for end-of-line:

```
F000:FFA5 E8B7FA          CALL       FA5F
```

It finishes by restoring the DX value from the stack:

```
F000:FFA8 5A              POP        DX
```

Since it is starting a new line, the program has to increment the screen row number stored in the DH register (just as we did before with the column):

```
F000:FFA9 FEC6            INC        DH
```

and it then tests the incremented row against the value stored in the CH register to see if it has come to the end of the screen (again, just as we did for the column):

```
F000:FFAB 3AEE            CMP        CH,DH
```

If it is not at the end, it jumps back to the top of the loop:

```
F000:FFAD 75D0            JNZ        FF7F
```

And on it goes, around and around, until it has covered the entire screen. At the point when the program doesn't jump back, it is at the end of its duties. It is time to clean up after itself. Recall that the original cursor location was saved on the stack. This location is now recovered into the DX register so that the cursor can be repositioned at its place on the screen at the start of the program:

```
F000:FFAF 5A              POP        DX
```

We prepare to ask for video service number 2, which moves the cursor:

```
F000:FFB0 B402            MOV        AH,02
```

and we then invoke the video interrupt, hex 10:

```
F000:FFB2 CD10            INT        10
```

For the next piece of housekeeping, the program needs to set the control byte at segment paragraph hex 50 to indicate that the print-screen routine is finished. Recall that at the beginning of the program, this byte was set to 1. Now, it is reset to 0:

```
F000:FFB4 C606000000    MOV         BYTE PTR [0000],00
```

Next, the program jumps over some instructions that will turn out to be the error handler for printer errors:

```
F000:FFB9 EB0A          JMP         FFC5
```

Remember that while going through its loop, the program tested for a printer-error code and if there was one, jumped to location FFBB. This is the location of the next instruction. First the cursor position is recovered from the stack just as before:

```
F000:FFBB 5A            POP         DX
F000:FFBC B402          MOV         AH,02
F000:FFBE CD10          INT         10
```

and then the control byte is set to the error code, hex FF:

```
F000:FFC0 C6060000FF    MOV         BYTE PTR [0000],FF
```

Next comes the program's exit routine. This is the routine that the program jumped to at the very beginning if it found that a print-screen was already in progress. It is also the place it jumped to when skipping over the error handler. This exit routine has the job of restoring the registers that were saved at the very beginning of the program. When the contents of the five registers were pushed onto the stack, it didn't matter what order they were pushed in; any order would have saved them equally well. Now that it is time to restore the registers, they have to be popped back in exactly the reverse order, since the stack works on a last-in, first-out basis. So the program does five pops, like the five pushes:

```
F000:FFC5 5A            POP         DX
F000:FFC6 59            POP         CX
F000:FFC7 5B            POP         BX
F000:FFC8 58            POP         AX
F000:FFC9 1F            POP         DS
```

Finally, as the very last step of the routine, the program returns the computer to whatever it was doing before the print-screen interrupt was requested. This is done with a special interrupt-return instruction:

```
F000:FFCA CF            IRET
```

and that completes the work of the print-screen program.

Going over this program has taken some time, but it should give you quite a bit of insight into what assembly-language coding is like and how registers work. As you have seen, the details can be very tedious, and this is why assembly language is usually avoided unless really necessary. You have also had a chance to see how all sorts of instructions are used, how a subroutine is called, how other interrupt services are invoked, and how logical tests and branches are performed, as well as how a loop can be used. That's quite a lot, for such a quick tour through assembly language.

SOME OTHER THINGS TO LOOK AT

There are other interesting things in ROM that you can explore when you have a little time. For example, one interesting thing to check is the ROM-BIOS release marker. IBM wisely marks each version of the ROM-BIOS for its personal computers with a date indicator that will tell us which version is installed in any IBM personal computer. Here are the commands to get DEBUG to show us the release marker and DEBUG's response:

```
A>DEBUG
-D F000:FFF5 L 8
F000:FFF5 30 36 2F-30 31 2F 38 33        06/01/83
-Q
```

This display shows the date, 06/01/83, of the very first IBM PCjr ROM-BIOS. If you perform this operation on your own PCjr, you'll find which BIOS date you have; it might be a later revision. The release markers are always put at segmented address F000:FFF5, which is the location we asked DEBUG to display. If it mattered, we could have our programs routinely inspect this area for a particular date. For example, if a program only worked properly with a particular version of ROM-BIOS, we would want the program to check the BIOS date indicator to make sure it was working with the right one.

For your own information, the original PC's ROM-BIOS was dated 04/24/81 and a revision was released on 10/19/81. The XT was released with a marker of 11/08/82, and the replacement ROM-BIOS that is used when an IBM fixed disk is added to a PC is marked 10/27/82. There is not a whole lot of significance to these revisions and revision dates, but they are interesting to know about. And if IBM ever goofs up and gives us an error-ridden ROM-BIOS (which is very unlikely, indeed), we now know how to find out if we have the original ROM, or a later replacement.

We can use DEBUG to do all sorts of looking around in the ROM. For example, we can hunt through the ROM-BASIC and display its messages, or we can disassemble its code to figure out how parts of it work. If we start DEBUG like this:

```
A>DEBUG
```

and then ask it to display data from the beginning of the ROM-BASIC, like this:

```
-D F600:0000
```

it will show us the contents of the first location where ROM-BASIC is stored. If we repeatedly key in the D command, DEBUG will show us succeeding chunks of memory, without our having to specify the addresses we want to see. If we keep at it for a while, we'll run across the error messages that are incorporated into BASIC. While knowing about these messages isn't particularly useful, it still is interesting to poke around and explore them. The skills that we acquire this way come in handy later if we have to do some patching or advanced debugging of programs.

8
CONNECTING WITH THE CARTRIDGES

The cartridges for the PCjr work in a very simple way: If they're there, they're there; if they're not, they're not. It is simple, quick, and efficient for programs to check for, test and use cartridges.

Unlike the diskette drive, which reports an error when you try to use it without having first inserted a diskette, the cartridge slots simply accept read only memory on cartridges that plug into one or another of the four predefined memory locations.

The job of seeing whether a cartridge is present and of checking it out falls to the software that looks at the cartridges. While it can take a while for a diskette drive to signal that no diskette is inserted, checking for cartridges takes place at the speed of a few 8088 instructions.

When a cartridge is plugged in, the data that are stored in the cartridge's ROM are directly present in its part of the PCjr's memory map. All Junior needs to do to check for a cartridge is to read from those memory locations. If there is a program to be run on a cartridge, our PCjr can pass control to the program, just as it would to any other program.

Programs on cartridges are stored in ROM and must use part of Junior's memory for their stack and other working storage—but this is quite normal business. After all, the segmented-address architecture of the 8088 is set up to have programs, data, and stack all independently located, each under the control of its own segment register. The ROM-BIOS and ROM-BASIC each operate in ROM, so there is nothing difficult about making games and other programs work this way as well.

For cartridges to be used successfully, there have to be some conventions about how they are marked and their contents indicated. In the next section we'll take a look at how this is done.

CARTRIDGE LAYOUT

There is a standard coding called a *header* at the beginning of each cartridge, so that it can be recognized and its features made known. The header starts with a 2-byte *signature*, hex 55AA; if it's found at a cartridge memory location, that tells the computer that a cartridge is present. Hex 55AA seems to be used by IBM for many similar purposes. For example, the special ROM-BIOS used by the IBM fixed disk system contains the same signature, and the boot record on disks ends with this signature.

After the 2-byte signature comes a 1-byte size indicator that tells the computer in units of 512 bytes, or ½K, how much memory there is in the cartridge. While the maximum memory size of a PCjr cartridge is 64K, this coding scheme allows for sizes up to 256 times 512 bytes (½K), or 128K. In practice, you'll find that the cartridges have a multiple of 2K bytes, so this size code will be some multiple of four (four times ½K equals 2K bytes).

The fourth through sixth bytes of the header are set aside for a 3-byte jump instruction. This jump instruction is used to allow the cartridge to participate in the computer's start-up process. Here is how it works. When the computer is started up, or *"booted,"* the bootstrap program in the ROM-BIOS checks the cartridge address locations for the cartridge signature. If a cartridge is found, then the ROM-BIOS uses the CALL instruction to pass control to the cartridge, so that the cartridge can do any *initialization* it wants to do.

The cartridge could do any of several things. One is that it could ignore the opportunity, and immediately return control, using the RET instruction, to the ROM-BIOS. Another possibility is that the cartridge could immediately take charge of the computer, and never return control to the ROM-BIOS; this approach can be used by game cartridges that control the computer directly, without the help of DOS. The third thing a cartridge might do is perform some initialization and then return control to the ROM-BIOS, which would then carry on with the bootstrap operation. The BASIC cartridge works this way for a very simple reason. When we boot our computers, if there is nothing to take charge of the computer, such as a DOS diskette or a game cartridge, the bootstrap program activates the ROM-BASIC program by using interrupt 24 (hex 18). This is all fine, except that when we have the BASIC cartridge plugged in, we'd rather use the cartridge BASIC, with all its features, instead of the ROM-BASIC, which has fewer features. To make this possible, the BASIC cartridge does one simple bit of initialization when it is given the opportunity: It replaces the interrupt hex 18 vector (which normally points to the ROM-BASIC), to point to the address of the BASIC inside the cartridge. This makes it possible for the BASIC cartridge to put itself in the place of the ROM-BASIC, and yet not interfere with the bootstrap process.

So, the reason why each cartridge has a 3-byte jump instruction at its beginning is to make these tricks possible. The jump instruction just passes control to whatever location inside the cartridge is the actual initialization program. Putting the jump at the beginning of the cartridge gives the bootstrap program a standard place to pass control, no matter where the actual working initialization program is.

By the way, recall that the PCjr is automatically restarted, or booted, whenever we insert or remove a cartridge. This makes sure that the computer has a chance to respond to any change in the cartridges, and that every cartridge gets a chance to do its initialization.

After these six beginning bytes comes a *table of the DOS command programs* on the cartridge. The table is very simple: There are as many entries as are needed, and there is no fixed limit to its size. The end of the table is marked by a zero byte after the last entry. Each entry in the table consists of one byte indicating the length of the name of the program, followed by the name of the program, which contains as many bytes as the length byte specified. The last part of the table entry is a 2-byte word that shows the offset of the command

Code	Meaning
Header:	
55AA	Signature
40	Length 64 * 512 = 32K bytes
E9 1D 00	Jump instruction to which the interrupt hex 18 vector points; in this case a jump to initialize BASIC
Table:	
05 BASIC E9 82 01	BASIC command program
06 BASICA E9 78 01	BASICA command program
00	End of table

Figure 8-1. Header and command-program table from the BASIC language cartridge

within the cartridge, which can be used to pass control to that particular command program.

A sample of the header and command-program table is shown in Figure 8-1.

One use of cartridges for the PCjr is to provide DOS commands right on tap. As you know, DOS comes with a large number of commands. Some are internal, meaning that they are kept in memory with the command interpreter, COMMAND.COM. All other commands are external; they must be found elsewhere, and customarily that means looking for them on the disk. But with the PCjr, DOS will quickly check any cartridge that is plugged in, and if the name of the requested command is in the cartridge's command-program table, DOS will use it immediately. The BASIC language cartridge contains two entries in its DOS command table, *BASIC* and *BASICA*, which are the names of the two original versions of BASIC on the IBM PC.

BASIC is set up to work with cartridge programs, so that games and other programs can be delivered in cartridge format. These are BASIC *program* cartridges, which are used with the BASIC *language* cartridge; be sure not to mix them up.

To keep from confusing DOS, BASIC program cartridges have the standard header for cartridges, with nothing in the table of DOS commands. There is one thing that is special about the header on BASIC program cartridges, so that BASIC can recognize them, but this special coding is incorporated into the standard format. Here is how it's done:

Three bytes are set aside in the cartridge header for a jump instruction to any initialization program that the cartridge has. BASIC program cartridges, and some other cartridges, don't have any initialization program, so instead of a jump instruction in these three bytes, the cartridges have a RET (return) instruction, as we mentioned before. This RET only takes up one byte, leaving the other two bytes unused. On a BASIC program cartridge, these two bytes are set to the signature code hex AA55; if BASIC finds that signature in these two bytes, it knows that the cartridge contains a BASIC program.

Following the cartridge header is the cartridge's program. On a BASIC program cartridge, that's a BASIC program in the same format as a BASIC program stored on a diskette. The program itself is stored in BASIC's compressed, or "tokenized," format, and the first byte indicates whether or not the program is protected, which keeps us from listing the program code. A protected program begins with hex FE, and an unprotected program begins with hex FF.

CARTRIDGE MEMORY LOCATIONS

We've just covered how the contents of a cartridge are coded. How about where they are located in memory? We'll discuss that in this section, and show you how the answer takes on a different look when we consider it from different perspectives.

As we've mentioned, it is the cartridge itself, and not the cartridge slot, that determines where in memory the cartridge's data appear. It doesn't matter

Code	Meaning
Header:	
55AA	Signature
XX	Length of this cartridge
CB	Return instruction
AA55	2nd signature, indicating BASIC program
00	End-of-table marker, indicating no DOS commands
Program:	
FE or FF	Is program protected or not?
XX YY XX	BASIC program in tokenized format

*Figure 8-2. Header and program from a
     BASIC program cartridge*

which slot we plug a cartridge into; the information inside the cartridge will appear in the same place in the computer's memory.

The coding of the cartridge's contents, which we just looked at, has nothing to do with specifying the cartridge's memory location. That is done with the hardware circuitry inside the cartridge. The PCjr's cartridges are designed to plug into any one of six different memory locations.

We mentioned when we covered Junior's memory that 128K of memory has been set aside for use by the cartridges, the combination of the two 64K blocks that are located at segment addresses D000 and E000. Just above that area is the 64K block, at segment address F000, where the PCjr's ROM-BIOS is located. The circuitry in Junior's cartridges is designed so that it can plug into memory at either the beginning or the middle of any of these three blocks. In the area that is set aside for ordinary cartridge use, the addresses would be any of these four:

D000 (beginning of D-block)
D800 (2nd half of D-block)
E000 (beginning of E-block)
E800 (2nd half of E-block)

As an example, the PCjr's BASIC language cartridge plugs into the E800 memory address, the highest of these four addresses.

Those four locations are where cartridges are normally supposed to appear. But a cartridge can also be addressed into the ROM-BIOS area, at either F000 or F800. When a cartridge is addressed into this ROM-BIOS area, it overrides the ROM-BIOS that is built into the computer. This makes it possible for a cartridge to change the computer's most fundamental programming, temporarily. The ordinary software cartridges that we buy for our PCjrs don't do this—they use the D and E memory addresses that are intended for software cartridges. But it is possible for a cartridge to use the ROM-BIOS's F-block of memory as well.

In the overall design of the IBM personal computers, the 128K of memory in the D and E address areas is set aside for cartridges, to be used in any way that is desired. While our Junior's specific circuit design only allows ordinary cartridges to appear at the four memory locations listed above, the general design for all the IBM personal computers is more flexible. The software that searches through memory to see if a cartridge is actually plugged in looks at other locations besides these four. In the next section, we'll show you a program that searches for cartridges; we will have it check more memory locations, to illustrate the idea.

MORE SNOOPING

In this section, we are going to show you how to do some exploring, snooping, poking around in the PCjr's cartridges. We'll create the BASIC program shown in its entirety in Figure 8-3. This program will enable us to explore any cartridge and find out what is in it. I could just give this to you as a program listing that you could key in and use. However, instead, I'm going to talk you through its development to help you understand what is going on, and to demonstrate good, structured BASIC programming.

```
1000 ' cartridge exploration program
1010 ' from Exploring the IBM PCjr Home Computer
1020 ' authored by Peter Norton, 1983
1100 '
1110 ' main program outline
1120 '
1130 GOSUB 2000                       ' initialize
1140 FOR CARTRIDGE = 1 TO 2           ' loop thru both
1150    GOSUB 3000                    ' check cartridge
1160 NEXT CARTRIDGE
1170 GOSUB 4000                       ' finish up

2000 '
2010 ' initialization subroutine
2020 '
2030 KEY OFF
2040 CLS
2050 PRINT "Cartridge exploration program"
2060 PRINT
2070 TRUE = 1                         ' a handy name
2080 FALSE = 0                        ' a handy name
2090 RETURN

3000 '
3010 ' check out one cartridge
3020 '
3030 PRINT
3040 PRINT "Checking cartridge number ";CARTRIDGE
3050 BASE.SEG = &HE000 - &H1000 * (CARTRIDGE - 1)
3060 ' loop thru every 1K boundary in the area
3070 FOR K = 0 TO 63
3080    DEF SEG = BASE.SEG + K * 64
```

(continued)

Figure 8-3. A program to check the contents of a PCjr cartridge

```
3090    GOSUB  5000         ' check for signature
3100    IF SIGNATURE GOTO 3140     ' if found, good
3110 NEXT K
3120 PRINT "No cartridge signature was found."
3130 RETURN
3140 PRINT "A cartridge is in this slot with ";
3150 PRINT PEEK (2) / 2;"K bytes of memory."
3160 OFFSET = 6
3170 LIST.COUNT = 0
3180 PRINT "These commands are on this cartridge:"
3190 WHILE PEEK (OFFSET) > 0
3200    NAME.LENGTH = PEEK (OFFSET)
3210    OFFSET = OFFSET + 1
3220    LIST.COUNT = LIST.COUNT + 1
3230    ' if ok, skip over error handling
3240    IF NAME.LENGTH < 20 THEN 3270
3250    PRINT "Cartridge not coded as expected."
3260    RETURN
3270    PRINT " ";
3280    WHILE NAME.LENGTH >0
3290      PRINT CHR$ (PEEK (OFFSET));
3300      OFFSET = OFFSET + 1
3310      NAME.LENGTH = NAME.LENGTH - 1
3320    WEND
3330    PRINT
3340    OFFSET = OFFSET + 3         ' skip past jump
3350 WEND
3360 PRINT LIST.COUNT;" commands were found."
3370 RETURN

4000 '
4010 ' finish up subroutine
4020 '
4030 PRINT
4040 PRINT "End of the exploration program."
4050 PRINT
4060 PRINT "Press 'B' to return to BASIC,"
4070 PRINT "or any other key to return to DOS."
4080 ' wait for keystroke
4090 IKEY$ = INKEY$
4100 IF IKEY$ = "" GOTO 4090
```

(continued)

*Figure 8-3. A program to check the contents of
a PCjr cartridge (continued)*

```
4110 IF (IKEY$ = "B") OR (IKEY$ = "b") GOTO 4150
4120 PRINT
4130 PRINT "Returning to DOS..."
4140 SYSTEM
4150 PRINT
4160 PRINT "Returning to BASIC..."

4170 END
5000 '
5010 ' check for 55AA signature
5020 '
5030 SIGNATURE = FALSE
5040 IF ((PEEK (0) = &H55) AND (PEEK (1) = &HAA))
     OR ((PEEK (0) = &HAA) AND (PEEK (1) = &H55))
     THEN SIGNATURE = TRUE
5050 RETURN
```

*Figure 8-3. A program to check the contents of
a PCjr cartridge (continued)*

First, let's look at the main outline of the program. One of the basic principles of *structured programming* is to write programs with simple, logical outlines, breaking the program down into *modules*. This approach takes a little extra time, but it makes programs more understandable and easier to write, debug, and improve. Here is our outline:

```
1110 ' main program outline
1120 '
1130 GOSUB 2000                    ' initialize
1140 FOR CARTRIDGE = 1 TO 2        ' loop thru both
1150   GOSUB 3000                  ' check cartridge
1160 NEXT CARTRIDGE
1170 GOSUB 4000                    ' finish up
```

To get the housekeeping out of the way, we'll take care of initialization (the subroutine at line 2000) and clean-up (the subroutine at line 4000) first. These routines can be anything we want.

Initializing

A natural thing to do is to start by clearing the screen, announcing what we are going to do, and setting up true and false variables, to help make the program clearer.

```
2000 '
2010 ' initialization subroutine
2020 '
2030 KEY OFF
2040 CLS
2050 PRINT "Cartridge exploration program"
2060 PRINT
2070 TRUE = 1                    ' a handy name
2080 FALSE = 0                   ' a handy name
2090 RETURN
```

Cleaning Up

A good way to finish up is to give the program's user a choice of going to command-level BASIC or to DOS, so we end like this:

```
4000 '
4010 ' finish up subroutine
4020 '
4030 PRINT
4040 PRINT "End of the exploration program."
4050 PRINT
4060 PRINT "Press 'B' to return to BASIC,"
4070 PRINT "or any other key to return to DOS."
4080 ' wait for keystroke
4090 IKEY$ = INKEY$
4100 IF IKEY$ = "" GOTO 4090
4110 IF (IKEY$ = "B") OR (IKEY$ = "b") GOTO 4150
4120 PRINT
4130 PRINT "Returning to DOS..."
4140 SYSTEM
4150 PRINT
4160 PRINT "Returning to BASIC..."
4170 END
```

Checking for a Cartridge

Our next task is to build the 3000 subroutine, which will explore one of the cartridges. We begin by reporting what we are doing and by calculating the segment address of the memory block where a cartridge should be located.

```
3000 '
3010 ' check out one cartridge
3020 '
3030 PRINT
3040 PRINT "Checking cartridge number ";CARTRIDGE
3050 BASE.SEG = &HE000 - &H1000 * (CARTRIDGE - 1)
```

We use the formula in line 3050 because we want to be able to use this subroutine to check for both cartridges. Had we only wanted to check for the one located at segment address E000, we could simply have said BASE.SEG = &HE000.

Next we check for the signature, hex 55AA. We'll need to do this several times so we might as well make it a subroutine. We'll make the subroutine *tolerant,* that is, have it accept either a signature of 55AA or of AA55. (Signatures have been known to get mixed up, partly because the 8088 stores words in memory "backward," so that what we would write as 1122, it stores as 2211.) Also, we need to search within the 64K block set aside for the cartridge, to see exactly where it is. Here is how we do it:

```
3060 ' loop thru every 1K boundary in the area
3070 FOR K = 0 TO 63
3080    DEF SEG = BASE.SEG + K * 64
3090    GOSUB 5000                    ' check for signature
3100    IF SIGNATURE GOTO 3140    ' if found, good
3110 NEXT K
3120 PRINT "No cartridge signature was found."
3130 RETURN
3140 PRINT "A cartridge is in this slot with ";
3150 PRINT PEEK (2) / 2;"K bytes of memory."
```

This PEEK command tells the computer to look at the size-code byte located at the offset address 2 and, since the size code represents how many units of 512 bytes (½K) of memory there are, to divide the size code by two to get the number of K in the cartridge.

Here is the subroutine called in line 3090 to test for the signature. If the right signature is found, the presence of a cartridge in the first slot and its size is announced; if it is not found, the program will return to line 1150 and test for a signature in the next cartridge slot.

```
5000 '
5010 ' check for 55AA signature
5020 '
5030 SIGNATURE = FALSE
5040 IF ((PEEK (0) = &H55) AND (PEEK (1) = &HAA))
     OR ((PEEK (0) = &HAA) AND (PEEK (1) = &H55))
     THEN SIGNATURE = TRUE
5050 RETURN
```

Checking the Contents of the Cartridge

If we find a cartridge, we search for the two possible things that might follow the cartridge header: the table of any command programs and the

101

identifying signatures of any BASIC programs. We set the offset we are going to use for our next PEEK instruction past the signature and other header bytes to the seventh byte (which, since we address the bytes starting with offset 0, is offset 6), where the length of the command name is stored. We then set a counter, LIST.COUNT, to 0 so that we can use it to count the number of commands in this particular cartridge's command table.

```
3160 OFFSET = 6
3170 LIST.COUNT = 0
3180 PRINT "These commands are on this cartridge:"
```

and then we start searching. The table (even if there is nothing in it) ends with a zero byte, so our search will be a WHILE loop checking for that end mark:

```
3190 WHILE PEEK (OFFSET) > 0
```

Then we take a look at the byte at offset 6 to get the length of the name of the command and set the variable NAME.LENGTH equal to the value of that byte. We also increment LIST.COUNT.

```
3200   NAME.LENGTH = PEEK (OFFSET)
3210   OFFSET = OFFSET + 1
3220   LIST.COUNT = LIST.COUNT + 1
```

For safety, we test for a reasonable length. In this case, a command name 20 bytes or longer would be considered unreasonable and would cause the program to return to line 1150 and start looking for another cartridge.

```
3230   ' if ok, skip over error handling
3240   IF NAME.LENGTH < 20 THEN 3270
3250   PRINT "Cartridge not coded as expected."
3260   RETURN
```

If the name length is reasonable, the name of the command is printed one character at a time and the jump instruction then moves the program to the next entry in the table.

```
3270   PRINT " ";
3280   WHILE NAME.LENGTH > 0
3290     PRINT CHR$ (PEEK (OFFSET));
3300     OFFSET = OFFSET + 1
3310     NAME.LENGTH = NAME.LENGTH - 1
3320   WEND
3330   PRINT
3340   OFFSET = OFFSET + 3        ' skip past jump
```

When the end-of-table zero byte is encountered, the program exits the loop through the command names and prints out the number of commands in the table.

```
3350 WEND
3360 PRINT LIST.COUNT;" commands were found."
3370 RETURN
```

THE BASIC COMMAND CARTRIDGE

When we use this program to check out the PCjr's BASIC command cartridge, it reports two programs: BASIC and BASICA. Actually, there is only one program in the cartridge. Since the disk BASIC used on the IBM PC came in two versions, BASIC and BASICA (meaning Advanced BASIC), the PCjr cartridge needs to have both versions to maintain compatibility with the PC. In actual fact, though, the PCjr has only one BASIC program, which can be used under either name.

Oddly enough, this has undermined compatibility with the PC model in a very small way. In the original PC version, BASICA had a few features not found in BASIC. It is possible for programs to check to see if these features are working. (They do this by setting an ON ERROR trap and then trying to use any BASICA feature; if an error occurs, then BASIC, rather than BASICA, is in use.)

There is one extra program on the BASIC cartridge, the *TERM* program, which isn't visible in the cartridge's table of DOS commands. Large mainframe computers usually talk to many *terminals* of various types. One standard and relatively unsophisticated type is called an ASCII terminal, or "dumb" terminal (dumb because it has no sophisticated features). The TERM program in the BASIC cartridge makes the PCjr act like (emulate) an ASCII terminal, and many PCjr users who also work with mainframe computers will find TERM very useful. For some people, the features of TERM are almost worth the entire price of the PCjr itself.

The TERM program is activated by first getting to BASIC, and then entering the BASIC command TERM. What happens then is fascinating. The ASCII terminal emulation program, which is written in BASIC, is transferred from the cartridge to BASIC's working memory and then run, just as if we had LOADed it from diskette, or typed it in. The TERM program is written in BASIC so that it can make use of BASIC's abilities, and also so that we can use it even on an entry-model PCjr, without needing a diskette drive, or DOS. TERM is a little marvel, which we've been given as a bonus with the BASIC cartridge.

9
HIGHER EDUCATION: FUNDAMENTALS OF DOS

We pointed out earlier in this book that the computer's programs represent its education. Programs fall into two categories—*application programs*, such as an accounting program, and *system programs*, such as DOS.

Application programs are the computer's practical education, while system programs are the fundamental education a computer needs to be able to go into the world and do a job. These system programs come in various types and work at various levels.

As we have already pointed out, the ROM-BIOS programs that are built into the PCjr are the computer's elementary education—the foundation that the computer needs to be able to continue on to more sophisticated things. In the same vein, we can say, without stretching the analogy too far, that the cartridge programs we just covered are elective courses. Cartridges, particularly the BASIC cartridge, can supplement the elementary education, enriching Junior's capabilities—but they don't take the computer's education much further.

For the computer's higher education, we turn to *DOS*, the Microsoft® *Disk Operating System*, which provides the facilities needed to make the PCjr a complete working computer. With DOS to help it, Junior can use a spreadsheet program to become a skilled accountant, a word-processing program to become a writer, or a host of other application programs to acquire many different professional skills.

WHAT DOES DOS DO?

From the simplest point of view, the disk operating system is what we need to run our programs on the computer. Programs need an environment, an operating framework, to work in. The task of the disk operating system is to provide the framework, the working environment that programs need to get their work done.

Each individual program could, if necessary, take care of its environment by itself. But there are two major things wrong with that. First, the environmental needs of programs are pretty uniform and it would be a foolish duplication of effort for each program to include these facilities within itself. Second, we need to maintain some standards for the way programs operate, so that they can work together. This kind of continuity is especially important in disk formats; if each program were to use diskettes in its own unique way, then we wouldn't be able to pass data easily from one program to another. For example, a word-processing program might not be able to pass its information on to a spelling-checker program. Incompatibility is enough of a problem as it is; without a standard disk operating system like DOS, things would be a lot worse.

So what does a disk operating system, such as the PCjr's DOS, do to provide a standard environment for programs? Although we may not realize it when we are using DOS on our Juniors, the operating system does three main things for our programs: task management, memory management, and storage management.

Task Management

Task management is the job of controlling the actual execution, or use, of programs. For our DOS, this means loading our programs into memory and getting them started properly. In more sophisticated computers, task management also involves the complex job of keeping track of many programs that are running simultaneously. In the largest computers, the number of independent programs, or "tasks," can be in the hundreds or even thousands and in this case the job can become hair-raising indeed. For our DOS, however, only one program is running at a time, so the job of task management is much simpler.

Memory Management

The second main job of an operating system is *memory management*. The computer's memory is one of its most important resources, and it needs to be carefully husbanded and controlled. DOS takes care of this for us by choosing which parts of memory will hold our programs and by telling the programs how much memory they can use. As part of this memory management, DOS has the ability to give extra memory to programs that are running and to take it back, as needed. It can also reserve sections of memory for a program to use, even after the program seems to be finished, through a trick called "terminate but stay resident." We will talk more about programs that terminate but stay resident later in this chapter.

Storage Management

The third and most visible job for the disk operating system is *storage management*, the control of the data and storage space on our disks. Storage management itself breaks down into two main parts: file management and space management.

File management involves locating and using the data that we have in our disk files. When our programs open files, as with the OPEN statement in BASIC, it is the job of file management to find the files and keep track of them. When we read or write data to the files, file management takes care of that as well.

Closely related to file management is *space management*. Each diskette has a certain amount of usable storage space on it where the data in files can be kept. The job of space management is to make sure that nothing goes wrong with the space—that each file is kept separate, that none of the data in the files gets lost, and, as much as possible, that we do not run out of space when we are using a disk.

All of these jobs come together in the disk operating system, DOS. Some things happen actively, with DOS taking the initiative on what is to be done, and some things occur passively, with DOS simply providing a service that one of our programs has requested. Either way, DOS is responsible for managing the tasks, the memory, and the storage in our PCjr.

Let's now take a look at how the various system programs fit together. In the next two sections, we'll see these programs from two perspectives: how they are brought into the computer and set to work, and how they work together when they are in operation. We'll begin with how the parts work together.

BUILDING A PYRAMID

Like an acrobatic team building a human pyramid, DOS puts on its show by supporting one part on top of another. The very lowest part of the pyramid, the ROM-BIOS, is not really part of DOS at all, but is, as we have seen, a fundamental part of the design of the PCjr. DOS, or any other operating system, must start with the very basic services that the ROM-BIOS provides—the foundation that the operating system builds on.

First Level—the ROM-BIOS

The ROM-BIOS is a set of programs; literally, it is software. But in effect, the ROM-BIOS represents a transition between hardware and software; it bridges the gap between the computer's circuitry—the hardware—and its more conventional programs—the software. The ROM-BIOS may literally be software, but we will understand it best if we think of it as half software and half hardware, because it works so closely, so intimately, with the hardware. This is where the entire fabric of software for the PCjr begins. As the first and lowest layer of system software, the ROM-BIOS becomes the foundation and the first level of DOS's pyramid.

Second Level—the DOS-BIOS

The ROM-BIOS serves everyone, and therefore is tailored to no one. Any disk operating system can use the ROM-BIOS services as the starting point for its connection with the computer. Providing DOS with BIOS-type services tailored to its particular needs is the job of the next level of the operating system pyramid, the *DOS-BIOS*. While the ROM-BIOS is built into the computer, DOS-BIOS is stored on diskette, like the rest of DOS. The DOS-BIOS program adds extra features and control to the ROM-BIOS. It adapts the universal ROM-BIOS to provide what DOS needs in the way of BIOS services.

To give you an idea of what the DOS-BIOS does, let's look at one particular service: reading a chunk of data from a diskette. The disk routines in the ROM-BIOS give our programs simple services to read data (or write data, or perform other disk operations). If we ask the ROM-BIOS to read from a diskette, it makes a single attempt at reading and then tells us if it succeeded or failed. There are many reasons why reading the diskette might fail; in fact, there are about ten main errors that could occur. Some are very simple. For example, if the diskette is not already spinning when our program asks the ROM-BIOS to read from it, it has to start spinning; if it is not turning fast enough by the time the ROM-BIOS attempts to read from it, the ROM-BIOS will report a failure to read.

Since the ROM-BIOS provides very basic and primitive services, it only reports errors; it does not try to recover from an error. The DOS-BIOS, though, has more smarts. It inspects the error codes that the ROM-BIOS passes back and tries to take appropriate action. For example, if ROM-BIOS fails to read data from a diskette, DOS-BIOS tries to read it three times before reporting a read error. This increased capability takes care of the problem of the diskette that starts to rotate and is not yet up to speed at the time of the first read attempt. It also solves other problems as well.

The DOS-BIOS routines do much more than we've discussed here, but you now have an idea of their main function: They take the ROM-BIOS services as a starting point, and add whatever sophistication and window-dressing is needed to take them to the next level of reliability and service.

Third Level — the DOS Services

So far we have the low-level BIOS (the ROM-BIOS) and the high-level BIOS (the DOS-BIOS) in our pyramid. The next level is the *DOS services*, which provide all the main operations that programs need from the operating system.

Following the principle that each level of the pyramid builds more sophisticated and complicated services onto the levels below, the DOS services add an enormous amount to the DOS-BIOS. For example, the DOS-BIOS is only able to read data from a diskette, but the DOS services are able to decode that information so that they can see the names of the files and find where each file is on the diskette.

Although we still have two more levels to go in completing the DOS pyramid, the level we are at here, the DOS services, is the one single part that can best be called DOS itself—the heart of DOS. If a technical distinction were ever made between the disk operating system per se and its minor parts, then this part, the DOS service routines, would be considered DOS proper.

Fourth Level—the Command Interpreter

The next level of the pyramid, the *command interpreter,* is what you and I work with; it is the part we tend to think of as DOS when we use our computers.

The job of the command interpreter is both to ask for our commands and to act on them. The command interpreter asks for commands by giving us its command prompt, like this:

```
A>
```

It then accepts as our response the name of a program we want to use. The main job of the command interpreter is to find the program we have asked for, get it ready to run, and then run it.

There are three places the command interpreter can look to find the programs to be executed. Two are common to all IBM personal computers, and one is new to Junior. The first place the command interpreter looks is inside itself. Some of the simplest and most important command programs, such as DEL, COPY, and TYPE, are actually incorporated into the command interpreter and, naturally, are called *internal commands.* As part of the command interpreter, they are always ready to be used.

All other commands are *external* and the command interpreter has to find them somewhere else. Functionally, then, there is a big difference between internal and external commands: The internal ones can always be used; the external ones, maybe yes and maybe no—depending upon whether they are available at this moment.

On the PCjr, the command interpreter can look in two places for external commands. The first place, which is new to Junior, is in the table of command programs on any cartridge inserted in the cartridge slots. The second place is on the diskette. On the larger IBM personal computers, which can hold several diskettes at the same time, the command interpreter can be told to look in all sorts of places—different disks, and even different parts of different disks. On our PCjr, however, there is only one diskette drive, and normally all the commands on any diskette are kept in one place.

When the command interpreter finds the requested command program, it executes the program. In other words, the command interpreter temporarily turns over control of the computer to the program. Before it can do that, though, the program must be in memory, ready to be executed. In the case of internal commands, which are part of the command interpreter, or cartridge commands, which are in ROM, the program is already there and the command interpreter has nothing special to do. But command programs that are located

110

on a diskette must first be loaded—read from the diskette into memory and generally prepared for use. Once this preparation is done, the program is run, or executed. Finally, when the program is finished, the command interpreter takes back control of the computer and asks for another command.

Fifth Level—the Command Programs

The final level of the DOS pyramid is made up of the *command programs*. There are more than a dozen commands that come with DOS and that we rightly think of as a basic part of DOS. A good example is the FORMAT command, which prepares blank diskettes for use. Although FORMAT is an external command program, it would be very hard for us to use DOS without being able to format diskettes; so FORMAT is, for all practical purposes, a key part of DOS.

In fact, any program that can be executed with DOS is a command program—including the BASIC interpreter and all sorts of application programs, such as word processors, games, and spreadsheets. These application programs are not part of DOS but are built on top of DOS to give us a fully functional computer pyramid.

So, we have seen that there are five levels to the DOS pyramid: First, the ROM-BIOS, which is built into the PCjr and is actually part of the computer, to provide the most basic control. Second, the DOS-BIOS to customize the ROM-BIOS to DOS's needs. Third, the DOS services to make up the heart of DOS. Fourth, the command interpreter to make the connection between DOS and us, the users of the computer. And fifth, the DOS command programs, to enable us to perform computer magic.

GETTING DOWN TO WORK

Now that we have seen how the DOS pyramid is built, let's see how DOS gets down to work. Starting up a computer always presents special problems. It is sort of like the explorer's problem of where do you live while you build yourself a grass hut to live in? For disk operating systems, the business of starting up is called bootstrapping, or booting, and it involves some intricate tricks.

When the computer is first turned on, it performs its power-on self test (POST) and then tries to boot, or start up, a disk operating system. Booting involves reading the very first *sector,* or block, of data from a diskette. As we will see in the next chapter, there is a boot record at the very beginning of every diskette. If the ROM-BIOS start-up programs succeed in reading this boot record, then that sector is used as the first part of the disk operating system's own start-up routine. The job of the boot record is to begin loading the real working parts of DOS; the boot record itself is not used in DOS, and it is discarded after DOS gets going.

Each sector on a DOS diskette is 512 bytes in size—roughly enough room for 150 instructions. Within that amount of programming space, the boot record manages to check the diskette's format and determine if it is a *system diskette*; that is, if the diskette has a copy of DOS on it. If so, it reads into memory the two files that contain the DOS-BIOS and the DOS services programs, which are stored under the file names of IBMBIO.COM and IBMDOS.COM. With this done, the boot record has finished its work and it passes control over to an initialization program in IBMBIO.COM.

The IBMBIO initialization program checks out the computer's equipment, sets up whatever information it needs, and then passes control to IBMDOS. IBMDOS then does its own initialization, which includes figuring out where in memory the command interpreter should be placed. Control is then passed back to IBMBIO. IBMBIO reads the command interpreter, which it finds in a diskette file named COMMAND.COM, and the command interpreter is then allowed to do its initialization.

Finally, the command interpreter looks to see if we have set up an AUTO-EXEC.BAT file, a file of special instructions that we want the computer to carry out when it is first turned on. This file of DOS commands is known as a *batch command file*. If it finds this file, the command interpreter carries out our commands; if we have not set up an AUTOEXEC file, the command interpreter executes its own default commands, which are to ask us for the date and time and then to display the DOS starting messages, which look like this:

```
The IBM Personal Computer DOS
Version 2.10 (C)Copyright IBM Corp 1981, 1982, 1983
```

At this point, DOS is at work, ready for our commands. In the next section, we'll see more about how this work is performed.

DOS AT WORK

To help you understand what goes on when DOS is in operation, we'll go through a short outline of DOS at work. Obviously we'll be skipping over literally hundreds of technical details, but you will see the essence of how DOS works.

We begin at the point where the command interpreter writes the command prompt A> to the display screen and asks the DOS services to fetch our complete line of input from the keyboard. This request is similar to the

```
10 ' a program to act like the command interpreter,
20 ' that rejects all commands
30 CLS
40 ' turn off function key explanation line
50 KEY OFF
60 INPUT "A>", COMMAND$
70 PRINT "Bad command or file name"
80 PRINT
90 GOTO 60
```

*Figure 9-1. A program to imitate a command interpreter
that rejects all commands*

following line in a BASIC program:

```
10 INPUT "A>", COMMAND$
```

which writes the prompt A> on the screen and then waits for an input line.

As an aside, Figure 9-1 is a little bit of devilry to confuse your friends. Try keying it in. It creates a convincing imitation of the command interpreter, except that no matter what command is entered, this program acts as though the command is improper.

When the command interpreter receives our command line from the DOS services, it separates the command program's name from any parameters. Next, it goes looking for the command program, first in the internal list, then in the cartridges, and finally on the diskette. If the command is on diskette, the command interpreter loads the program, does any preparatory work needed (such as setting up the segment registers, storing the command parameters, setting aside a section of memory for a stack, and so forth), and then passes control to the program.

While a program is running, the command interpreter is not active. However, the DOS services, the heart of DOS, are usually busy beavers, doing all sorts of work for the program.

When the program is complete, it passes control back to the command interpreter, at which point something very interesting happens. Before I can explain it, we need to look at a fundamental problem.

DOS is in a special bind. On the one hand, the command interpreter needs to be full of rich facilities in order to perform all sorts of magic for us — the more of the DOS commands that are internal to the command interpreter, the handier the interpreter is for us. On the other hand, a big command interpreter

113

uses up a lot of memory that we might need for our programs and their data. If we happen to have loads and loads of memory in our personal computers, there is no problem. But what if we have only a limited amount? After all, our Junior is essentially limited to a maximum of 128K of memory, and after the amounts needed for the display screen and for DOS are subtracted, there are only about 88K left. If the command interpreter is very big, it just cuts into the amount of memory left for us to use.

To resolve this conflict, the command interpreter works in a very clever way: It breaks itself up into essential and nonessential parts. The essential part, which absolutely must be in memory, is kept in low memory locations, right next to the DOS services program (IBMDOS.COM). But the nonessential part of the command interpreter, which is not needed when a program is executing, is placed in the highest available memory locations and is considered disposable. This part of the command interpreter includes all the internal command programs, since we aren't using them when we are running another program, anyway.

If it turns out that there is plenty of memory for everyone, any program that we run will leave the disposable part of the command interpreter undisturbed. When the program ends, the disposable part can then be used again. However, if there is a shortage of memory space, the program that is being run can use the part of memory occupied by the disposable command-interpreter programs. This overwriting occurs automatically and, in fact, no one knows when it is happening.

When the program ends and the nondisposable part of the command interpreter takes back control, it checks the contents of the high memory locations to see whether all of its other half is still there. Because Junior has only 128K of memory, the other half will be wiped out a lot of the time. If the disposable part of the interpreter has been disturbed, the nondisposable section goes to the system diskette, searches for the COMMAND.COM file, and loads it in. If it can't find COMMAND.COM, then it displays a message telling us to load a system diskette. (This is why it is a good idea to have a copy of COMMAND.COM on all our diskettes, even when the diskettes don't have the rest of DOS on them.)

Once the disposable part of the command interpreter has either been found intact in memory or been reloaded from a system diskette, the cycle of command execution has been completed and the DOS once again gives us the command prompt A>.

QUICKLY THROUGH THE SERVICES

As we've mentioned several times, DOS provides all sorts of services to programs. In this section, we'll take a quick tour through them. We won't cover them in great detail, since this book is about the IBM PCjr itself, rather than a technical book on the inner workings of DOS. What we will do here is give you a good idea of the nature of the services that DOS provides, partly to give you a better understanding of how the PCjr works with DOS, and partly to show you what services are available to your programs if you should need them. To learn more about the DOS services in detail look to the *IBM Disk Operating System (DOS 2.10) Technical Reference* manual.

Before we tantalize you with some of the power of the DOS services, you should be aware that most programming languages don't give you direct access to these services. Just as you need an assembly-language interface routine to make the connection between a programming language, such as BASIC or Pascal, and the ROM-BIOS, you need assembly-language connections to the DOS services. In addition, such interface routines usually have to be custom-written for the exact needs of both the particular DOS service and the programming language that is being used. However, most programming languages provide us with features that are equivalent to many of the DOS services— after all, the programming languages build their features out of the services that DOS provides. In broad general terms, then, direct use of these DOS services is only for sophisticated, assembly-language programmers who understand quite a bit about the inner workings of DOS.

The DOS services are divided, somewhat arbitrarily, into three groups. The first group includes the *DOS interrupts*, each of which is invoked by its own interrupt number. The second and third groups both include the *DOS functions*, which are all invoked by a common interrupt number, 33 (hex 21). This interrupt number is combined with a distinct service code to indicate which DOS function is desired. (The mechanism is very much like that used by the ROM-BIOS, where an interrupt is used to invoke a range of services and a service code indicates which one is wanted.)

We ought to pause for a second to get our terminology straight. In the IBM DOS manual, and in other DOS literature, you will find the terms DOS interrupt and DOS function or function call used. For our convenience, in this book we use the general term DOS services to refer to both interrupts and functions.

The two groups of DOS functions are the *traditional* and the *extended*. When DOS was first created, it was designed and organized in a certain way. With experience, a better way was found to make DOS work and to organize the DOS functions. All versions of DOS include the traditional services. The level-2 versions, such as DOS 2.00 and DOS 2.10, also have the extended functions which, among other things, look forward to the needs of faster versions of IBM personal computers and more sophisticated operating systems. The importance of the extended services is that they help guarantee a solid future for the IBM personal computer family, for DOS, and for the programs we use with both of them. The design of the extended services ensures that, as computing progresses, we won't be stuck in a blind alley.

With that introduction out of the way, let's look at the services themselves.

■ Two services, one an interrupt and one a function, are used to terminate a program and return control to DOS. Programmers can decide which service is most appropriate for their programs.

■ A related and very important service, called "terminate but stay resident," ends the operation of a program but reserves the part of memory where the program is stored so that it will not be overwritten by other programs. This service is used mostly by special interrupt handlers, which are loaded as command programs. Having set themselves up with an interrupt vector pointing to them, they then return control to DOS. ProKey, a keyboard-enhancing program, uses this technique.

■ Three interrupt services are used to tell DOS the location of a subroutine to be used under special circumstances: One is invoked if the Fn-B, or Break, key combination is pressed; another is invoked when DOS detects an error with a hardware device, such as the printer or diskette drive; and the third directs DOS when the program ends.

■ Two interrupt services, known as absolute disk read and write, are used to read or write sectors of data directly from or to the diskette. All the other diskette services work on files and the data in the files, but these services allow any part of the diskette to be read or written to directly.

■ Several function services support the use of the keyboard and display screen. A variety of features is provided: Some keyboard services report whether or not anything has been keyed in; others wait for a keystroke; and still others wait for the Enter key to indicate that a complete line has been entered. Keyboard input may be automatically echoed on the display screen or it may not, depending upon which function is used. Single characters or complete messages can be written to the display screen. One of the choices provided by these services is whether or not DOS is to check for the Fn-B, or Break, key combination, which breaks into the execution of a program.

■ A large variety of service functions is provided for the diskette drive. One service allows the diskette to be reset, cleaning up any operations in progress. Another service selects the diskette drive to be used. (Our Junior has only one diskette drive, but the other IBM personal computers can have more than one.) One service indicates which diskette drive is the current DOS default, and another gives information about the format of the diskette being used.

■ Various file services are used to find, create, or delete diskette files. There are services to open a file (ready it for reading or writing), close a file, or search the file directory for an entry that matches a generic file name. Another service deletes a file from a diskette.

■ For working with the data in files, there are function services to read and write data sequentially, or to skip to a specified location in a file and read or write the data there. Other services allow files to be created or renamed.

■ To allow fancy footwork with programs, there is one function service that will set any interrupt vector, and another that will create a program segment, which is needed for one program to load another from disk.

■ For the date and time records kept by DOS, there are services to find out what they are and to change them.

All of the function services mentioned so far are part of the traditional DOS services provided by DOS-1 as well as DOS-2 versions. Next come the new, extended DOS functions, which can only be used with DOS-2 versions, such as DOS 2.00 and 2.10.

■ There are services to do all the basic directory operations, such as creating a subdirectory, removing one, or changing the current directory. These services allow ordinary programs to perform the functions of the DOS commands CHDIR, RMDIR, and MKDIR.

■ Following a new DOS-2 scheme for managing files, there is a full range of file services (opening, closing, reading, writing, renaming, and so forth), similar to the traditional services, but all using the DOS-2 methods.

■ To manage memory, there are extended services to request the use of memory from DOS, or to hand some memory back to DOS.

■ For dynamic subprogramming, there is an execute function, which will load a program from diskette and run it under a main program.

This has necessarily been only a brief outline of what the DOS services— interrupts, traditional functions, and extended functions—can do for our programs, but it should give you some idea of the tremendous operational power that DOS provides to the programs that it executes.

10
EXPLORING
THE DISKETTES

Disk storage is at the heart of the
effective operation of a computer.
Our Junior can operate without using
diskettes, thanks to its cartridges, its
built-in ROM-BASIC, and its ability
to use a cassette recorder for data.

But to make full use of it, we need a disk operating system, like DOS, and we need disk storage. For the PCjr, the disk storage comes in the form of a single diskette drive. In this chapter, we'll look at the most important aspects of our PCjr's diskettes.

ANATOMY OF A DISKETTE

Diskettes themselves are circles of thin, flexible, mylar plastic covered with the same sort of magnetic coating used on recording tape. The type of diskette used by the PCjr is 5¼ inches, or about 13 centimeters, in diameter.

As you can see in Figure 10-1, the diskette is held in a square, protective jacket, inside which is a felt liner that protects the diskette, acts as a dust catcher, and contains a lubricant to help the diskette turn easily.

There are four openings in the diskette jacket. The hub opening in the center allows the diskette drive to grab and spin the diskette inside the jacket. The oval opening in the front of the jacket lets the recording heads get close enough to the diskette to read or write data on it by magnetizing its surface. Just to one side of the hub opening is a small *index hole* that is used by the diskette drive to find a matching hole on the diskette itself. This index hole indicates the beginning and end of a *track*, or circle, of data on the diskette. The final opening is the *write-protection notch* on the side of the jacket, which controls whether or not the diskette drive has permission to write on the diskette. On the sort of diskettes used with our PCjr, when we cover the notch

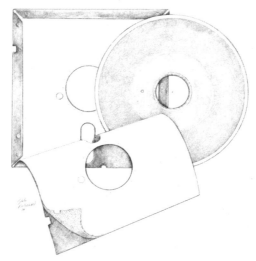

Figure 10-1. Anatomy of a diskette

the diskette may not be written on, and when we leave the notch open the diskette can be written on.

There are myriad ways to store data on diskettes. Diskettes can be *hard sectored*, meaning that their format is fixed. Hard-sectored diskettes are not used by the IBM personal computer family. Instead, our PCjr uses diskettes that are *soft sectored*, which means that they can be formatted in various ways. Soft-sectored diskettes offer flexibility but require that we run the FORMAT program each time we use a new, blank diskette. Our soft-sectored diskettes have just one index hole. In contrast, a hard-sectored diskette has a separate index hole for each sector around the circumference of the diskette.

The term sector refers to the actual space occupied by data records stored on the diskette. The number of sectors on a track and the size of the sectors can vary, depending on the standards established by an operating system. Our DOS uses only one sector size, 512 bytes, or ½K, in each sector. The number of sectors on each track can be eight or nine. Eight sectors per track—which gives us 4K bytes of data on each track—was the standard with DOS-1 versions, and nine sectors—or 4½K bytes per track—is the standard with DOS-2 versions. On any particular diskette, all the tracks will be either eight- or nine-sector format, and our DOS 2.10 can work with either format.

Our diskettes are *double density*, which means that they are recorded with the tracks spaced at 48 to the inch. There are 40 tracks to a diskette, so all our data are stored within a band less than an inch wide, just under 21 millimeters.

The magnetic, read-write *heads* of the diskette drive move in and out to go from track to track. The rate at which they move is under software control, so it varies with the performance of the drive. Our PCjr's heads take 6 milliseconds per track, so the longest they would take to move from one part of the diskette to another is about a quarter of a second. The diskette itself spins at 300 rpm, so it takes one-fifth of a second for a complete revolution. In practice, the computer has to wait an average of one-tenth of a second for the desired part of the diskette to rotate into place.

A diskette drive can have recording heads on one or both sides; that is, it can be *single* or *double sided*. Our PCjr's drive is double sided, so it can use either single- or double-sided diskettes. Since the original PC came with only single-sided drives, most programs are distributed on single-sided diskettes to ensure that any IBM personal computer can use them. (A single-sided drive cannot work with a double-sided diskette, since it can't see half of what is recorded on the disk.) In fact, though, most IBM personal computers, including our Junior, now come with double-sided drives.

Incidentally, there is a reversible, or *flippy*, variety of diskette that is recorded on both sides, but it is not recorded like a double-sided diskette. Instead, a flippy diskette is used as if it were two separate, single-sided diskettes. To use the second side, you turn the diskette over. To make this kind of use possible, flippy diskettes have two sets of index holes and two write-protect notches.

DISKETTE FORMATS

There are four different diskette formats that can be used by DOS on the PCjr. They differ only in detail, not in the main way they operate. We will concentrate on the common ground of the four formats, but you need to know what the four are, so that we can refer to them.

The four diskette formats come from the combinations of the two different choices we have already covered. First, diskettes can be single- or double-sided, depending upon whether or not they are recorded on one or both sides. Recall that single-sided drives naturally can work only with single-sided diskettes; but double-sided drives, like the one used in our PCjr, can work with either diskette format. Second, diskettes can have either eight or nine sectors of data on each track. Any diskette drive can work with both eight- and nine-sector diskettes; however, DOS-1 versions cannot work with nine-sector diskettes, while DOS-2 versions can.

The very first version of DOS, 1.00, used only single-sided, eight-sector diskettes. The next release, 1.10, added the double-sided format, but still used only eight sectors per track. With DOS 2.00, the single- and double-sided, eight- and nine-sector formats appeared, so that there are now the full four formats. The PCjr can work with any of the formats. Our main version of DOS, 2.10, uses the same four formats as 2.00.

The basic layout of a diskette is the same in all four formats. There are 40 tracks, or concentric circles, of data on the diskette. When they are referred to individually, the tracks are numbered from track 0 on the outside to track 39 on the inside. Normally the track numbers and all other details of the diskette format are more or less hidden from us by DOS; we only discover these details when we do some technical poking around.

On a double-sided diskette, there are two sides of data numbered 0 and 1. On a single-sided diskette, the one side is referred to as number 0. The sectors, either eight or nine of them, are on each track on each side. The sectors are numbered from 1 through 8 or 9 (and not numbered beginning with 0, the way tracks and sides are).

The storage spaces on a double-sided diskette are used in sequence from outside to inside, starting with sector 1 of side 0 of track 0, and moving to sector 1 of side 1 of track 0, and so on. After side 0 is used for one track, then side 1 is used next. The very last space on a double-sided, nine-sector diskette is sector 9 of side 1 of track 39. Thus, on double-sided diskettes, both sides of track 0 are

	Single Sided	Double Sided
8-sector	160K	320K
9-sector	180K	360K

*Figure 10-2. Storage capacity of the
four diskette formats*

used before the computer moves on to track 1, to reduce the amount of recording-head movement from track to track.

Space on the diskette is used in full sectors. On single-sided diskettes, the 512-byte sectors arc allocated to files one at a time, while on double-sided diskettes the sectors are allocated in pairs, two at a time. As many sectors, or pairs of sectors, as are needed are allocated to a file. At the end of a file there will usually be some space left unused in its last sector.

Figure 10-2 shows, in terms of raw storage capacity, how much data storage space is on each of the four diskette formats. Not all of that space can be used to store our data, though. A certain amount is taken up by system control information. We'll look at that now.

SYSTEM CONTROL INFORMATION

Each diskette begins with a boot record in its first sector. The boot record, as we have seen, is the first part of the program that loads DOS from a diskette. Even if a diskette does not have DOS on it, its first sector holds the boot record.

Following the boot record is an item called the *file allocation table*, or *FAT*, which is used by DOS to manage and control the storage space on the diskette. The FAT keeps track of what part of the space is being used by files and what part is available. DOS always uses the first available space for storing data, so that our files are stored as close to the FAT as possible.

The very first byte of the FAT contains a code used to indicate which of the four diskette formats is being used. When DOS is working with a diskette, it checks this format code first to learn how to interpret the rest of the diskette. The four format codes are shown, in hexadecimal, in Figure 10-3.

The size of the FAT varies: For the 8-sector formats it occupies less than one sector; for the 9-sector formats it needs slightly more than one sector and therefore occupies two, since space can only be allocated in complete sectors. Because the FAT is used to control the entire usable data-storage portion of the

	Single Sided	Double Sided
8-sector	FE	FF
9-sector	FC	FD

Figure 10-3. Diskette format codes

diskette, two identical copies of it are stored in the hope that, if one is damaged, the other might still be usable. So altogether, the FAT occupies either two or four of the sectors immediately following the boot record on the diskette.

For the moment, we'll skip over the details of how the FAT works, until we come back to it later in this chapter, where we cover how data are stored.

The next item stored on the diskette is the file *directory*. A record is kept in the file directory for each file on the diskette, giving the file's name, size, location, and so forth. Each diskette has a *root*, or main, directory, and with DOS 2.00 and later versions, each diskette can have *subdirectories* that expand the size and structure of the directory. Although subdirectories can be used with any IBM personal computer, they are best used with a fast, high-capacity disk system like the one on the XT.

The diskette's root directory occupies a fixed number of sectors and there is thus a limit to the number of entries, and therefore the number of files, that can be stored on each diskette. However, the number is usually more than enough. Each directory entry occupies 32 bytes, so there are 16 entries in each 512-byte directory sector. A single-sided diskette has four directory sectors, for a maximum of 64 entries or files; a double-sided diskette has seven directory sectors, for a maximum of 112 entries or files.

You will notice that, while the size of the directory varies with single- or double-sided format, the size of the FAT varies with eight- or nine-sector format. If you are working with the directory and the FAT, take care not to get their sizes confused.

Following the directory comes the data portion, which takes up the rest of the diskette. The overhead portions that we have mentioned (the boot record, the FAT, and the directory) take up only about 2 percent of the diskette—not very much at all.

If a diskette contains a copy of DOS—that is, if it is a system diskette—then the first three files in the data storage space of the diskette will be IBMBIO.COM, the special BIOS for DOS; IBMDOS.COM, the DOS service routines; and finally, COMMAND.COM, the command interpreter. The two "IBM" files are hidden system files that will not appear in the diskette's file directory listing. The command interpreter, COMMAND.COM, is an ordinary file that can be copied or erased, and it will appear in the directory listing.

Before we go into more details about diskette data storage space, let's take a closer look at the file directory.

THE DIRECTORY IN DETAIL

The file directory is used to keep basic information about each file. It is a simple table of 32-byte entries, one for each file. There are eight parts, or fields, to each directory entry.

First Field—the File Name

The first eight bytes are the file name. If a file name is less than eight characters long, it is filled out with blanks (CHR$(32)). Letters must be uppercase (capitals); if they aren't, DOS won't be able to handle the directory entry properly. (When we enter file names at the keyboard, DOS always converts any lowercase letters to uppercase.) There shouldn't be any spaces embedded in the file name, though there is a trick in BASIC that makes it possible for you to use spaces. In a DOS command, such as COPY, there is no way to use a file name with blanks inside it; but since BASIC puts quotation marks around file names, like this:

```
OPEN "A B" AS #1
```

you can work with files that other programs won't normally touch. Using tricks like this isn't a good idea, but if you have a need for it, BASIC lets you do it.

There are three special codes that may appear in the first byte of the file-name field. They are used to indicate special situations. If the byte is 0, the directory entry has never been used before. This special code was introduced with DOS 2.00 to provide a way to speed up DOS's operation by indicating when the last entry in a directory had been found. Before DOS 2.00, unused directory entries were marked just like erased files.

If the first byte of the file-name field is hex E5, the directory entry is marked as not in current use. With DOS-2 versions, this code always has the same meaning: A file has been erased. With DOS-1 versions, it can mean either that a file has been erased or that the directory entry has never been used.

When a file is erased, the space that was allocated to it is released to the pool of available space in the FAT, and the directory entry is marked with this hex E5 byte. When a file is erased, though, its data are not immediately overwritten, nor is any of the information in the directory lost, except for the

125

first character of the file's name. This makes it possible, under favorable circumstances, to recover an erased file.

The third and last of the special codes for the file-name field is the period character, hex 2E. One or two periods are used to mark two special file entries in subdirectories; we'll discuss the significance of this period character in our discussion of subdirectories later in this chapter.

Second Field—the File-Name Extension

After the file name, the next field in the directory entry is the file-name extension. It is three bytes long and, like the file name, it is padded with blanks if it is less than the full length. While a file name must have at least one ordinary character in it, the extension can be all blanks.

Third Field—the File Attribute

The third field of the directory entry is one byte, each bit of which is used to indicate whether or not a file has a certain attribute. When the bit is 1, or set, the file has that feature and when the bit is 0, or not set, it does not.

■ *Bit 0*, the lowest-order bit, is used to mark a file as read only. This protects it from being changed or erased. The read-only bit is new to DOS-2 versions and is not handled properly by DOS-1 versions.

■ *Bit 1*, the next bit, marks a file as hidden. We could use bit 1 to hide our secret files from others who might have access to our diskettes, since hidden files cannot be seen by ordinary directory searches, including the DIR command.

■ *Bit 2* marks a file as a system file, such as the IBMBIO and IBMDOS files we've already talked about. System files are invisible in the same way that hidden files are. However, our programs can gain access to hidden and system files by using programming tricks, which include special manipulation of some information known as a *file control block*.

■ *Bit 3* marks a directory entry as the diskette *label*, which identifies the diskette internally the same way the paper labels we stick on the diskette jacket identify it externally. This type of directory entry is also new to DOS-2 versions.

■ *Bit 4* is used to identify subdirectories—another new item for DOS-2 versions, which we'll discuss shortly.

■ *Bit 5* is used to mark files as to-be-archived. This feature is intended for use with the XT's fixed hard disk to indicate files that have been changed since the last archive copy was made. It really doesn't apply to the diskettes used by our PCjr.

■ *Bits 6 and 7* are not presently used; they are available in case future versions of DOS might need them.

Even though each bit of the attribute byte has its own independent meaning, the bits can't be used arbitrarily. A file can have any combination of the read-only, hidden, system, and archive bits set, but if the label or subdirectory bits are set, none of the other bits should be. Subdirectories could possibly be read only or hidden, but my experiments show that DOS doesn't intend for us to use these exotic combinations of attribute bits. If you know how to modify diskettes with tools such as DEBUG, you can experiment with different attribute combinations—the results are interesting.

Fourth Field—Ten Empty Bytes

Moving on, the next field in a directory entry is an unused string of ten bytes that have been set aside for future needs.

Fifth and Sixth Fields—Time and Date

The next two fields are each unsigned, 2-byte values that indicate the time and date the file was last written to. This is the information that is displayed when we do a DIR directory listing.

The time is stored as hours (in a 24-hour clock, ranging from 0 through 23), minutes, and seconds; but because the 2-byte word used to store the time is one bit too short to store all the seconds, they are divided by two and indicated in 2-second increments. The DIR command doesn't show us the seconds, but they are actually recorded. The date is stored as year, month, and day, with the year compressed by subtracting 1980 from it. The year code can range from 0 through 119, indicating 1980 through 2099.

We don't have any ordinary, practical reason to know how the date and time are coded, but it's interesting to see. Their parts are combined, following these formulas, to produce two 16-bit words:

$$\text{TIME} = \text{HOUR} \times 2048 + \text{MINUTE} \times 32 + \text{SECOND} \times 2$$
$$\text{DATE} = (\text{YEAR} - 1980) \times 512 + \text{MONTH} \times 32 + \text{DAY}$$

The way these formulas are worked out and the order in which they are stored makes it possible to treat them as a single, 4-byte, unsigned number that can be compared directly with similar numbers from other files; a larger number indicates a later date and time.

Seventh Field—
the Starting Cluster Number

The next field in the directory entry is the starting *cluster* number, which indicates the beginning of the file's storage allocation in the FAT. This starting cluster number is the entry point to the FAT for this file. We'll learn more about clusters in a minute.

Eighth Field—the File Size

The last field of a directory entry is a 4-byte integer indicating the file's size in bytes. Normally, this field indicates the file's exact size but the size is sometimes fudged a little. For example, text files are often stored in 128-byte increments and so the true end of the text data could be anywhere within the last 128-byte storage block. Although the files on Junior's diskettes can't be larger than 354K, the size field is made large enough to hold the size of files created with large storage devices, such as the XT's 10-million-byte, fixed hard disk.

DISK STORAGE STRATEGY
AND THE FAT

DOS uses a simple and efficient storage strategy for its disk space based on two main rules: First, no space is reserved for files other than the space that is actually in use. Second, all space is used on a first-come, first-served basis.

As a file is created, DOS allocates space piece-by-piece, as it is needed for the growing file. The space is allocated in units known as clusters. For single-sided diskettes, a cluster consists of a single sector; for double-sided diskettes, there are two sectors in a cluster. (On the fixed disk used by the XT, clusters are normally eight sectors.) However big a cluster is, it is the unit of storage that is allocated to a file. As a file grows and needs more space, it is assigned the first available cluster.

When things are quite simple, each file is stored on one contiguous part of the diskette; this is ideal for fast and efficient access. However, when files are created and then erased or added to, the storage space can become fragmented and files can be scattered over several parts of the diskette. There is no real harm in this, but accessing the data can be slightly slower.

If you are curious, there are two ways you can learn whether a file is broken into more than one piece: First, you can use the CHKDSK command to have DOS check a specific file and report whether it is fragmented. Second, you can use a program such as DiskLook™ (see Appendix C) to see a graphic map of the location of each file on your diskette.

In order for DOS to manage the space on the diskette, each cluster of sectors is given a reference number. Since the reference numbers are maintained in the FAT and the first two entries (0 and 1) of the FAT table are set aside for the format-descriptor byte, the cluster numbers run from 2 to one higher than the number of clusters. Figure 10-4 shows the total number of clusters for each diskette format.

The cluster reference numbers are stored in the FAT as a simple table, with one entry for each cluster. The table entries are each three hex digits in size, or 1½ bytes each. The FAT entries are scrambled in pairs, so that each pair of entries takes up three bytes altogether. While it was interesting and informative to pore over the details of the directory, trying to understand the FAT format could be described as complicated and annoying—so we'll leave that for the most technical book in this series, *Mastering the IBM PCjr Home Computer.*

Since the FAT entries are three hex digits (or 1½ bytes), they can range from 000 through FFF, allowing the table to have over 4,000 unique entries.

If a cluster is free for use, the FAT entry for that cluster is zero. All DOS has to do to find the first available cluster is scan the table for the first zero entry.

When clusters are in use for a file, their FAT entries act as a chain, with each entry giving the cluster number of the next cluster belonging to the file. The end of this chain of allocated space is indicated by a high value, usually 4095, hex FFF. To trace through a file, then, all DOS has to do is follow the chain of space allocation for the file in the FAT—very quick, efficient, and simple.

The FAT values hex FF0 through FF7 are reserved for special uses. Currently, they have only one special use. When a diskette is formatted, some of the surface of the diskette may not be usable. So that the entire diskette is not wasted, the unusable portion is marked as a bad cluster with the FAT value hex FF7. In the first version of DOS, version 1.00, another trick was used: A

	Single Sided	Double Sided
8-sector	313	315
9-sector	351	354

Figure 10-4. Number of clusters for each diskette format

special, hidden file was created under the name BADTRACK and the unusable clusters were allocated to it.

The way that the FAT is organized—with each file's space allocated in a chain of FAT entries—makes the FAT vulnerable to several kinds of mishaps. Although it doesn't happen often, a disk's FAT can become scrambled. Fortunately for us, there is a DOS command called CHKDSK that will test for any errors, and repair them (as much as possible).

What could go wrong with a FAT? Mainly three things: First, a space allocation chain could double back on itself, and repeat forever, without end. Second, two different files could have their allocation chains point to the same FAT entry—this is called cross-linking. And third, a cluster, or chain of clusters, might not be marked as available space (FAT value 0), and yet also might not belong to any file—becoming, in effect, orphans.

While these exotic FAT errors are rare, they can occur. You can use CHKDSK to test for them, and you can use DiskLook (described in Appendix C) to give you a diagram of what is wrong.

When a file is erased, its space is deallocated. The FAT entries are reset to zero to indicate that they are available for use, and the directory entry for the file is marked as erased by replacing the first byte of the file name with hex E5. All the data in the file are still stored where they were on the diskette sectors and all the information about the file is still in the directory, including the starting cluster number, which points to the beginning of what was the file's space allocation chain in the FAT.

Eventually, when other data are written to the diskette, the erased file's data will be overwritten and the directory entry will be reused, wiping out the remaining traces of the erased file. However, before that happens it is possible to recover an erased file completely. All that is needed is first, to restore the first byte of the file's name (the easy part) and second, to discover which sectors used to belong to the file and to reallocate them (the tricky part). A clever program can make this possible; for example, UnErase™ (see Appendix C).

There are two reasons why we have covered what happens when a file is erased: The first is to provide a better understanding of how Junior's diskettes work; the other is more practical. One of the common horrors in personal computing is accidentally erasing some important files; it happens too easily and much too often. If you have not yet inadvertently erased a file, consider yourself blessed. Of all the handy programs you should probably buy for your PCjr, some sort of unerase program ought to be one of the first on your list.

I have delayed talking about two interesting special features of diskettes: diskette *volume labels* (volume as in book, not volume as in capacity), and *subdirectories*. Labels are a very useful item on diskettes, and all PCjr owners ought to know about them and use them. Subdirectories, on the other hand, are mostly used with large, high-capacity, hard-disk systems like the one on the

XT. We can use subdirectories on our Juniors if we want to, though, and besides, we should all understand subdirectories, whether we use them or not. We'll start with labels.

VOLUME LABELS

A volume label is a special directory entry used to give an identifying name to a diskette. While we can't see these labels, DOS can, and will tell us what they say when we use commands like DIR and CHKDSK.

By themselves, volume labels are nice to have to help us keep track of which diskette is loaded in our PCjr's diskette drive. After all, we can't see the paper label we attached to the outside of the diskette once the diskette is in the drive. But the greatest benefit of volume labels comes when they are used with a diskette *librarian*.

A librarian is a program that keeps a record of which files are stored on which diskettes. This record is particularly useful when we keep several copies of our data files, both current and older versions. And it is particularly important with business data, so that if a major mistake is made, we know where to go to find the next most recent version. Having volume labels on our diskettes is essential to effective use of a diskette librarian, and labels can be quite useful even if we don't have a librarian program.

I recommend putting labels on all diskettes. Some people will want to use the label as a diskette serial number, such as DISK-0034, but I feel it is best to give diskettes functional names, such as GAMES, PROG-TOOLS, and PHONE-LIST.

As we saw when we went over the details of directory entries, a directory entry is marked as a label when it has an attribute byte of hex 08; that is, by having only bit 3 of the attribute byte set. The entry's file-name and extension fields are then used as a single, 11-byte field where the label is stored. Thus, while the names of files and subdirectories are broken into two parts, the name and the extension, a label is treated as a single, unified name. As with file names and extensions, a diskette label is padded with blanks if the label name we choose is shorter than the length allotted.

Normally, if a diskette has a label, the label is the first directory entry. But when DOS goes looking for a label, it will look through all the active part of the diskette's directory. Unfortunately, though, for those of us who want to make use of labels, DOS is very limited in the way it lets us control them. DOS lets us set a volume label only when we format a diskette, and then only if we format the diskette with nine sectors per track. (This is the automatic default for our DOS 2.10 version; we have to ask to use eight-sector format.) DOS gives us no way to change or remove a label, or to add one to an existing diskette. However, there is a way to add, change or remove labels, as you'll see in Appendix C.

SUBDIRECTORIES

Now we come to subdirectories, one of the most interesting aspects of diskettes. A subdirectory is an addition to a diskette's root directory. While the root directory is kept in a fixed, standard location at the beginning of each diskette, a subdirectory is stored just like any other file. Space for each subdirectory is allocated from the diskette's data storage space, exactly as for any ordinary file. Files can grow in size, and so can subdirectories—as more and more file entries are added to a subdirectory, it expands to accommodate them. While a diskette's root directory is fixed in size and limits the number of files it will keep track of, subdirectories have no size limit other than the diskette's storage capacity.

Subdirectories are always attached to a parent directory, which can be either the root directory or another subdirectory. There can be directories branching off directories branching off still other directories, forming a tree structure.

A parent directory has one entry for each of its subdirectories that is like the entry for any other file, with two exceptions. First, of course, the attribute byte marks the entry as a subdirectory. Second, the file-length field is set to zero; the actual size of the subdirectory is found by tracing its allocation chain through the FAT. In principle, a program can read a subdirectory like any other file, and there is some mention of how to do this in the *DOS* manual. In practice, the file length of zero presents an obstacle to reading the directory. When it reads a file, DOS uses the file length to know when it has come to the end. Since a subdirectory has a file length of zero, DOS thinks it has come to the end before it's even begun, and refuses to try to read any data from the file.

Each subdirectory is created with two special entries, named " . " and " .. " (one or two periods). These two entries help DOS manage directories by providing the starting cluster number of a related directory. The " .. " entry has a starting cluster number that is the beginning of this subdirectory's parent directory. This gives DOS a way to trace its way back up the directory tree. If the starting cluster number field contains a zero, that indicates that the parent of this directory is the root directory.

The other special entry, the " . " entry, points to the subdirectory itself; that is, the starting cluster number of the " . " entry indicates where this directory is stored. Curious. I am certainly puzzled about why an entry like this is needed, but there it is. DOS must have a need for it that I haven't really figured out.

I have mentioned before that subdirectories aren't particularly useful on the diskettes that our PCjr uses, and this calls for some explanation. There are two reasons not to use subdirectories with Junior. First, the main point of having subdirectories is to separate and isolate groups of files from one another; this kind of organization is important when you have a lot of disk storage capacity and many, many files—like on the XT's hard-disk system. For example, my XT has, as I write this, 651 files on its 10-megabyte, fixed disk; I can't keep track of them all in one group, so I have them organized into 27 subdirectories, mostly by subject matter.

Diskettes, on the other hand, do not have enough space for so many files that it is really necessary to divide them into subdirectories, though you may want to for your own reasons. With the PCjr's diskettes, the same purpose is best served by putting files on different diskettes, rather than into different directories.

The second reason for avoiding subdirectories on the PCjr concerns performance and is probably the strongest reason for not using them. To work with files that are in subdirectories and to trace its way through subdirectories, DOS has to read much more from the diskette and generally hunt around on many more tracks. On a fast, hard-disk system, all this reading causes only a slight delay, but with diskettes, which are much slower anyway, you are likely to find that using subdirectories causes more loss of speed and more annoyance than you are willing to put up with.

We've talked about how diskettes and directories are organized. What about the files themselves? That's the topic of the next section.

FILE FORMATS

Each of us could organize the data we put into diskette files for our own use any way we wanted. But for all of us to be able to use common programs, we have to use some standard file formats that make it possible for our computers to work cooperatively. With standard file formats, different programs can safely and reliably share information through diskette files.

In this section we'll look at the most common file formats. One word of warning, though: As far as I know, there aren't any published definitions of these "standard" file formats, so they are rather informal. Since there are no published rules, the players have to play the game cooperatively and that means that when we get into the interpretation of the finer points, things can get a little uncertain. If you want to understand the basics of diskette files, what we cover here should serve you well.

We are going to cover four basic file formats, with some interesting variations. The four are: two ways of storing programs (known as COM files and

EXE files); the most common way of storing text (known as ASCII text files); and a catch-all, general file format (which I'll call data files). In addition, we'll cover some special formats that BASIC uses for its programs.

Program File Formats

When executable programs are stored on diskette, they are kept in one of two formats known by their file-name extensions as *COM* and *EXE*. COM and EXE files are programs that are ready to be used by the computer and basically just need to be loaded into memory and run.

Programs as you or I think of them can have many forms. If we are writing in an interpreted language, such as BASIC, then in a strict, technical sense our programs are never actually executed. Instead, the BASIC interpreter—which truly is a program—is executed and it carries out line by line the steps that our BASIC programs call for. If we are writing in a compiled language, such as Pascal, C, COBOL, or FORTRAN, or in assembly language, then what we write is called *source code*. This code must pass through several translation stages before it appears in one of the two executable formats, COM and EXE.

With the compiled languages, here is what happens: First, a compiler or assembler translates our source code into an intermediate form known as *object code*. Object code consists of the machine-language instructions that will carry out our program, but the format of object code requires further preparation before it can be executed directly. Object code is stored in diskette files with a file-name extension of OBJ. To translate object code into the EXE executable format, we use the *LINK* program that is part of DOS. When appropriate, we can then translate EXE format into COM format, with the DOS program *EXE2BIN*. Only when we have a program in COM or EXE format do we have what DOS considers a finished, executable program.

COM

Let's look at the COM format first. COM is an abbreviation of the word "command"—COM files are command files, meaning that they contain the programs needed to carry out the commands, such as FORMAT and LINK, that we give DOS. A COM file is an exact image of the program as it will appear in Junior's memory when the program is run. In terms of the program itself and the data that it carries with it, a COM file is not changed or prepared in any way when it is loaded into memory by the *loader program* (which is a part of DOS's command interpreter, COMMAND.COM).

When a COM file is loaded, the loader selects where in memory the program is to be located. In the first 256 (hex 100) bytes of that part of memory, the loader constructs a *program segment prefix*, or *PSP*. The PSP contains information that the program may need, including any parameters that were given when we asked DOS to execute the program. The loader then places the program itself in memory immediately after the PSP, exactly as it appears in its diskette file. Just before the program begins execution, the segment registers are set to point to the location of the PSP. The machine-language instructions in the program can include offsets to various program and data locations, all based on the fact that the segment registers point to 256 bytes before the program, where the PSP is located. When a program begins operation, it can tell where it is, thanks to the segment registers, and it can find its command parameters stored in the PSP.

There are some inherent limitations to COM programs. For one thing, since all the segment addressing registers point to the same location, the program, its data, and its stack must all fit within the 64K that can be addressed from one segment location. Of course, a program can do some fancy footwork to break out of that limitation, including resetting the segment registers. But barring that kind of tricky programming, a COM program is limited in size to a total of 64K.

EXE

To break out of the 64K limitation, we use the EXE file. While COM programs are loaded unchanged into memory, EXE programs are processed somewhat by the loader program. At the beginning of an EXE file there is a table of information indicating what needs to be done to the program to prepare it for execution. This information includes the size of the stack that the program wants, the data segment needed, and also what is called a *relocation table*. When the loader places the program in memory, the program can contain specific references to memory locations within itself or within its data. Since the actual memory locations aren't known until the program is loaded into memory, the loader uses the relocation table to set the proper addresses in the program.

All this is special setup work that can be performed for a program in EXE format. If a program needs these extra services, it is kept in EXE format. If it doesn't, the program can be converted to COM format, which takes up less space on diskette and loads into memory faster.

Only these two formats, COM and EXE, can be used to store executable programs. They are the only formats that DOS's loader program can recognize and use. As a result, you can easily see which executable programs are stored on any diskette by asking for two DIR listings: DIR *.COM and DIR *.EXE.

Text File Formats

The next file format we'll look at is the ASCII text file, or just text file. Text files are used to store written information, such as the words you are now reading. (They happen to be stored on my computer's disk in a text file named CHAPTER 10.)

Text files are the most universal file format for personal computers. They are used for many, many purposes. Text-editor programs, including the EDLIN program that comes with DOS, use the text file format; so do many word processors. When we write programs that will be compiled or assembled, the program source code has to be stored in text file format. When we create batch-processing files with the extension name BAT to be carried out by DOS, they are also in text file format.

Text file format starts out very simply. First, the data consist of letters of the alphabet, digits, and punctuation just like the text you are reading. The data are coded by the computer using the ASCII coding scheme. Each character of the text occupies one byte and is coded numerically; for example, the capital letter A has the byte value 65, or CHR$(65). To mark the end of the text file, a special code, CHR$(26), is used. (This code is also called Ctrl-Z, since that is one way it can be typed in on the keyboard.)

Text file format divides the text into lines. At the end of each line are two characters known as carriage return, which is CHR$(13), and line feed, which is CHR$(10). If there were a special end-of-line character, like the end-of-file character, then a single character would do the job. But since there really is no end-of-line character per se, these two print-formatting characters are used. On a printer or typewriter, a carriage return and a line feed end one line and begin another, so they are used in text files as the standard end-of-line marking.

Since the end of a line is marked by these two special characters, a line could, in theory, be very, very long. However, many programs that work with text files set limits on how long lines can be: Most set a limit of 255 bytes; a few limit lines to the width that can be shown on the display screen—40 or 80 characters.

There are actually quite a few formatting characters in the ASCII coding scheme, including one, CHR$(12), to mark the end of a page. A text file may include these page markings and other formatting codes as well. Word processors usually need special codes to indicate such things as where a word can be hyphenated, which words are to be underlined, and which lines can be changed when a paragraph is reformatted. There are no universal standards for how these things are done.

Lack of uniformity can cause quite a bit of trouble if we try to transfer files between a word processor that uses lots of special markings and programs that expect very ordinary data, such as a compiler. To avoid putting yourself through some real grief, test for compatibility before you invest lots of effort. It would be awful to spend the time needed to write a large program, only to discover that your compiler won't accept the format used by your text editor or word processor.

There is one oddity that should interest you about the length of text files. DOS keeps track of the length of a file and stores the information in the file's entry in the diskette directory. If a program passes data into a file byte-by-byte, DOS has an exact record of the length of the file. But many editors and word processors pass data in blocks of 128 bytes in the interests of efficiency— passing data this way reduces the number of calls to DOS over a hundredfold. When we come to the end of a text file, these programs mark the true end of the file with CHR$(26); DOS, on the other hand, thinks that the file continues to the next multiple of 128 bytes. So there can be a discrepancy between the actual file size and the record in 128-byte units that DOS keeps of the file's size.

Since so many programs and all programming languages work with data files in text format, there is a major advantage to keeping all our data in this format: We will be able to use our data with more programs than we could if we kept them in another format. When deciding which format to use for storing your own data, you should consider using text files if at all possible to make your use of the data more flexible.

Data File Formats

The next file format is the ordinary data file format. The data file format can be used with any data that we wish to store on diskette. It is really a general-purpose, open-ended format. With this kind of file, a program reads and writes data in records of a fixed size, determined by the program according to its needs. DOS takes care of the job of fitting records into the 512-byte storage sectors with no wasted space, no matter what the record size.

By writing fixed-length records, we can read and write our data in two ways: We can either work sequentially from beginning to end, or we can jump to any location in the file, using the file randomly. Since the records in the file are all the same size, DOS can calculate the location of each record by multiplying its relative record number by the record size.

If we are working with a file sequentially, all the records don't actually have to be the same size; they can vary, as long as our programs have some way of determining how long each record is. Usually, though, sequential-file records are also kept uniform in size, since we then have the added advantage of being able to work with the file randomly, jumping, if we want, to any record that we need without having to work our way to it from the beginning. With fixed-size records, the location of any record can be easily calculated, without having to search through the records that precede it.

We mentioned before that many editor programs store text files in blocks of 128 bytes. In effect, these programs translate the format of the data. When talking to DOS and the diskettes, they use 128-byte, fixed-length data records. The difference between these records and data files is simply that, when they talk to us, the editor programs present the data as text, formatted into lines, just as we expect text files to be.

Special File Formats Used by BASIC

To finish this discussion of file formats, we'll look at some special formats that BASIC uses. When BASIC stores its programs on diskette, it uses three different formats. One of the three is our standard text file format. If we save a BASIC program with the A option, like this:

```
SAVE "FILENAME",A
```

the program will be stored as a standard text file. (The A in the SAVE command stands for ASCII format).

Normally, though, BASIC stores its programs in what is called a *tokenized format*. A large part of any BASIC program consists of standard BASIC key words, such as REM, INPUT, and PLAY. To save space, the tokenized format replaces each key word with a token that takes only one or two bytes to store. This one trick alone can save about one-fifth in the size of the file.

BASIC can also store programs in a *protected format* coded to prevent them from being listed. The protected format is roughly the same as the tokenized format, but in addition it is scrambled, so that it is not easy to decipher.

When BASIC writes a program to diskette, we must specify which format we want; if we don't ask for text or protected format, tokenized is used. When BASIC reads a program, it checks the first byte for a format code. Tokenized files begin with hex FF and protected files begin with hex FE. If a file begins with any other byte, BASIC assumes that it is in text format.

There is one more disk file format used by BASIC that we ought to know about—the *BLOAD format*. BASIC can copy data between memory and diskette files with the commands BLOAD and BSAVE. These statements are used mostly for two purposes: to load assembly-language programs into memory, where they can be called with the CALL statement; and to store a picture of our screen on diskette. The data in a BLOAD-format file are the exact image of what is in memory, but BASIC adds a header and a trailer to the file to indicate what is what. In case you want to work with these files, we will go over the format here.

The file begins with a 7-byte header. The first byte is a signature, hex FD. The next four bytes indicate where in memory the data are to be loaded. With the BLOAD statement, you can specify where a file is to be loaded; if you don't specify an address, the address stored in the file when it was created with the BSAVE statement is used. (When a file is created with the BSAVE statement, the location is stored in the file as a complete segmented address with segment

Code	Meaning
FD	1-byte signature
SSSS	2-byte segment address
OOOO	2-byte offset address
LLLL	2-byte length of data
Data	As many data bytes as needed
1A	1-byte signature

Figure 10-5. Summary of a BLOAD-format file

and offset locations.) The last two bytes of the header indicate the length of the data. The data themselves follow this 7-byte header, and the file ends with a 1-byte trailer, a signature of hex 1A. A summary of the file format is given in Figure 10-5.

ROM-BIOS DISKETTE SERVICES

As we mentioned in Chapter 6, the ROM-BIOS contains a wealth of services for our programs to use. Six of these services are for diskettes. These ROM-BIOS services are low-level, very basic, and primitive. They don't involve anything like finding files; that sort of thing is a high-level service that belongs to DOS.

In this section we'll go through the ROM-BIOS services for diskettes, both to give you an idea of what they do, and also to cover the interesting subject of copy protection.

Our PCjr provides the same ROM-BIOS diskette services as the other IBM personal computer models, but there is much more programming in the ROM-BIOS to accomplish them. One reason for Junior's lower price is its use of ROM-BIOS software to do the work of more expensive hardware. The PCjr's diskette-controller circuitry is not nearly as smart as that of the PC and XT, but its ROM-BIOS makes up for the missing intelligence in the controller.

There are six diskette services, numbered with service codes 0 through 5.

■ *Service 0* is used to reset the diskette system and might be used when the diskette drive has reported an error—resetting the system will sometimes cause problems to go away.

■ *Service 1* reports the status code from whatever operation was last performed. Each time a diskette is used, a code is returned to indicate what happened. This code is one of many possible values, each of which indicates a different event, such as "read successful" or "disk is write protected." We can use service 1 to repeat the last status code so that an error-recovery routine can find out exactly what happened.

■ *Service 2* reads sectors into memory. The locations of the sectors must be specified by track, head (meaning diskette side), and sector number. More than one sector can be read at a time, which is good for bulk operations; for example, DISKCOPY uses this service when it's reading the source diskette. Although I have not found anything that says so, I suspect that if you are going to read more than one sector, they would all have to be on the same track and side.

■ *Service 3* writes sectors, just as service 2 reads them.

■ *Service 4* verifies sectors. The verify operation checks that the disk data are recorded correctly; that is, that all the disk codes are good. Verify doesn't compare the data on disk with the data in memory to check that they match.

■ *Service 5* formats a diskette track. When we use the FORMAT command to *format* a new, blank diskette, DOS relies on this ROM-BIOS service to do the job. Once a track has been formatted, it can be read or written to.

MORE ABOUT FORMATTING

With the soft-sectored diskettes our PCjr uses, there is more information written on the diskette than just our data. There is also reference information that identifies each sector. Formatting is really the writing of this reference, or framework, information. The process is the equivalent of ruling guidelines onto a blank piece of paper so it will be easier for us to write.

When we use the FORMAT command to format our diskettes, DOS supplies the information the ROM-BIOS format service needs to do its job. When we use the ROM-BIOS service directly, we have to specify reference information for each sector, and it uses four bytes for each. The first byte gives the track number (0 through 39) for confirmation of the right track. The second gives the head, or diskette side number (0 or 1), also for confirmation. The third gives the sector number (1 through 8 or 9). The fourth specifies the length of the sector (128 to 1,024 bytes); for DOS, sectors are always 512 bytes.

Formatting for Copy Protection

On an ordinary DOS diskette, tracks are formatted in the conventional way. To *copy protect* a diskette, though, some unconventional formatting may be used. Copy protection is a complex technical issue—as well as a delicate ethical and commercial issue—and I am far from being an expert in how copy protection is accomplished. But from looking at the ROM-BIOS format service, we can see some of the ways that diskettes can be copy protected.

One way to copy protect a diskette is to format at least one of the sectors on the diskette a different length than the DOS standard; then special methods must be used to read or write data to that part of the diskette.

Another way to copy protect is to change the order of the sectors. When a diskette is being formatted, the diskette drive uses the diskette's index hole to find the start of the track. After that, the index hole is never used—the diskette drive finds each sector not by counting its location from the beginning of the track, but simply by looking for the sector number ID in the reference data. DOS places the sectors in consecutive order, but they could be written in a shuffled order and still work just fine. Sectors formatted in that way would work the same, but there would be a timing difference between reading ordinary sectors and these special sectors, since the diskette would be rotating for a longer or shorter time between sectors. A clever program could use this timing difference to detect an unauthorized copy. This method is tricky as a copy-protection scheme. For one thing it depends partly on the performance of the specific diskette drive. But then, all copy-protection schemes are tricky.

There are many more copy-protection schemes than the two we have mentioned here. But now, at least you have some idea of how it can be done.

11
AN INTRODUCTION TO VIDEO DISPLAYS

Nothing is more important to our use
of the computer than video display
screens. Display screens are
fundamental to the interaction
between people and computers.

Many people refer to the display screen as the computer itself—and in a sense they are right, for the display screen is our window to the computer.

The subject of video displays is so interesting and so important that we'll devote the next three chapters to it. This chapter will cover most of the basics of how the PCjr's display screen works, while the next two chapters will focus on the specifics of the two different modes it uses: text and graphics.

To set the stage, let's start by considering the basic concepts of video display, so that we understand how the PCjr's screen works and how it differs from some other screens.

There are several different ways, mechanically and electrically, to make a display screen show an image. Among the newest and fanciest are liquid crystal displays and plasma displays. But the mainstay of computer displays is the same technology used in television sets: the *cathode ray tube*, or *CRT.* All the display screens that our Junior can use, including ordinary TV sets, are CRTs.

CRTs AND HOW THEY WORK

A CRT display screen always draws its pictures by directing a beam of electrons over a sensitive coating on the inside of the screen. Wherever the beam lands, the screen glows. The flying spot of the electron beam moves over the surface of the screen, drawing the entire display picture in a fraction of a second. As soon as the picture is complete, before it can fade away, the electron beam draws it again and then again, thus making sure that the picture stays bright.

No matter what a CRT is used for, it draws its picture with the spot of its electron beam. There are two basic ways it can draw. One is to move the beam around to just the parts of the screen that should be lit. This method is called *vector scan*, since the beam draws short, straight lines, or vectors. Vector scan is not used much, and it is not used for either our TVs or the other display screens used with Junior. But, if you visit a video-game arcade, you will probably find some games that have the distinctive appearance of vector-scan graphics.

The other basic way to draw a picture on a CRT is called *raster scan*, and it is used by TVs and by almost all computer display screens, including our PCjr's. With raster scan, the flying spot of the electron beam moves in a fixed trace over the entire screen. It usually moves in *scan lines* that go from left to right and from top to bottom, and usually the picture is painted in two halves: First every other line is drawn, from top to bottom, and then the lines in between are drawn, top to bottom. This double path gives us a more stable and flicker-free image than we would see if each line were drawn in turn. Our PCjr draws its picture with 200 lines, so the flying spot first draws the 100 even-numbered lines and then the 100 odd-numbered lines.

As the flying spot is tracing over the entire screen, it is given the signal to light up, or not light up, each part of the screen. While the spot on a vector-scan screen moves only to the places where the image is to appear, the spot on a raster-scan screen moves everywhere, turning on and off for each tiny dot on the screen.

HOW THE COMPUTER
CONTROLS THE DISPLAY

So far, we have talked about how the screen itself draws the picture. How a computer display screen works also depends on how the computer controls the screen image. Again, there are two basic ways. One way, which is particularly good when the display screen is located far away from the computer, is for the computer to issue commands to the screen, such as clear-the-screen, or write-one-character-at-such-and-such-a-location. Working that way, the screen is responsible for keeping a record of what is being displayed, and the computer has to send only those commands that make changes to the screen. The talk between the computer and the screen is minimal, a real advantage if the display screen is really far away and talks with the computer through a telephone line. This command method is used by most large, mainframe computers to talk to their display terminals, but our PCjr uses another, more intimate method.

The more intimate method for a computer and a display screen to work together is for them to share some memory. With this method, called a memory-mapped display, the display screen does not keep track on its own of what is being displayed. Instead, the record of what is to be displayed is stored in some memory shared with the computer. Each time an image is drawn, the display screen reads the memory to see what it should show. When the computer needs to change all or part of the display information, it simply writes changes into the shared memory locations, the display screen reads the changes, and a new image appears on the screen.

There are many advantages to using a memory-mapped display. It offers tremendous speed and flexibility. Mainframe computers have not been able to take advantage of memory mapping because they cannot count on having their display terminals close enough for the intensive interaction that memory mapping requires. But for personal computers like our PCjr, the display is never very far away from the computer, and we can get all the advantages of memory mapping. It is ironic that our inexpensive Junior can use memory mapping to generate snappier displays than those produced by multimillion-dollar mainframe computers.

THE PCjr's SPECIAL VIDEO DISPLAY

One of the most important things about our Junior is that it is fully compatible with the other IBM personal computers and can share their software. For the video displays, this compatibility is quite special—the PCjr is both completely compatible with the other IBM personal computers, and it is also uniquely different.

For the IBM personal computers, the display is an optional add-on. You have to have one, of course, but one is not built into the computer. For the PC and XT, there are two different display adapters, known as the *monochrome adapter* and the *color/graphics* adapter. A PC or XT can have either one, or both, installed. Part of the way in which the PCjr differs is that it comes with the equivalent of a color/graphics adapter built into it (and it doesn't have any way to accommodate the IBM Monochrome Display). To understand the PCjr's display better, and to see how it can make Junior both different and exactly the same as the PC and XT, we need to take a quick look at the two conventional display adapters.

(Before we get you confused, let's pause to note that we are talking about display adapter cards here; these are the interfaces, or translators, between the computer and the display screen itself. All sorts of display screens, including ordinary home TVs, can be plugged into a display adapter, but it is the adapter that defines what can be displayed.)

The original PC came with the choice of two display adapters for a simple, practical reason. Color/graphics are essential for games and other such uses on a personal computer, but there is one major problem with color displays: When you are using them for business applications such as word processing, the display quality just is not clear enough to stare at all day. To solve that problem, IBM created the monochrome adapter and a special monochrome display screen to produce extremely crisp, sharp, readable images. There are, as we'll discuss later, good monochrome display screens that can be connected to the PCjr, or to a color/graphics adapter; they are good, but not as superbly good as the IBM Monochrome Display.

The monochrome display adapter works with a screen made up of 25 rows of 80 characters, a common format for a computer terminal display screen. The color/graphics adapter—and our PCjr—can also display 25 rows of 80 characters, so the monochrome display does not add anything that the color/graphics display does not have; it just does it clearer and crisper. There is, however, one minor thing the monochrome display can do that the color system cannot: The monochrome display can show characters underlined. While the color display cannot ordinarily underline any text, it automatically uses the color blue when it displays anything that the monochrome system would show as underlined.

While the monochrome adapter can show only text, the color/graphics adapter has many operating modes. Two of these modes work exactly like the monochrome display, except that color replaces underlining. The color/graphics modes also provide several different ways to display text information, as well as several ways to display graphic drawings (which can be combined with written text, as we'll see later).

With the minor exception of underlining, the monochrome adapter gives PC and XT users just a subset of what the color/graphics adapter gives them. Thus, systems with only the color/graphics adapter can still use the same software, and do the same things that monochrome systems do. So, while many business and professional computer users are willing to forgo the dramatic capabilities of color systems for the clearer, easier-to-read monochrome display, anyone who wants the full, rich range of possible uses for the IBM personal computers should seriously consider getting a color/graphics adapter, or using our nice little PCjr.

As I have said, IBM designed the PCjr with a color/graphics adapter built right into it. From the point of view of an old PC and XT user, our Junior's color capabilities are right at home with those our programs are accustomed to using. But actually, our PCjr's video system is quite special and gives us some very interesting features that the others do not.

Obviously, the first thing that's special about the PCjr's adapter is that it is built-in; with the PC and XT you have to pay extra to buy a video adapter.

The next special thing about Junior is the fact that it has three video outputs. With the PC's color/graphics adapter, there are two outputs providing two kinds of connections to display screens. One is the RGB output, with separate signals for the red, green, and blue parts of the color picture, and the other is the composite video signal in which these colors are combined. A special RGB monitor can be connected to the RGB output; an ordinary color monitor, or an inexpensive monochrome monitor, can be connected to the composite video output. Our PCjr has these two outputs, plus one more.

With the PC, if you want to connect a home TV to the color/graphics adapter, it has to be connected to a special RF (radio-frequency) modulator that is plugged into the composite video output. So, to use your TV with the color/-graphics adapter, you have to buy an RF modulator as a converter. The PCjr's adapter cable for TV sets includes an RF modulator. With the PCjr, then, we can also use a TV as a monitor, without any special adapter. As an extra benefit, the sounds that Junior generates are fed right into our TVs as well.

In addition, the PCjr's video system adds some extra features that the color/-graphics adapter for the PC and XT doesn't have. As I've mentioned, there are both text and graphics modes of operation for these displays. The PCjr enriches the modes available on the PC and XT by adding three new, enhanced, graphics drawing modes.

The final thing that is special about Junior's video is that its memory mapping works quite differently from the memory mapping in the other IBM personal computers (although, by a trick, it appears to be just the same). A few pages further on, we will cover how the memory mapping works and explain the special trick.

MORE ABOUT MODES

There are 11 different modes of operation for the PCjr's displays, and in this section we will take a look at what they are, how they work, and how they are controlled one way in the ROM-BIOS and another way in BASIC.

The various video modes, which are numbered 0 through 10, are controlled by the ROM-BIOS programs. To avoid confusion, remember that the ROM-BIOS mode numbers are not the same numbers used by BASIC in the SCREEN statement; although BASIC gives us full control over the video modes, BASIC refers to them in its own way.

Of the 11 modes, numbers 0 through 7 are part of the original design of the PC and XT; modes 8, 9, and 10 are new to our PCjr.

Mode 7 is the code for the monochrome adapter. Since our PCjr has a built-in color/graphics adapter, mode 7 does not apply here. If a program asks the PCjr's ROM-BIOS to change the mode to 7, the request will be rejected, just as it would be on a PC that had the color/graphics adapter and not the monochrome adapter. All the other modes, 0 through 6 and 8 through 10, apply to our PCjr; the last three, as we've said, are Junior's alone.

Text Modes

Modes 0 through 3 (and, on a PC or XT with monochrome adapter, mode 7) put the display in text mode, where characters can be shown on the screen but graphics cannot. As Figure 11-1 shows, these five modes represent different combinations of two factors: either with or without color, and with either 40 or 80 characters on each screen line. Mode 0 is 40-column, black and white; 1 is 40-column, color; 2 is 80-column, black and white; and 3 is 80-column, color. (Mode 7 is 80-column, black and white, for the PC and XT.)

The 40-column modes were originally created for use with TV sets, which do not have enough resolution to show 80 columns of characters well. There is an additional benefit for our PCjr in using the 40-column modes: Since the display memory is taken out of our main working memory space, 40-column mode reduces the memory needs of the display by half.

The black-and-white modes are intended to be used when a display screen does not show color well. This is true of many of the inexpensive monochrome

		Columns				
Model	Mode	80	40	Rows	Colors	Black and White
All	0		x	25		x
All	1		x	25	16	
All	2	x		25		x
All	3	x		25	16	
PC/XT	7	x		25		x

Figure 11-1. Five text modes

monitors that are used with IBM personal computers. (Don't confuse these monitors with the IBM Monochrome Display, which is connected to the monochrome adapter and which cannot be used with our PCjr. The monochrome monitors we are talking about here are plugged into the composite color output of a PCjr or the color/graphics adapter of a PC or XT. Using this kind of monitor is one of the cheapest ways to get a good display screen for an IBM personal computer, but it is done at the sacrifice of color.)

Modes 0 through 3 and mode 7 are all text modes; that means the display screen is divided into *character positions*. There are 40 or 80 character positions (columns) across the screen and 25 character positions (rows) down, for a total of 1,000 or 2,000 character positions per screen. Since the PCjr's display screen has 200 horizontal scan lines, each character position is the equivalent of eight scan lines high.

Into each character position we can place a character, such as A. When we place characters with a programming language, as with the BASIC statement:

```
PRINT "A"
```

the ASCII code for the letter A, which happens to be the number 65, is placed into the part of the memory that the display uses for its information. The display sees the ASCII code for A, and shows an A on the screen.

In the text modes, we can only show characters on the screen. Although there are some special characters (lines of various sorts) that allow us to make simple drawings, we can only make crude drawings with characters.

Graphics Modes

Modes 4, 5, and 6, plus the PCjr's own, unique 8, 9, and 10, are all graphics modes. In text mode, the screen is made up of character positions, but in the graphics modes, the screen is reinterpreted as a grid of closely spaced dots, called *picture elements*, *pixels*, or *pels*. Each pixel, or dot on the screen, can be controlled individually. In graphics mode, drawings are made by lighting up the appropriate pixels. If we use some of the BASIC drawing commands, such as:

```
CIRCLE (160,100),60
    or:
LINE (0,0) - (100,100)
```

BASIC will figure out which pixels are on the circle or line and will turn them on. Even though BASIC appears to let us draw quick circles, lines, and boxes, what actually goes on behind the scenes is that a series of dots is lit up to make the picture we want.

When we are in graphics mode, it is still possible to write characters on the screen. Not only does BASIC give us this ability, but the ROM-BIOS itself can write characters on the screen. What is unusual about writing characters on the screen in graphics mode is that the display can't just be told to display a character—as far as the display is concerned, the only thing appearing on the screen is a drawing made up of pixel dots. The interesting trick here is that when the display is in graphics mode, the ROM-BIOS routines actually draw the characters we want displayed. Just as BASIC draws a line by turning on the appropriate pixels, so the ROM-BIOS writes a character by turning on the pixels that make up the character.

How does the ROM-BIOS know what to draw? A table of character drawings is stored in ROM. We can't change these drawings, but we can, if we wish, override half of them. The design of the PCjr doesn't let us override the first half of the character table, which contains the alphabet and other ordinary text characters, but it does let us change the drawings for the second half, CHR$(128) through CHR$(255). To override half the table in ROM, we set up another table of our own drawings and place its address in the interrupt vector table so that the ROM-BIOS knows where to find it.

All told, there are six graphics modes, three old and three new, detailed in Figure 11-2.

We have not yet gone into how the color possibilities work with either text or graphics modes; we'll get into that and other interesting details in the next two chapters.

VIDEO AND BASIC

Before we finish up here, we need to see how BASIC gives us control over the video modes. Through a combination of statements, BASIC allows us to select any of the modes, as shown in Figure 11-3. In the text modes, the

		Pixels			Black and White
Model	Mode	Columns	Rows	Colors	
All	4	320	200	4	
All	5	320	200	(suppressed)	x
All	6	640	200	2 or	x
PCjr	8	160	200	16	
PCjr	9	320	200	16	
PCjr	10	640	200	4	

Figure 11-2. Six graphics modes

WIDTH statement sets 40 or 80 columns. The SCREEN statement selects between the various text and graphics modes, while the second, or burst, parameter of this statement allows us to choose whether the mode will operate in color or not. Matching all these elements to the list of ROM-BIOS screen modes can be a bit complicated, so Figure 11-3 is a summary of BASIC statements to help out.

MEMORY TRICKS FOR VIDEO DISPLAYS

With a memory-mapped display, the IBM personal computers have to have some part of memory set aside for the use of the displays. The PC and XT have

Mode	BASIC Statements to Get There SCREEN (mode), (burst) : WIDTH (columns)
0	SCREEN 0, 0 :WIDTH 40
1	SCREEN 0, 1 :WIDTH 40
2	SCREEN 0, 0 :WIDTH 80
3	SCREEN 0, 1 :WIDTH 80
4	SCREEN 1, 1
5	SCREEN 1, 0
6	SCREEN 2
7	(Doesn't apply to the PCjr)
8	SCREEN 3
9	SCREEN 5
10	SCREEN 6

Figure 11-3. BASIC statements to select ROM-BIOS video modes

blocks of memory dedicated solely for this purpose. The PCjr adds an extra trick; it works differently, but at the same time closely mimics the way the others operate. In order to understand the difference, let's look at both types of memory mapping—the original (PC and XT) and the unique (PCjr).

In the original PC design, two separate areas of memory are used—one for the monochrome adapter and another for the color/graphics adapter—to make it possible for the computer to have both types of display at the same time. Each of these reserved areas of memory is 32K in size, although not that much is needed. The monochrome adapter needs only 4,000 bytes, or a little less than 4K, and the color/graphics adapter needs just 16K. Each of these memory spaces is located in the B000 memory block; the monochrome adapter uses the first half, from segment address B000, and the color/graphics adapter uses the second half, from B800.

Each of the display adapters used by the PC and XT comes with the memory needed by the display. While logically this memory is a part of the computer's total 1,024K memory space, physically the display memory is located on the display adapter board, separate from all the other memory. Electronically, there is one thing special about this memory—there are two electronic doorways into it so that both the computer and the display screen can be working with the memory simultaneously, without getting in each other's way as they pass information through the doorways.

When the PC or the XT needs to write something on the display screen, it simply stores the information in the appropriate memory locations for the display. If a program finds that it needs to read information from the display screen, it can simply look at what is stored in the shared display memory.

Now, so far we have described the memory-mapping magic of the PC and the XT, which is closely related to the PCjr's own magic. How is its display different?

First, Junior has no dedicated memory for its display screen; this is one of the many ways that its cost has been held down to make it so inexpensive compared with its bigger brothers. Instead of using special dedicated memory, the PCjr uses part of its 64K or 128K of main working memory.

Second, there is no fixed amount of memory used, nor even a fixed location for the memory given to the display. While the monochrome adapter places its display memory at the fixed location of paragraph hex B000, and the color/graphics adapter puts its memory at paragraph B800, our Junior varies in the memory location it uses. The display memory is always at the highest end of the RAM storage, but the address varies depending upon how much memory there is, 64K or 128K, and how much is set aside for the display. The amount of display memory needed varies with the video mode, as shown in Figure 11-4.

One thing that we lose on our PCjrs is the dual-path memory of the PC and XT. In the PCjr, both the computer and the display are competing for the use

Video Mode Number	Corresponding BASIC SCREEN Mode Number	Minimum Memory Used (in K)
0	0	2
1	0	2
2	0	4
3	0	4
4	1 or 4	16
5	1 or 4	16
6	2	16
7	n/a	n/a
8	3	16
9	5	32
10	6	32

Figure 11-4. Amount of memory needed by each video mode

of the same resource, the path into the memory. This slows the performance of our PCjrs down a little—they do not run at the full speed of a PC or XT. On the average, the loss should be about 15 percent.

In the original PC, the ROM-BIOS knows which display adapter is being used, and so it knows where to store information in memory in order to have it appear on the display screen. Our PCjr's ROM-BIOS also knows which part of memory is set aside for the use of the display and where to store information. However, there are loads and loads of programs written for the PC and XT that think *they* know where the display memory is. These programs were built around the design of the PC and XT and place information on the display screen by writing directly to the computer's dedicated memory locations. Unfortunately, the PCjr doesn't use those locations; instead, it uses lower, ordinary memory locations for its display.

This difference would have made all those PC and XT programs unusable on our PCjr if IBM had not come up with a very special trick. They have installed a special bit of circuitry called a video gate array, or VGA, in Junior's memory. The VGA is kept aware of the part of memory that is being used for the display. Whenever any program running on the PCjr uses any part of memory, the VGA checks to see if the program is referring to the PC/XT display memory locations at segment addresses B000 and B800. If it is, the VGA translates the segment-address reference to the part of memory where the PCjr's display is located. The program is completely unaware that its attempts to use the old display locations are being rerouted to new locations. All the magic goes on behind the scenes, without the program being any the wiser.

153

So, if we want our programs to display information by placing it directly into memory, we have two choices: We can calculate the actual location of Junior's display memory; or we can use the VGA to pretend that Junior has a color/-graphics adapter, and we can place our information into the color/graphics memory addresses that begin at paragraph B800. I would strongly recommend using paragraph B800 for two reasons: One is that we don't have to bother trying to figure out just where the movable location of the PCjr's display memory is. The other is that if we write programs that use the PCjr's unique memory locations, we can't use them on a PC or XT.

SOME HORSING AROUND

For fun, let's horse around in BASIC with the video modes. We can do a little experimenting with the various video modes, seeing what they look like and how they display characters, and we can also get a rough idea of what they do with the bits in the memory map with a little program we'll evolve here.

What we want to do is try all the video modes, write something out in them, and then POKE a value into memory to see what it looks like. Here's the program outline:

```
1000 ' Horsing around with video modes
1010 ' from Exploring the IBM PCjr Home Computer
1020 '
1030 CLEAR , , , 32768           ' needed for modes 9-10
1040 GOSUB 2000                  ' other initialization
1050 FOR MODE = 0 TO 10          ' loop through modes
1060    GOSUB 3000               ' try each mode
1070 NEXT MODE                   ' finish the loop
1080 END                         ' finish the program
1090 '
```

To initialize the program, we clear the screen and set a working color (let's set a rather glaring red on blue). We also set the segment register to B800, the location in memory used by the PC/XT color/graphics adapter.

```
2000 ' initialization subroutine
2010 ON ERROR GOTO 2110          ' prepare for color errors
2020 DEF SEG = &HB800            ' color segment location
2030 KEY OFF
2040 COLOR 14,1,1
2050 CLS
2060 PRINT
2070 PRINT " Exploring the PCjr's video modes "
2080 PRINT
2090 INPUT " Press enter, to explore ... ", A$
2100 RETURN
2110 RESUME NEXT                 ' handle color errors
```

Then for each mode, we set the mode with the BASIC SCREEN statement and print out what mode we are in. We POKE a value into the memory and show how the value is treated by each mode (the value appears at the top right of the screen). The program then waits for a keystroke telling it to continue, giving us time to inspect each mode carefully. The value we'll poke is 119—a sneaky choice, since it is the ASCII code for lowercase w, and has lots of bits set: Six of the eight bits in the byte are on.

```
3000 ' subroutine to act on each mode
3010 '
3020 IF MODE =   0 THEN SCREEN 0, 0 : WIDTH 40
3030 IF MODE =   1 THEN SCREEN 0, 1 : WIDTH 40
3040 IF MODE =   2 THEN SCREEN 0, 0 : WIDTH 80
3050 IF MODE =   3 THEN SCREEN 0, 1 : WIDTH 80
3060 IF MODE =   4 THEN SCREEN 1, 1
3070 IF MODE =   5 THEN SCREEN 1, 0
3080 IF MODE =   6 THEN SCREEN 2
3090 IF MODE =   7 THEN SCREEN 0, 1 : WIDTH 80
3100 IF MODE =   8 THEN SCREEN 3
3110 IF MODE =   9 THEN SCREEN 5
3120 IF MODE = 10 THEN SCREEN 6
3130 COLOR MODE+1, MODE+2 : CLS
3140 PRINT " -- Look here for POKE results"
3150 POKE 0, 119 ' here we put a 'w' into memory
3160 PRINT
3170 PRINT " This is mode number"; MODE
3180 PRINT
3190 PRINT "Press any key to continue... "
3200 IF INKEY$ = ""GOTO 3200 ' wait for keystroke
3210 RETURN
```

The complete program is shown in Figure 11-5.

```
1000 ' Horsing around with video modes
1010 ' from Exploring the IBM PCjr Home Computer
1020 '
1030 CLEAR ,,, 32768              ' needed for modes 9-10
1040 GOSUB 2000                   ' other initialization
1050 FOR MODE = 0 TO 10           ' loop through modes
1060    GOSUB 3000                ' try each mode
1070 NEXT MODE                    ' finish the loop
1080 END                          ' finish the program
1090 '
```

(continued)

Figure 11-5. A program to demonstrate video modes 0 through 10

155

```
2000 ' initialization subroutine
2010 ON ERROR GOTO 2110          ' prepare for color errors
2020 DEF SEG = &HB800            ' color segment location
2030 KEY OFF
2040 COLOR 14,1,1
2050 CLS
2060 PRINT
2070 PRINT " Exploring the PCjr's video modes "
2080 PRINT
2090 INPUT " Press enter, to explore ... ", A$
2100 RETURN
2110 RESUME NEXT                 ' handle color errors


3000 ' subroutine to act on each mode
3010 '
3020 IF MODE =  0 THEN SCREEN 0, 0 : WIDTH 40
3030 IF MODE =  1 THEN SCREEN 0, 1 : WIDTH 40
3040 IF MODE =  2 THEN SCREEN 0, 0 : WIDTH 80
3050 IF MODE =  3 THEN SCREEN 0, 1 : WIDTH 80
3060 IF MODE =  4 THEN SCREEN 1, 1
3070 IF MODE =  5 THEN SCREEN 1, 0
3080 IF MODE =  6 THEN SCREEN 2
3090 IF MODE =  7 THEN SCREEN 0, 1 : WIDTH 80
3100 IF MODE =  8 THEN SCREEN 3
3110 IF MODE =  9 THEN SCREEN 5
3120 IF MODE = 10 THEN SCREEN 6
3130 COLOR MODE+1, MODE+2 : CLS
3140 PRINT " -- Look here for POKE results"
3150 POKE 0, 119 ' here we put a 'w' into memory
3160 PRINT
3170 PRINT " This is mode number"; MODE
3180 PRINT
3190 PRINT "Press any key to continue... "
3200 IF INKEY$ = ""GOTO 3200    ' wait for keystroke
3210 RETURN
```

Figure 11-5. A program to demonstrate video modes 0 through 10 (continued)

12
FUNDAMENTALS OF TEXT VIDEO

In this chapter, we will look at how our Junior works with the display screen in text mode. Just to avoid confusion, let's remind ourselves that text mode can only display characters; it can't do any drawing, except for the drawings that we can make with characters.

To Get to Mode	SCREEN Statement	Burst Parameter	WIDTH (columns)	BASIC Command
0	SCREEN 0	0	WIDTH 40	SCREEN 0,0 : WIDTH 40
1	SCREEN 0	1	WIDTH 40	SCREEN 0,1 : WIDTH 40
2	SCREEN 0	0	WIDTH 80	SCREEN 0,0 : WIDTH 80
3	SCREEN 0	1	WIDTH 80	SCREEN 0,1 : WIDTH 80

Figure 12-1. BASIC commands to move to four text modes

Our PCjr normally operates in text mode. When we turn it on, it is in text mode. If we are programming in BASIC and have put the computer into graphics mode to play games or draw pictures, when we leave BASIC with the SYSTEM command, the computer will go back to text mode before DOS takes charge.

As we have seen, there are four different text modes: with or without color, and with a 40- or 80-column screen width. If we are programming in BASIC, the SCREEN command will switch us between text and graphics modes, as shown in Figure 12-1.

To get to text mode, we ask for mode 0, with the command:

SCREEN 0

We can control which of the four text modes we are in by using the WIDTH command, specifying:

WIDTH 40

or:

WIDTH 80

and combining it with the *burst* parameter of the SCREEN command to control color, specifying:

SCREEN , 0

or:

SCREEN , 1

With these BASIC commands, we have quick, easy control over the video modes. With other programming languages, we would probably have to set the video mode through an assembly-language interface routine that would request the mode change from the ROM-BIOS services. Whether we use BASIC or any other language, in the end it is the ROM-BIOS that actually switches the mode.

What is special about the text mode for our video display is that the data in the memory-mapped storage consist of the actual ASCII codes for each character that we want displayed. The display circuitry in our PCjr does the work of making the characters that the codes represent appear on the screen. This is another way of saying that the display circuitry has a built-in *character generator.* The character generator has the job of determining what each character should look like.

When we are in text mode, the character generator is active, building our display characters. If we want to display characters when we are in graphics mode, there has to be a drawing of the character in memory in order to have the character appear on the screen. In graphics mode, the character generator can take a break while the display shows a direct image of the picture stored in memory.

No matter what mode our video display is in, the information on the display screen is controlled by the data stored in the memory map. The data stored in memory specify two things: what is to be displayed, and how it is to be displayed. In text mode, the *what* is the codes of the characters that are to be displayed; the *how* is the colors that are to be used and whether the characters are to blink.

For each character position on the screen, there are two bytes in the memory map. The first, the character byte, gives the ASCII code for the character to be displayed; the second, the color attribute byte, gives the color attributes for the character. Thus, every single position has an independently controlled color and if we need to, we can give each of our program's messages (or even each character of each message) its own distinctive color. This can be very useful for making error messages stand out, or for adding emphasis in the same way books use italics or typewriters use underlining.

Later in this chapter, we will learn how these two bytes work, but for a little fun right now, you might want to try the short program shown in Figure 12-2. It will quickly run through all the color possibilities, at the top corner of your PCjr's display screen. For such a simple program, the appearance of so many colors is quite dramatic.

This program runs through all the color attributes. If you would like to see the same action, but with all the possible characters that can be displayed, just change one line of the program. In line 200, set OFFSET = 0, instead of 1. Don't worry if the logic of this change is a little unclear to you right now; I'll explain it later on. For now, just watch the program change the characters displayed, instead of the color attributes of the characters. The result will look a bit like a dancing chorus line.

Most programming languages do not give us any direct control over the color of what we display, for the simple reason that the kind of color our Junior uses is not a common, universal feature of computers. But our PCjr's ROM-BASIC has special commands to support most of these special features. (One of the most important characteristics of our PCjr's BASIC is that it is closely in tune with the PCjr's features. This isn't true of other programming languages.) So in BASIC, we can use the COLOR statement to control how each message we write on the screen appears. To see it in action, try keying in the program in Figure 12-3.

Now it's time to look at the color attributes more closely.

```
100 ' show the attributes in action
110 ' from Exploring the IBM PCjr Home Computer
120 ' authored by Peter Norton, 1983
130 '
140 KEY OFF
150 SCREEN 0, 1
160 WIDTH 40
170 CLS
180 ' use PC/XT color/graphics segment location
190 DEF SEG = &HB800
200 OFFSET = 1
210 PRINT "ABC—watch this space."
220 PRINT
230 PRINT "Press any key to stop."
240 PRINT
250 WHILE 1                           ' continue forever
260    FOR I = 0 TO 255
270       POKE OFFSET + 0,I           ' change 1st character
280       POKE OFFSET + 2,I           ' change 2nd character
290       POKE OFFSET + 4,I           ' change 3rd character
300       ' check for a keystroke
310       IF LEN (INKEY$) 0 THEN GOTO 350
320       FOR J = 1 TO 50 : NEXT J    ' kill some time
330    NEXT I
340 WEND                              ' end of forever loop
350 PRINT
360 PRINT "End of demonstration program."
370 END
```

Figure 12-2. A program to demonstrate all the color attributes

```
100 KEY OFF
110 SCREEN 0, 1
120 WIDTH 40
130 CLS
140 COLOR 1
150 PRINT " Colors ";
160 COLOR 2
170 PRINT " can be ";
180 COLOR 4
190 PRINT " dramatic "
200 END
```

Figure 12-3. A program to demonstrate color combinations

COVERING THE COLORS

In text mode, each character on the screen has its own, individual attribute byte that controls how the character will be displayed. A byte, of course, has eight bits, and each bit in the attribute byte acts independently to control a different aspect of how the character is displayed. Before we look at each bit, let's start by breaking the color attributes into their main parts.

There are four main parts to the color attributes. First, there is the foreground color, the color of the character itself. Then there is the background color, the color of the area surrounding the character—on a printed page like this, the background is the white space around the black ink. There are also two special properties that the foreground (the character itself) can take on: It can be intense or not, so that the character's color is bright or dim; and it can be blinking or steady.

Not all color display screens can show the difference between intense and dim colors, but for those that can, there are 16 possible colors; without the distinction between bright and dim, there are only eight possible colors.

The colors themselves, foreground and background, break down into three parts each. A color display, whether it's a TV set or a special color monitor for a computer, builds its colors out of three components: red, green, and blue—the three colors that give RGB color monitors their initials. On our PCjr, each of these three color components works independently; so when the attribute byte specifies the foreground and background colors, there are three bits—one for red, one for green, and one for blue—dedicated to each. Bit numbers 0 through 2 control the foreground color and bit numbers 4 through 6 control the background color.

R	G	B	Color
0	0	0	Black
0	0	1	Blue
0	1	0	Green
0	1	1	Cyan
1	0	0	Red
1	0	1	Magenta
1	1	0	Yellow
1	1	1	White

Figure 12-4. Eight colors created from combinations of red, green, and blue

With three bits controlling three colors, there are eight possible combinations (16 counting both intense and dim ones). With all bits/colors off, we have black; with all on, we have white. With one of the three bits on, we get an intense, pure red, green, or blue. With any two of the bits on, we get a composite color: cyan (blue and green), magenta (red and blue), or yellow (red and green). A quick summary of the eight basic colors used by the PCjr is given in Figure 12-4.

As you may recall from science classes, the pigment in ink or paint makes colors by subtracting color. In contrast, the light from a CRT screen makes colors by adding color. So the combined colors, such as cyan, are brighter than the pure colors, such as blue. Brightness is one of the things we have to take into account in choosing the colors that our programs will use.

The layout of the eight bits of the attribute byte is shown in Figure 12-5.

Bit	Attribute Controlled	Color
0	Foreground	Blue
1	Foreground	Green
2	Foreground	Red
3	Intensity	
4	Background	Blue
5	Background	Green
6	Background	Red
7	Blinking	

Figure 12-5. Layout of eight bits of the attribute byte

Color	Dim	Bright	Dim/Blinking	Bright/Blinking
Black	0	8	16	24
Blue	1	9	17	25
Green	2	10	18	26
Cyan	3	11	19	27
Red	4	12	20	28
Magenta	5	13	21	29
Yellow	6	14	22	30
White	7	15	23	31

Figure 12-6. Parameter numbers for the BASIC
COLOR statement

When we use the COLOR statement in BASIC, the foreground parameter, which is a number from 0 through 31, sets the foreground color bits, the intensity bit, and the blinking bit. The background parameter, which is a number from 0 through 7, sets just the background color. For example, COLOR 26,7 gives us a bright, blinking green foreground on a white background, which is remarkably difficult to read. If you play around with color, you'll find some combinations that are lovely (COLOR 7,1,1) and some that are diabolical (COLOR 17,4,4). Figure 12-6 shows the parameter numbers for the COLOR statement.

Figure 12-7 gives a program that will demonstrate the full range of possible color attribute combinations for the PCjr. Other than satisfying curiosity, there are two good uses for this program. First, it lets you check whether your display screen makes use of the intensity bit. If the bright colors differ from the ordinary colors, you will know that the intensity bit works with your display. Second, this program gives you a chance to see all the color possibilities and thus helps you choose the ones you might want to use in your own programs.

While our Junior has a full range of colors to use, the PC and XT may or may not have the same range. If they have the color/graphics adapter, they can use color just like our PCjr. If they use the monochrome adapter, there is no color, although the monochrome adapter still makes use of the attribute byte to display characters in different ways. These special characteristics of the monochrome adapter don't apply to Junior, but we need to understand them for two reasons: first, to better understand all the IBM personal computers; second (and more to the point of this book), so that if we are writing programs, we can select our color choices so that they work well on a monochrome PC or XT, as well as on a color computer like our PCjr. For these reasons, let's look briefly at the "color" attributes of a monochrome display.

```
1000 ' demonstrating all the color combinations
1010 ' from Exploring the IBM PCjr Home Computer
1020 ' authored by Peter Norton, 1983
1030 '
1040 ' main program outline
1050 '
1060 GOSUB 2000                    ' initialize
1070 ' loop through blinking/not blinking
1080 FOR BLINKING = 0 TO 1
1090 ' loop through background colors
1100    FOR BACKGROUND = 0 TO 7
1110    ' loop through high/low intensity
1120      FOR INTENSITY = 0 TO 1
1130      ' loop through foreground colors
1140        FOR FOREGROUND = 0 TO 7
1150        ' display information about the color
1160          GOSUB 3000
1170          NEXT FOREGROUND
1180        NEXT INTENSITY
1190    NEXT BACKGROUND
1200 NEXT BLINKING
1210 GOSUB 6000                    ' finish-up

2000 '
2010 ' initialization subroutine
2020 '
2030 KEY OFF
2040 SCREEN 0, 1
2050 WIDTH 80
2060 COLOR 2, 0 ,0
2070 CLS
2080 PRINT "Color demonstration program"
2090 PRINT
2100 PRINT "from Exploring the IBM PCjr"
2110 PRINT "authored by Peter Norton, 1983"
2120 PRINT
2999 RETURN

3000 '
3010 ' report on one color combination
3020 '
3030 COLOR FOREGROUND + INTENSITY * 8
     + BLINKING * 16, BACKGROUND
3040 PRINT
```

(continued)

*Figure 12-7. A richer program to demonstrate
all the color attributes*

```
3050 PRINT " ";
3060 IF FOREGROUND = BACKGROUND THEN COLOR 7, 0:
     PRINT "(This would be ";
3070 IF BLINKING THEN PRINT "blinking ";
3080 IF INTENSITY THEN PRINT "bright ";
3090 COLOR.NUMBER = FOREGROUND
3100 ' get the number translated into a name
3110 GOSUB 4000
3120 PRINT "on ";
3130 COLOR.NUMBER = BACKGROUND
3140 ' get the number translated into a name
3150 GOSUB 4000
3160 IF FOREGROUND = BACKGROUND THEN PRINT ")";
3170 PRINT " ";
3180 GOSUB 5000 ' check if time to pause
3999 RETURN

4000 '
4010 ' translate a color number into its name
4020 '
4030 IF COLOR.NUMBER = 0 AND INTENSITY = 0
     THEN PRINT "black ";
4040 IF COLOR.NUMBER = 0 AND INTENSITY = 1
     THEN PRINT "gray ";
4050 IF COLOR.NUMBER = 1 THEN PRINT "blue ";
4060 IF COLOR.NUMBER = 2 THEN PRINT "green ";
4070 IF COLOR.NUMBER = 3 THEN PRINT "cyan ";
4080 IF COLOR.NUMBER = 4 THEN PRINT "red ";
4090 IF COLOR.NUMBER = 5 THEN PRINT "magenta ";
4100 IF COLOR.NUMBER = 6 AND INTENSITY = 0
     THEN PRINT "brown ";
4110 IF COLOR.NUMBER = 6 AND INTENSITY = 1
     THEN PRINT "yellow ";
4120 IF COLOR.NUMBER = 7 THEN PRINT "white ";
4999 RETURN

5000 '
5010 ' check if time to pause
5020 '
5030 IF FOREGROUND < 7 THEN RETURN
5040 COLOR 2, 0
5050 PRINT
5060 PRINT
5070 PRINT "Press any key to continue."
```

(continued)

*Figure 12-7. A richer program to demonstrate
    all the color attributes (continued)*

```
5080 IF LEN (INKEY$) = 0 THEN GOTO 5080
5999 RETURN

6000 '
6010 ' finish up subroutine
6020 '
6030 PRINT
6040 PRINT "End of demonstration program."
6050 PRINT
6060 PRINT "Press 'B' to return to BASIC,"
6070 PRINT "or any other key to return to DOS."
6080 IKEY$ = INKEY$
6090 IF LEN (IKEY$) = 0 GOTO 6080
6100 IF (IKEY$ = "B") OR (IKEY$ = "b") GOTO 6140
6110 PRINT
6210 PRINT "Returning to DOS."
6130 SYSTEM
6140 PRINT
6150 PRINT "Returning to BASIC."
6160 END
```

*Figure 12-7. A richer program to demonstrate
all the color attributes (continued)*

Color on a Monochrome Display

The monochrome adapter provides some limited equivalents of colors. For one thing, both the intensity and blinking bits work with the monochrome adapter, so we can make monochrome characters bright and/or blinking. There are also two special "colors" for monochrome characters: underlined and reverse video. If we set the attribute colors to blue foreground and black background, the monochrome adapter will show characters as underlined. This is done by setting the attribute byte to hex 01, or using the BASIC statement COLOR 1,0. If we set the colors to black foreground and white background, the monochrome adapter will use *reverse video*, or black (unlit) characters on a white (lit) background (which is a green phosphor in IBM's Monochrome Display). This is done by setting the attribute byte to hex 70, or using the BASIC statement COLOR 0,7. All other foreground and background color combinations are treated by the monochrome adapter as if they were the default combination of white on black, which is an attribute value of hex 07, equivalent to the BASIC statement COLOR 7,0.

Although we can use the BASIC COLOR statement to control the color attributes, any program can manipulate the attribute byte directly in the memory-mapped storage. That's what the attribute program in the first section of this chapter does. In the next section, we'll see how the memory-mapped storage works, so that we'll understand how our programs can work with it directly.

USING THE MEMORY MAP

To understand the memory mapping in the PCjr, we have to understand three separate elements, each of them rather complicated: the mapping of a single screen image, or *page*, as it is called; the use of multiple pages; and the PCjr's special mapping of video in RAM. Let's start with the mapping of a single page—a single image of the display screen.

Mapping a Single Screen Image

As we've mentioned, each position on the display screen has two corresponding bytes in memory where the character code and the color attributes are stored. These bytes are next to one another, with all the character bytes in even-numbered memory locations and each corresponding attribute byte in the adjacent odd-numbered memory location. Let's suppose we have ABC displayed in blue-on-black. The six bytes that display these characters are shown in Figure 12-8.

Byte Number	Hex Code	ASCII Code	Binary Code	Meaning
1	41	65		Character A
2	01	—	b f 0000 0001	Foreground = 1 = blue; background = 0 = black
3	42	66		Character B
4	01	—	b f 0000 0001	Foreground = 1 = blue; background = 0 = black
5	43	67		Character C
6	01	—	b f 0000 0001	Foreground = 1 = blue; background = 0 = black

Figure 12-8. Bytes for ABC displayed in blue on black

The "attributes in action" program in Figure 12-2 raced through all the possible color attributes by poking the attribute values at an OFFSET = 1 (that is, one byte) from where the character codes were located. When we changed the address to OFFSET = 0, the POKE statements changed the character codes themselves. Thus, with OFFSET = 1 we saw the colors change; with OFFSET = 0 we saw the characters change. So that simple program *really* demonstrated what we have just learned about the memory map.

Wherever the map of the display begins in memory, the first byte, at offset 0, is the first character of the top line of the screen; the third byte, at offset 2, is the second character in that line, and so forth until we reach the end of the first line on the screen (which could be 40 or 80 characters long and would take up either 80 or 160 bytes in memory). The very next even-numbered byte of memory is then the first character of the second line on the display screen. This sequence continues until we reach the bottom right corner, at the end of the memory map for the display screen.

There are always two bytes for each character, and there are always 25 lines on the screen. The width of each line can vary, as we know. If the width is 40, the display page will take:

$$2 \times 25 \times 40 = 2,000 \text{ bytes}$$

and if the width is 80, the display page will take:

$$2 \times 25 \times 80 = 4,000 \text{ bytes}$$

We can calculate the offset address, within the memory page, of each character by using the following formula, counting the rows from 1 to 25 and the columns from 1 to 40 or 80:

$$\text{CHARACTER.OFFSET} = ((\text{COLUMN-1}) + ((\text{ROW-1}) \times \text{WIDTH})) \times 2$$

The offset address of the attribute byte would be just one higher.

Notice that since the memory is mapped continuously from one row to another, the memory location that would be the first character of the second line in 40-column mode would be the 41st character in the first line in 80-column mode.

Mapping Multiple Screen Images

So far, what we have seen applies to one display page—one image of the screen. Junior can keep more than one screen image in memory; so can the other IBM personal computers, when they use the color/graphics adapter. (The monochrome adapter, though, has only enough display memory for a single screen image.) The basic color/graphics adapter has 16K of memory, and our PCjr sets aside 16K of memory for the display. In 40-column text mode, our display screen needs only 2,000 bytes (or roughly 2K), and in 80-column text mode it needs only 4,000. So there is much more memory available than the display needs at any one time. To make good use of this memory, it is divided into display pages, each of which is an image of the display screen with which our programs can work. Only one of the pages actually appears on the screen at any one time, but our programs can be building information in one page while another is being shown.

We can figure the number of display pages by dividing the size of a page into the amount of memory that is set aside for the display screen. In our PCjr, unlike the other IBM personal computers, we can vary the amount of display memory from as little as 2K to as much as 32K; the standard amount, though, is 16K, and so we'll use that to figure with. If we are using our screen in 40-column text mode, each page takes 2,000 bytes, which the system rounds up to 2K (2,048) bytes; in 80-column text mode, a page takes 4,000 bytes, or 4K (4,096) bytes. So, with 16K of display memory, 40-column mode gives us eight display pages, and 80-column gives us four pages.

The pages are referred to by number, and they are always numbered from 0 through 3, or 7, or however many pages there are. The pages are stored in memory with page 0 first, at the beginning or lowest address in the display memory. Since memory is set aside for each page in even increments of K, there is an unused slack of 48 or 96 bytes following the end of each page.

The ability to have more than one screen image in memory can be a tremendous advantage. Sometimes it takes a program an annoyingly long time to put together all the information that needs to appear on the display screen. Instead of having us watch the process in action (and wonder when it will be finished), our programs can do all their work offstage, so to speak, and then present us with the finished display, by simply changing the display page that is being actively shown.

BASIC gives us a way to control these display pages with the SCREEN command. Two of the parameters of the SCREEN statement control the pages. The *vpage*, or visual page, parameter controls which page is shown, and the *apage*, or active page, parameter controls which page receives any output from the program. We can write into the different pages either by changing the apage parameter, or, if we are sophisticated in our knowledge of memory, by putting our data directly into the various memory locations with the POKE statement. Other programming languages can use similar methods.

Mapping Screen Images in RAM

Our PCjr operates its display in a unique way, as we've already seen. Instead of having a dedicated display memory, it borrows part of its main memory for display use. One of the goals of the PCjr is to pretend successfully to be a color/graphics adapter. To be as compatible as possible with the PC and XT, our PCjr must provide a very convincing imitation of the color/graphics adapter, and this must extend to its 16K of display memory. Thus, by default, Junior sets aside exactly 16K of its working memory to simulate the color/-graphics adapter's 16K of dedicated memory.

However, since our PCjr is using its main memory for the display, it can be much more flexible about how much memory is used. If we want to have more display pages, we can increase the amount of memory set aside for the display. On the other hand, if we don't need so many pages (and few programs use the display pages to their full advantage), we can reduce the amount of display memory and gain back more usable, general-purpose memory. This flexibility can be very valuable, since one of the main limitations of the PCjr, in comparison to its bigger brothers, is a lack of memory. In BASIC we can use the CLEAR command to set the amount of memory used for the display, for example:

```
CLEAR,,,2048
```

sets it to the minimum amount of 2K.

That wraps up the memory map for us. Now it is time to move on and look at all the characters the PCjr lets us display on its screen.

ALL THOSE CHARACTERS

Junior has a wealth of characters it can display, 256 in all. There are lots and lots of wonderful things in this character set, and we'll take a look at them in this section.

Before we go any further, you might like to know that you can find pictures of all the PCjr's characters in Appendix D. The program in Figure 12-9 will also display all these characters on your PCjr's screen, so that you can see exactly what they look like on your display.

The PCjr's character set is based on the ASCII characters. ASCII was designed using only a 7-bit code, so there are only 128 *true ASCII* characters. Our PCjr, like most computers, stores characters in an 8-bit byte. IBM, therefore, had an additional 128 characters that it could design for its personal computers.

The complete set of 256 characters is sometimes called *extended ASCII*, and it's often just called ASCII, as well. But, properly speaking, only the first 128 characters are true ASCII.

We'll look at the true ASCII characters first.

True ASCII Characters

The first 128 characters, with byte codes CHR$(0) through CHR$(127) are the ASCII character set, including the characters we are most familiar with: digits 0 through 9, CHR$(48) through CHR$(57); capital letters A through Z, CHR$(65) through CHR$(90); lowercase letters a through z, CHR$(97) through CHR$(122); and ordinary punctuation characters, scattered about with various code values. You will find a chart of these ASCII character codes in Appendix D.

The first 32 ASCII codes, CHR$(0) through CHR$(31), are special formatting codes (such as the carriage return, the line feed, and the form feed) and special communications control codes (such as the codes known as start-of-text and acknowledge). When the PCjr is working with a printer or with a communications line, these special codes are used as they were originally intended. But IBM also gave these character codes special display shapes, such as the four card suits (spades, hearts, diamonds, and clubs) and certain musical notes. These character codes can be used to produce some fancy effects on our display screens. But, be forewarned: They can't be used indiscriminately, since they also have their special meanings in the ASCII coding scheme. Generally speaking, our programs can't write these characters on the screen with ordinary output statements. The program in Figure 12-9, however, shows how we can display these characters by putting them directly into the display memory.

Additional Characters

The second half of the 256-character set is both more complex and more interesting. It is designed to take care of several needs. First, it provides the most commonly used scientific and mathematical symbols; for example, CHR$(236) is the infinity knot. Second, it provides the accented letters used in languages other than English. Currency symbols are provided as well: the cent, the pound, the franc, the yen, and the Spanish peseta. (The dollar sign is included with the true ASCII characters.) The part of greatest interest to most of us, though, is the graphics character symbols.

Graphics Characters

To make it possible to produce simple drawings in text mode, the PCjr has 48 graphics characters. These characters fall into three groups. The first group of 40 characters makes it possible to draw boxes of single and double lines. This is one of the nicest features of the IBM personal computers' character set and one that many, many programs have used to good advantage. The other two groups are oriented toward drawing bar charts: One consists of four characters

171

that occupy the entire character space, but fill it in such a way that either one-quarter, one-half, three-quarters, or all of it is solid. The other set consists of four characters that are each half solid and half blank, divided horizontally or vertically, with the top, bottom, left, or right half of the character space showing. To see the full glory of all these characters, run the program in Figure 12-9, and see Appendix D as well.

```
1000 ' display all the characters
1010 ' from Exploring the IBM PCjr Home Computer
1020 ' authored by Peter Norton, 1983
1030 '
1040 GOSUB 2000                      ' initialize
1050 FOR CHARACTER = 0 TO 255
1060    GOSUB 3000                    ' display character
1070 NEXT CHARACTER
1080 GOSUB 4000                       ' finish up

2000 '
2010 ' initialization
2020 '
2030 KEY OFF
2040 SCREEN 0, 1
2050 WIDTH 80
2060 CLS
2070 DEF SEG = &HB800
2080 PRINT
2090 PRINT " Displaying all characters . . ."
2100 LOCATE ,,0
2110 RETURN

3000 '
3010 ' subroutine to display each character
3020 '
3030 ROW.NUMBER = CHARACTER MOD 16
3040 COL.NUMBER = CHARACTER \ 16
3050 OFFSET = (ROW.NUMBER + 3) * 160 +
     COL.NUMBER * 6 + 26
3060 POKE OFFSET, CHARACTER
3070 LOCATE 2,38
3080 PRINT "character number ";CHARACTER;
3090 PRINT " hex code ";HEX$(CHARACTER)
3100 RETURN
```

(continued)

*Figure 12-9. A program to print the complete
text-mode character set*

```
4000 '
4010 ' finish up subroutine
4020 '
4050 LOCATE 21, 1, 1
4060 PRINT "Press 'B' to return to BASIC, ";
4070 PRINT "or any other key to return to DOS.";
4080 IKEY$ = INKEY$
4090 IF LEN (IKEY$) = 0 GOTO 4080
4100 IF (IKEY$ = "B") OR (IKEY$ = "b") GOTO 4120
4110 SYSTEM
4120 END
```

Figure 12-9. A program to print the complete
text-mode character set (continued)

Next let's look at the ROM-BIOS services used to support the text display.

ROM-BIOS TEXT DISPLAY SERVICES

The ROM-BIOS programs provide services to support all the operations of the PCjr's display screens. In this section, we'll take a look at all the service routines, except those that are special to the graphics modes; those we'll put off until the next chapter. If your programs need to be in complete control of the display screen, they can use these services through an assembly-language interface routine.

The ROM-BIOS display services are all invoked with interrupt 16 (hex 10) and are numbered, like the other services, with service codes beginning with 0.

■ *Service 0* is used to set the video mode, using the mode codes 0 through 6 and 8 through 10, as we outlined in the last chapter. Mode 7, remember, is for the PC/XT monochrome adapter and can't be set on the PCjr.

■ *Service 1* is used to set which scan lines the cursor will appear on. Since a character position is eight scan lines high on the PCjr, the cursor could be placed on any one of the eight, or could encompass a block of several lines. This service underlies the cursor-setting part of the BASIC LOCATE statement. When the LOCATE statement is used with start and stop parameters to indicate which scan lines the cursor is to appear on, BASIC uses this ROM-BIOS service to do the work. (When program compatibility with the PC matters to you, keep in mind that a monochrome adapter PC has 14 scan lines for the cursor.)

Service 2 sets the position of the cursor—both in its row and column, and also in a particular display page. Putting the cursor onto a display page other than the one that is being shown on the screen prepares the way for writing information to a page that we cannot currently see. Using the page part of this service is equivalent to setting the apage, or active page, in the BASIC SCREEN statement, while the row and column part of this service is equivalent to the BASIC LOCATE statement.

Service 3 is used to find out the current cursor position (row and column), and also which scan lines it appears on. In effect, service 3 is the opposite of services 1 and 2 combined.

Service 4 is used with the light pen, which we will discuss later.

Service 5 is used to change the page being displayed on the screen. To avoid confusion, we should give you one word of warning here: If you look these services up in the *Technical Reference* manual, you will find references to the active page; what the ROM-BIOS listings call the active page is the same thing BASIC calls the visual page. What BASIC calls the active page is the page where the cursor is located, which is set by service 2. If you followed that, give yourself two points.

Services 6 and 7 are used to scroll a *window*—a rectangular part of the whole display screen—up or down. Service 6 scrolls up and 7 scrolls down. In scrolling, the rectangular window is defined by its four corners, and we can make it any part of the screen we want. All the information in that window is moved up or down one line, and a blank line is inserted at the bottom or top of the window. This is a marvelous pair of services that can be used for all sorts of wonderful effects, but few programs take advantage of them.

Service 8 is used to read a character out of a display image. The BASIC equivalent of this service is the SCREEN function (not the SCREEN statement). We specify a location on the screen, and Service 8 tells us what character is written there.

Service 9 writes a character into a display page, with the color attribute specified. This service also allows us to specify the number of times the same character is to be repeated. The replication feature can be useful for writing blanks in the display or for any other character that we might want to repeat, such as the horizontal lines of a box that our programs are drawing.

Service 10 writes a character, like service 9, but uses the existing color attributes at that screen location. (With Service 9 we have to specify the attribute.)

■ *Service 11* applies mostly to the graphics modes, but it has one feature that also applies to the text modes. This is the service that is used to set the *border* color on the screen, as in the border parameter of the COLOR statement in BASIC; for example:

```
COLOR ,,7
```

■ *Service 14* provides another way of writing characters to the display memory. Service 14 is mostly used when the screen is being treated like a printer or typewriter.

■ *Service 15* gives information about the current state of the display, including the current mode number, column width (either 40 or 80), and active page number.

The remaining ROM-BIOS video services (12 and 13) apply to the graphics modes; we will cover them in the next chapter.

13

FUNDAMENTALS OF GRAPHICS VIDEO

In this chapter, we'll cover how the PCjr works in graphics mode. The fundamental difference between text mode and graphics mode is that text mode is set up solely to display characters, while graphics mode is organized to display a screenful of dots that can be used to draw pictures.

In text mode, our programs display characters by placing ASCII character codes into memory and using the display circuitry's character generator to produce the shapes of the characters on the screen. But in graphics mode, our programs produce drawings by setting bits in memory that correspond to dots on the screen. Each individual dot is controlled by manipulating data stored in the memory that are mapped to the display screen. As we've mentioned before, graphics mode can easily display characters on the screen, but it does so by producing drawings of the characters.

The color/graphics adapter for the original PC has exactly 16K of display memory on it, so the number of display-image pages is fixed. Each of the graphics modes for the PC and XT uses 16K, so these models have only one graphics display page. Our PCjr is more flexible, since we can choose how much memory to dedicate to display support. So, for our PCjr, there can be more than one graphics page, just as there can be more than one text page. That's something new that the PC didn't have. On the other hand, memory is in somewhat short supply in the PCjr, so we aren't likely to use multiple graphics pages much.

While the text screen is made up of 25 rows of either 40 or 80 character positions, the graphics screen is made up of dot positions, called picture elements, pixels, or pels, arranged in 200 rows of 160, 320, or 640 dots. There are six distinct graphics modes: Three are common to the PCjr, the PC, and the XT, and three are newly introduced with the PCjr.

In text mode, each screen position holds a character with two parts: the character itself, called the foreground, and the space around the character, called the background. The foreground is one color and the background another. In graphics mode, though, each pixel is complete in and of itself. It is fully shown in one color or another, so there is no foreground or background specification for graphics modes. You may be perplexed by that last statement, because the *BASIC* manual clearly states that there is a foreground and a background in the graphics modes. The confusion stems from two different approaches to the screen.

As the screen actually works, each pixel is set to display a particular color, and it is fully that color—no foreground, no background. This is the true nature of graphics mode. But when we work with graphics mode, we don't normally set the color of each dot on the screen separately—that would not only be extremely tedious, it would also obscure what we are really doing. When we work with graphics mode, we usually treat the screen like a piece of paper on which we are drawing things; and from this point of view, there is a background (the paper) and a foreground (our drawing). To work this way, our programs simply set all the pixel dots to the "background" color first, and then draw in the desired "foreground" dots.

BASIC talks in terms of foreground and background in graphics mode to make life easier for us. By creating a working foreground and background, BASIC is saying to us, "For your convenience, I'll make all the pixels one color (the background), except where you tell me to make them some other color (the foreground)." This is simply a handy working convention, and not something fundamental to the way graphics mode works. If we want to understand what really underlies graphics on the PCjr, we have to realize that each pixel has its own individual color setting, and this setting might be what we think of as the foreground, or as the background.

If each pixel could only be either on or off, lit or not, we could control each one with a single bit set to 0 or 1. Instead, each pixel is set to some particular color that is selected from a palette of colors. If the palette has only two choices, then only one bit is needed to select from it. But with four choices in the palette, two bits are needed, and with a 16-color palette, we need four bits to indicate our choice.

THE GRAPHICS MODES

Figure 13-1 is a quick overview of the six graphic modes we will discuss in this section.

Original Graphics Modes			
Mode	Pixels	Colors	Notes
4	320 × 200	4	One color chosen freely, others from palette
5	320 × 200	4	Black-and-white version of mode 4
6	640 × 200	2	Black-and-white
New Graphics Modes			
Mode	Pixels	Colors	Notes
8	160 × 200	16	Full colors
9	320 × 200	16	Full colors
10	640 × 200	4	From a changeable palette

Figure 13-1. Six graphics modes

179

Why do we need six distinct graphics modes? One reason is to give us a choice of how detailed the picture is. The level of detail of a picture is called its *resolution*. Depending upon our purpose, we may want lots of detail—high resolution—or not much. If we have less resolution than we need, our display picture may be too crudely drawn; if we have too much resolution, our programs will just have more pixel dots to worry about. So there are graphics modes to give us three choices of resolution. Another reason is how much color we want. Some jobs may need lots of color; others may do best in black and white. So there are graphics modes to give us a choice of how much color is available (as well as which colors). Further, different kinds of display screens vary in how well they show colors in different resolutions. An ordinary TV set, for example, does a poor job of showing high-resolution color, while most RGB monitors do it splendidly. Finally, different combinations of color and resolution require different amounts of display memory—and it's good for us to have a choice of how much memory is dedicated to our display. All these factors add up to the reasons why there are six different graphics modes in the PCjr.

Let's take a tour through the six modes, and see what they can do.

The Original Graphics Modes

Mode 4 (which corresponds to BASIC's SCREEN statement modes 1 and 4) provides 320 pixels across and 200 down, which is known as medium resolution. (All the modes give a uniform 200 rows, or lines, of pixels.) Two bits, giving four color choices, control each pixel. With two bits per pixel, 320 by 200 (64,000) pixels, and eight bits per byte, it takes 16,000 bytes (rounded up to 16K) for a mode 4 screen image.

As we know, the IBM personal computers can show 16 distinct colors—eight basic colors each with bright or dim variations. When we have a mode that can select only four colors, we have to decide which four colors can be used. IBM has taken two approaches to the problem. The actual controlling circuitry for the display screens is capable of letting us freely choose which four of the 16 colors will be used. However, for the original PC's color/graphics adapter, IBM decided to predefine three of the four colors. To give us more flexibility, two predefined sets were created, called *palettes* 0 and 1. Palette 0 gives us the colors green, red, and brown (dim yellow), and palette 1 gives us cyan, magenta, and white. We can freely choose the fourth color in each palette from any of the 16 possible colors.

For the four color choices in the PCjr's mode 4, IBM has broken away from the fixed palettes of the original PC color/graphics adapter. Junior's color adapter and its supporting ROM-BIOS programs have been developed in a way that makes it possible for us to create our own palettes, freely chosen from any of the 16 possible colors. Since graphics mode 4 has only two bits for each pixel, there can still only be four colors on the screen when mode 4 is being used. But on the PCjr, these four colors can be any we choose, while on the original PC, we had to make do with one free color choice and the use of IBM's pre-defined palettes 0 or 1 for the other three colors.

The original graphics mode 4 is mode 1 in the BASIC's SCREEN statement. Since the PCjr has added new capabilities to graphics mode 4 (the ability to select all four colors in the palette), BASIC has adopted two SCREEN mode numbers to refer to this one graphics mode. SCREEN mode 1 invokes the original graphics mode 4 with its fixed palettes; SCREEN mode 4 unleashes the new capabilities of the PCjr's graphics mode. It is not really necessary for BASIC to make this distinction, but doing so helps maintain compatibility among BASIC programs, new and old. For example, suppose we are working in graphics mode 4 (SCREEN mode 4) on our PCjrs and have set the palette to something unusual; if we load an old BASIC program that expects to use IBM's predefined palettes, it will automatically get them when its SCREEN statement sets the mode to 1.

Next is graphics mode 5. You will recall that the text modes have versions with and without color, mostly to make it practical to use non-color monitors with the color/graphics adapter. Mode 5 was created with the same idea in mind. Mode 5 is mode 4 with color suppressed. When mode 5 is used, four "colors" will still be displayed, but they will be shades of light and dark, instead of distinct colors. BASIC turns color on or off with the burst parameter of the SCREEN statement, so there isn't any special BASIC SCREEN mode number for this graphics mode.

Mode 6, the last of the original graphics modes, doubles the number of pixels in each line of the screen from 320 to 640; this is called high resolution. The number of bits that control each pixel is cut in half, from two to one, so that this mode uses the same amount of memory (16K) as is used for modes 4 and 5. However, there are only two color choices, black or white. While mode 4 was changed on the PCjr to allow a free choice of colors in the palette, the same change was not made with mode 6; so graphics mode 6 only uses black and white for its colors. Mode 6 is known to BASIC as SCREEN mode 2.

The New Graphics Modes

The first of the new graphics modes for Junior is mode 8, which is known to BASIC as SCREEN mode 3. This is a low-resolution mode, with only 160 pixels across the screen. This new mode is particularly important for the PCjr, since many owners will use TV sets for their display screens, and 160 pixels is the most that can be successfully shown with full color on an ordinary TV. There is a full 16-color palette for mode 8, so the screen can show all the possible colors at once.

Mode 8 seems to be the most important graphics mode for games on the PCjr. With 16 colors, there are four bits for each pixel, and so 16K of memory is used for each display page. Since 16K is the normal amount of memory used for Junior's display, programs can take advantage of this mode without giving up some extra memory, which the next two modes require.

Mode 9, known to BASIC as SCREEN mode 5, is a combination of the medium resolution of mode 4 and the 16 colors of mode 8. Mode 9 offers 320 by 200 pixels, with a full 16-color palette. The memory requirement is higher—32K. This mode will not work with full success on many TV sets, but it will perform superbly on RGB monitors.

Mode 10, the last of the new modes, is known to BASIC as SCREEN mode 6. Like mode 9, it is a mixture of the capabilities of two other modes. It offers the high resolution of 640 by 200 pixels, like mode 6, combined with the four-color choice of mode 4. Mode 10 uses two bits for each pixel, for a total of 32K of memory for the one screen page. As with the PCjr's mode 4, we can freely choose the four colors. This mode calls for a very good quality monitor, so many PCjr owners will not make use of mode 10. On the other hand, the new component-type TV sets can usually work as high-quality RGB monitors, so owners of this kind of home TV will be able to see the spectacular results of graphics mode 10.

Resolution

In this discussion of the graphics modes, I have used the terms low, medium, and high resolution. When talking about the IBM personal computers, the 640-pixels-per-line modes are high resolution; the 320-pixel modes are medium resolution; and the 160-pixel modes are low resolution.

There is another 160-pixel mode that is sometimes mentioned; it has 160 pixels across, but only 100 lines from top to bottom. None of IBM's personal computers uses this mode, but some of the IBM technical literature refers to it as a possibility. In any event, if you run across any of the terms low, medium, or high resolution, you should know that they refer to 160, 320, and 640 pixels per line. I prefer to avoid using these terms, though, since they are vague and mean different things in contexts other than the IBM personal computers.

With that basic information about the PCjr's graphics modes taken care of, we can move on to how the memory-mapped display and the control of color is handled.

THE GRAPHICS MEMORY MAP

Like text mode, graphics mode on the PCjr uses part of the main, general-purpose memory for support of the display. Also as with text mode, the display uses the highest locations at the end of the 64K or 128K installed memory. The amount of memory set aside for the display can be varied, but the usual, default amount is 16K, the same amount as in the PC's original color/graphics adapter. The actual display memory can be reached either by calculating its true address location or by referring to the paragraph location hex B800 used by the color/-graphics adapter. In every way, Junior's graphics mode, like the text mode, produces a convincing simulation of the color/graphics adapter used by the PC and XT.

The various text modes use the same memory locations but the locations are interpreted according to the different needs of each mode. The same holds true for the various graphics modes. The use of the display memory in graphics mode resembles its use in text mode, but many of the details are quite different. Let's look at these differences now.

The memory used for the very first scan line of the screen begins with the first byte of the display memory and proceeds through memory for however many bytes are needed—so far, the procedure is no different from text mode. However, the next memory locations are not for the second scan line, but for the third or the fifth line, depending on which graphics mode is being used. For graphics modes 4, 5, 6, and the new PCjr mode 8, every other line is stored first; for the other two new modes, 9 and 10, every fourth line is stored first. So it goes like this: For modes 4, 5, 6, and 8, it begins with line number 0 (the first line), followed by 2, 4, and so on through line 198. Then come lines 1, 3, 5, and on to the very last line, 199. The same idea applies for modes 9 and 10, except that the lines are divided into four groups, like this:

```
First we have 0, 4, 8, .......................................... 196
then 1, 5, 9, ................................................. 197
then 2, 6, 10, ................................................ 198
finally 3, 7, 11, ............................................. 199
```

Why is mapping done this way? You will recall that display screens are scanned every other line at a time; so this memory-map format matches the actual order in which the display screen uses the data. As a moment's thought will show, mapping the graphics memory in this order, rather than with the lines in numeric order, is a trade-off between convenience for the programs and convenience for the hardware. It would be tedious for you or me to calculate the right memory location for the beginning of any line, but in assembly language it is very quick and easy—in fact, it takes only three instructions (two shifts and an add or a test, a jump, and an add). It is therefore more practical to make the programs do the work than to make the display circuitry smart enough to skip every other line in memory when it is scanning.

From line to line, the memory locations are used one byte after the other, just as in text mode. However, there is a gap between the two or four blocks of

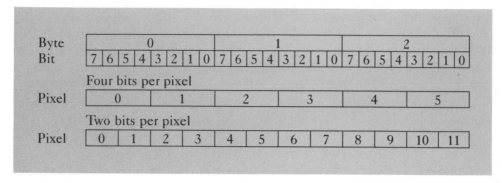

Figure 13-2. Graphics video modes pixel bits

scan lines to ensure that each block will start on an even 1K boundary. (This is just like the gap left between display pages that we mentioned earlier.)

With the exception of mode 10, which is quite special, the bits needed for each pixel follow each other in an orderly fashion. Whether one, two, or four bits are needed to specify the pixel's color, the bits in each byte are divided up in order so that the first pixel uses the highest-order bits in the first byte, followed by the bits for the next pixel, as shown in Figure 13-2.

Mode 10 is mapped out in a very odd way, though. Since mode 10 uses four colors, two bits are needed for each pixel. But the two bits are not adjacent within one byte. Instead, a pair of bytes at adjacent, even-odd locations provides separately the two bits needed for eight pixels. In the other modes, the eight bits of one byte would provide all the bits needed for two, four, or eight pixels, depending upon the number of color bits needed. But in mode 10, one byte provides one color bit for each pixel and the adjacent byte provides the other. The byte with the even address provides the higher order bit, and

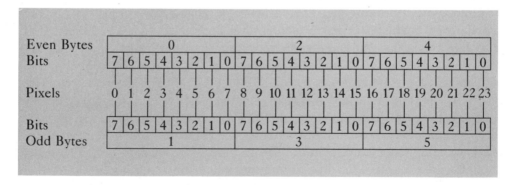

Figure 13-3. Video mode 10: interleaved bits

the odd byte provides the lower order bit needed for the pixel's color specification, as shown in Figure 13-3.

The reason for this unusual setup has to do with electronic hardware. Since the focus of this book is on understanding how the PCjr works, from the point of view of computer users like you and me, what we really want to discuss is functions—the things that make it possible for the software to go. While the details of how the hardware works are very interesting, those details are not functional in the sense of using and writing software. Here, though, since we've bumped our heads on the hardware, let's pause to understand what is going on.

Computer memory takes a certain amount of time to work and the speed of the memory is one of two main factors limiting the overall speed of the computer. (The other is the speed of the microprocessor.) There is, though, an interesting trick that can make computer memory work faster than it supposedly can: Many computer operations work with data located in adjacent memory locations; for example, the operation of reading out the bits that control the graphics display screen.

The computer's memory does not all have to be controlled by the same circuitry; there can be multiple sets of circuits operating in parallel (that is, at the same time). These multiple circuits don't control widely separated blocks of memory. Instead, they separate out and control adjacent memory locations by a technique known as *interleaving*. In the case of a PCjr with 128K of memory, the odd bytes are controlled by one circuit and the even bytes by the other. This allows the computer to use two adjacent bytes (each controlled by different circuits) much faster. Expensive mainframe computers use this interleaving idea, sometimes with many parallel circuits, not just the two that our PCjr has.

Even though interleaved memory is a fancy feature for top-of-the-line computers, our little Junior has interleaved memory when 128K is installed. With 64K, the PCjr has one memory circuit that is used in the ordinary way. But with 128K, it has two memory circuits that are used as two-way, interleaved memory.

This is remarkable for a home computer—not even the PC and XT use interleaved memory. The PCjr, though, has two special demands placed on its memory that the PC and XT don't. One is simply that the same memory is used for both program operation and display support, so the memory is exercised much more and needs to work faster. The other has to do with graphics mode 10. (See? We've come full circle, back to graphics.) To make it more practical to pull out all the data needed for mode 10, the bits are interleaved into even- and odd-byte pairs. The circuitry has to work very hard to produce the high-resolution colors that mode 10 gives us, and splitting each pixel's two bits onto separate bytes helps out.

185

COLORS FOR GRAPHICS

The colors used in graphics mode are selected from a palette of colors, and the colors are specified by the bits that belong to each pixel. In the six graphics modes, each pixel can have any one of two, four, or sixteen colors, which are specified by combinations of one, two, or four bits. The bit combinations are interpreted as binary numbers, starting at 0 and ranging up to 1, 3, or 15 (depending on the number of colors). This number selects from the colors available.

In the original PC and XT models, the colors available could not be varied, except to the limited degree that, in a four-color mode, we could select from two palettes of three colors each and then choose a fourth color. This capability was not just a function of BASIC; it was built into the computer itself. However, in the PCjr, we have much more control.

In the two-color mode, mode 6, we cannot vary the color choices—they must be either black or white. Although it might be interesting to use some other two colors, there is no compelling need for having a choice here. (And besides, if we really want to have 640-pixel, high resolution with two freely chosen colors, we can always use mode 10 and simply use only two of the four colors.)

In the four-color modes, we can set the four colors of our palette to any colors we choose from the full range of 16 colors. We make the choices in BASIC using the PALETTE USING statements, which are based on the palette ROM-BIOS services we will cover in the next section.

In the 16-color modes, we also are given a choice of colors by the PAL-ETTE USING statement. This might at first seem silly. With 16 colors to start with, we have no need for a palette the way we do in the four-color modes, where we are selecting the four colors out of 16. In 16-color, we always have the full use of 16 colors. What, then, does the PALETTE USING statement add to our use of color? It allows us to rearrange the way we are using our colors. By changing the palette, we can automatically change the colors of parts of our screen just by changing the palette colors. For example, if the same actual color is assigned to two seemingly different palette numbers, parts of a screen drawing can be made to disappear. A change in the palette can give a drawing the same color as its background, or a different color—making it disappear and reappear instantly, without being redrawn.

There is one final difference between text and graphics modes worth mentioning here. In the text modes, with the way the display attributes are set up, there is a difference between foreground and background. The foreground is chosen from the full 16 bright and dim colors, but the background is chosen from only the eight dim colors. In graphics mode, on the other hand, any pixel can be chosen from any color (except in the two-color, black-and-white mode), so we can if we choose work with bright-colored pixels in what we consider the background as well as bright-colored pixels in our foreground. We can, if we want, switch to a graphics mode even when we are doing all our work with characters, just to take advantage of this feature. (If we do that, though, we have to give up blinking characters and the cursor as well.) So, we don't have to be making drawings to have a good reason to use a graphics mode.

Now, with all that information about colors out of the way, let's look at the graphics services that are provided by the ROM-BIOS.

ROM-BIOS GRAPHICS DISPLAY SERVICES

The ROM-BIOS services for the graphics modes are similar to those for the text modes, and in fact services number 0 through 11 and 14 and 15, which we covered in the last chapter, are really common to both text and graphics. There are three services specifically for graphics that are common to the PC, the XT, and our PCjr.

■ *Service 11* is used to select the color being used in graphics. This same service is used to select between the two fixed palettes, or to set the one freely chosen color in the four-color palettes. Setting the one free color in the palette also sets the color of the border of the display screen—the area that is outside the working part of the screen. This border-setting operation works for both text modes and the graphics modes.

■ *Service 12* is used to write a pixel dot on the screen, specifying the row and column numbers and the color selection number. A variation on this service, used when the color number is over 128, does not replace the pixel's existing color—instead it ORs the new color number into the old color number. This can be useful in combining parts of a picture that is being drawn.

■ *Service 13* reads a pixel's color number from the screen, similar to the way that service 8, discussed in the last chapter, reads a character from the display.

CHARACTERS IN GRAPHICS MODE

There are always more tricks in the world than we imagine, and that certainly is true for the PCjr's graphics modes.

We've mentioned several times that Junior can write characters on the screen while it is in graphics mode, and that the characters are written by the simple expedient of creating a drawing of the characters. Let's go into the details of how this is done.

First, these drawings have to exist somewhere. The PCjr handles this in an interesting way. The complete 256-character set makes up a table of drawings divided into two parts: The first half is the 128 ordinary ASCII characters, and the second half is the 128 extra characters created by IBM. For the ASCII characters, the table of drawings is stored in the ROM in our PCjr and in the other IBM personal computer models. We can't change this table, and we can't change the pointer to the table, so these characters are fixed and protected from tampering.

The second half of the table of character drawings is more complicated and interesting. You'll recall from the last chapter, that the second half of our character set, from CHR$(128) through CHR$(255), is intended to add all sorts of special characters to the ordinary ASCII characters. In the original design of the IBM personal computers, these other characters were intended for use by the monochrome display, which doesn't have the graphics drawing abilities of our PCjr.

As originally set up, the PC's color/graphics adapter (on which our PCjr models itself) did not provide a character drawing table for these special characters. In text mode all the characters worked, but in graphics mode, only the ASCII half of the set of characters was provided. In our PCjr, though, IBM has added a table of drawings for the upper half of the characters set. This means that programs on our PCjr can freely use all the 256 characters, in graphics mode as well as in text mode; but it also means that if we write programs that use the special characters in graphics mode, they won't work on an ordinary PC.

In the original design, IBM provided a way for us to create a drawing table for these special characters. When our programs write characters in graphics mode, the ROM-BIOS service programs test whether these characters are ordinary (CHR$(127) and below) or special (CHR$(128) and above). For the ordinary characters, the computer's built-in and unchangeable drawing table is used. For the special characters, the ROM-BIOS looks to the interrupt vector table, takes the address for interrupt 31 (hex 1F), and uses it to provide the location of the drawing table for these characters. (You'll recall from our discussion of interrupts that three entries in the interrupt vector table were set aside for special uses that really had nothing to do with interrupts; this is one of those uses.)

Our PCjr has a character drawing table built into it, and the address in the interrupt vector table normally points to it. The original PC does not have this drawing table, and so the address for the interrupt vector is just set to zero, as a way of indicating that there is no drawing table.

The most interesting thing about the drawing table for these special characters is that we can create our own, if we want to. All we have to do is set up a drawing table somewhere in memory and then plug its address into the interrupt vector table. Once we set this up, we'll get our own character drawings whenever we use graphics mode to write a character of CHR$(128) or higher. As long as our drawing table and the interrupt vector are left undisturbed, our own drawings will be used.

Remember, this only works in graphics mode, since text mode uses a hardware character generator to produce its character shapes. And, of course, it only works if we perform the special magic needed to create a table of character drawings.

The characters in the table are stored as sets of eight bytes. With 128 characters, the whole table occupies 1K bytes. Each character is drawn within a box of dots, eight columns in eight rows. Each bit of the drawing bytes controls one dot in the box; the first byte controls the dots in the top row, and so forth. If a bit is set to 1, then the corresponding dot in the character box is set to the foreground color. Figure 13-4 shows how a character is coded, using IBM's own drawing for the question mark.

There are some interesting uses for these 128 characters. If we are writing a program that produces reasonably simple drawings, we may be able to reduce the drawings to modules of 128 shapes or less. If so, we could produce drawings by creating a table of shapes and having the ROM-BIOS perform the relatively messy job of moving those shapes into place on the screen. It may be laborious to define and create the table that we need, but once we have one, it can simplify the programming necessary to create a drawing.

There are two other potential benefits as well. First, the drawing may appear faster on the screen, since much of the work of setting the pixels is done by the fast, assembly-language routines in the ROM-BIOS. And second, storage of a drawing may be much more compact, since a character code can be used as shorthand to represent the eight bytes of drawing bits. To find out what the code means, the ROM-BIOS would simply look it up in the table and would then set the eight bytes of drawing bits accordingly. In the extreme, this method of storing drawings could reduce storage space thirty-fold, when you consider that a single graphics character fills a space that can take up to 32 bytes of pixel information. If we're using a 16-color graphics mode, each pixel dot uses four bits, or half a byte, and each graphics character fills 8 by 8, or 64, pixel dots, adding up to 32 bytes of display memory—all defined by one, single character byte.

*Figure 13-4. Character drawing for
the question mark*

14
COMMUNICATIONS AND THE MODEM

Everyone knows that there is a
revolution going on in personal
computing. The fast, even explosive,
growth in sales and use of personal
computers is visible to us all.

I believe, though, that most people don't understand the real significance of the personal computer revolution.

Many people think that the significance of this revolution comes from people having their own computers, computers dedicated to serving the needs of one person at a time. Isolated, unconnected, private computing is what most people consider personal computing to be. When you or I buy a personal computer, such as the IBM PCjr, we get computing power on tap, for our exclusive use. There is a great benefit to having our own source of computing power; by itself, though, it can only enhance the things that we might be doing ourselves—it does not enhance our connection with the rest of the world.

This part of the impact of personal computers is very important, but it is only the first half of the real revolution. The other half of the personal computer revolution is the connection of our own computing power to other computers. When we can talk to other systems with our PCjr, then we are plugged into both halves of the personal computer revolution—the revolution of private computing, and the revolution of computer connections.

In this chapter, we will cover the communications skills of the PCjr. Whether or not you plan to make use of Junior's ability to communicate over telephone lines, it is important to know about this half of the computer revolution.

The connection of our computer with others can take many forms; here are what I think are the three most important. First, there is talking "socially" to other personal computers. This is usually done on a basis of friend-to-friend, hobbyist-to-hobbyist, and it might, for example, involve sharing programs and data or using an electronic bulletin board for messages and the spreading of information.

Second, there is talking to other computers for work purposes. This might involve working at home and communicating with your employer's computers in what is called *telecommuting*—commuting to work by computer connection. Or using the computer connection for work can involve tapping into remote computer services; for example, an independent insurance agent might connect with a service that can quote insurance rates.

The third very important form of computer connection involves the use of information services, such as THE SOURCE and CompuServe, which let us connect into vast libraries that provide information ranging from ball scores and stock quotations to airline schedules.

Whatever form your use of communications on the PCjr might take, it is communications that fulfills and rounds out your computer's enormous potential.

Communications is a very complicated specialty subject all by itself. Since this book is about the workings of the IBM PCjr, we can't go into the details of communications, other than very superficially. There are places you can turn to for more information when you need it. For technical and practical information about communications, look to a technical book covering this subject, such as *Communications and Networking for the IBM/PC* by Jordan & Churchill (Brady).

A COMMUNICATIONS PRIMER

There are two main ways that computers can communicate, known as *asynchronous* and *synchronous*. Asynchronous communications is much less complicated and less expensive; naturally, it is also slower and less powerful. Although synchronous communications can be used as an expensive addition to the PC and XT, home computers normally use asynchronous communications, and that is all that is available on our PCjr.

One of the main problems to be solved in communications is that no one has very tight control over what is going on. Many pieces of equipment and considerable distances can be involved in communications, and the chance that something will go wrong or that data will be lost is considerable. For communications to work, common rules and conventions have to be used.

The convention for asynchronous communications is known as RS-232 or, more precisely, RS-232C. This is what our PCjr uses, whether we are working through the built-in serial port or using the smart modem attachment. In RS-232 communications, data are passed serially, which means bit-by-bit, one bit at a time. (In contrast, the standard printer connection for the PCjr passes eight bits in parallel, so that data move one byte at a time.) The transmission of the data is asynchronous, meaning that the sender and receiver of data don't expect bits to appear at certain precise times. Asynchronous transmission of data allows for reasonable delays and also lets the communications circuitry be sloppier about timing, which helps keep the cost of the equipment down.

The world of computer communications has a wealth of confusing terms that are all used to refer to basically the same thing, and we ought to straighten them out here. The sort of communications used by our PCjr and nearly all other personal computers is variously called asynchronous, RS-232, and serial. The computer's communications connection is usually called a port, so you will frequently hear the terms serial port and RS-232 port. All these terms refer, more or less, to the same thing. In this book, we'll mostly use the term serial port.

There is one more potential source of confusion that we ought to clear up. Although the main use of the serial port is for communication with other computers, this port can be used for many purposes. Any piece of equipment that follows the RS-232 conventions can be connected to the serial port. For example, the serial port offers an inexpensive way to connect a printer to a home computer, and many inexpensive computer printers are equipped to make this connection. The IBM personal computers, however, usually use a parallel interface to send data to a printer, because it is more efficient and better suited to printing.

In this chapter we'll be talking mostly about the use of the serial port in communications, but you should keep in mind that it can be used for many other purposes. The ROM-BIOS services we'll cover in the last section of this chapter apply to any use of the serial port. On the other hand, the smart modem attachment, which we will cover in the next section, is used only for true communications.

Although we can use communications on our PCjr very successfully without knowing anything technical about how it works, it is always better to know more than it is to know less. And in this particular area, as you have already seen, you are especially likely to run across perplexing technical terms. So, let's go through a simple outline of some of the main ideas and terms used in communications.

Communications Parameters

The RS-232 conventions allow for considerable variety in how data are transmitted. The first parameter, or variable, is speed. The speed of a communications line is expressed in *baud*, which is equivalent to one bit transmitted each second.

Numerous baud rates are used, from 110, which is the speed of an old teletype, to 9600, which is about the maximum that can be transmitted over a telephone line. The most common rate for personal computers is 300 baud, although 1200 baud is also used quite a bit on the more sophisticated models. The PCjr's modem attachment normally works at 300 baud; it can also work at 110 baud. To help you determine how much data this represents, here is a simple, practical rule of thumb: It takes about ten bits to transmit one character, including overhead (for example, the parity and start/stop bits we will discuss shortly). So it is easy to translate baud rates roughly into characters per second—300 baud, for example, is about 30 characters per second.

The amount of working data squeezed through any baud rate depends upon other communications parameters. One parameter is the character or byte size. Computers normally work with a size of eight bits per byte, though the ASCII code used to represent text in computers actually uses only seven bits per character. This is why we have 256 8-bit characters, even though there are only 128 true ASCII codes. With RS-232, we can transmit and receive either 7-bit (ASCII) or 8-bit (extended ASCII) characters.

The next communications parameter that varies is parity. Parity checking is not unique to communications—the memory used in the PC and XT (but not our PCjr) includes a ninth parity bit for each 8-bit byte. To guard against lost or

Start Bit	Character Bit	Parity Bit	Stop Bit	Total
1	7	0	1	9
1	7	0	2	10
1	7	1	1	10
1	7	1	2	11
1	8	0	1	10
1	8	0	2	11

*Figure 14-1. Number of bits transmitted per character
including variable overhead*

scrambled data in communications, our transmitted data can be checked with a formula that produces parity bits. The bits are calculated when the data are transmitted and checked when the data are received. This procedure allows the computer to detect most errors. With RS-232, there are three parity options: either no parity check or checking by one of two formulas known as even and odd parity.

The final communications parameter that we need to know about is stop bits. As part of the asynchronous scheme of transmitting data, distinguishing signals known as *start* and *stop bits* are needed to separate one character from another and to allow the receiver to get ready for each character. Each character has a single start bit before it and either one or two stop bits after it. The number of stop bits, one or two, is one of the communications parameters.

Including all the parameter bits, then, there are 9, 10, or 11 bits transmitted for each character (so 10 is a handy conversion factor when we want to translate between baud and characters per second). The minimum is nine: a start bit, seven character bits, and one stop bit. We get 10 or 11 bits, depending on the various combinations of stop bits, parity, and character length shown in Figure 14-1. The size never reaches 12 bits, because we aren't allowed to use a parity bit with 8-bit characters in communications.

When two pieces of computer equipment are communicating with one another, they have to agree on the setting for all these parameters: baud rate, character size, parity, and stop bits. On a few occasions we may have some choice in the matter, but usually the parameters are set by what we are doing, and we must conform to those standards. As an example of a common combination, THE SOURCE, one of the major communications services, uses 300 or 1200 baud, 8-bit characters, no parity, and one stop bit. The most common combination probably is 300 baud, 7-bit characters, even parity, and one stop bit, but if you look far enough, you'll find every combination in use.

As I've warned you, communications is a very complex subject, and for a deeper understanding you must now go elsewhere. With this very rudimentary knowledge, we are not experts on communications, but we're at least prepared to press on and look at the PCjr's smart modem.

THE SMART MODEM

One of the most interesting parts of the PCjr is the smart modem attachment. In order to communicate over a telephone line, a computer needs both a communications port, like the PCjr's RS-232 serial port, and a modem. A modem does the job of translating between the computer's signals and the telephone's signals. This translation is known as *modulation* (from computer to telephone) and *demodulation* (from telephone to computer). The basic work of a modem then, is to *mo*dulate and *dem*odulate.

Originally, that was all a modem did—direct translation from one signal format to another. But people using their computers for communications quickly discovered that much more help was needed. To communicate effectively, a computer needed to be able to answer the telephone, dial other numbers, and so forth. In several evolutionary steps, modems gained more and more capabilities, until there appeared the sort of smart modem that is available for our PCjr.

Our Junior's modem is an integrated, smart, 103 modem attachment. It is integrated because it contains all the components it needs and because it fits right into the PCjr's cabinet. In the past, most modems for personal computers have been external components that added to the clutter of equipment and wiring. Our integrated, internal modem is much more convenient. In addition, our modem is smart, because it accepts and acts on commands from the computer and because it can do everything that is needed for the computer to use the telephone. Finally, our modem is a 103, because it follows the specifications and features of Bell Laboratories' Model 103 modem, an early modem that set the standard for many of the conventions used in computer communications.

The PCjr's smart modem has a number of very important features and characteristics. It can work in *full duplex,* meaning data can pass in both directions at once, or it can work in *half duplex,* meaning data can pass either way, but only one way at a time. The smart modem can generate the multiple tones needed for touch-tone dialing, and it can also produce the pulses needed to mimic rotary-dialed telephones. To accommodate commercial long-distance telephone services, such as Sprint and MCI, and to accommodate information services, such as THE SOURCE and CompuServe, the smart modem can dial numbers many digits long, waiting for dial tones and providing service code numbers as necessary. Another useful feature is its ability to place calls or answer incoming calls, and do it either automatically or under manual control.

This smart modem is not fast. While data traffic on telephone lines can move at speeds of 1200, 4800, or 9600 baud, our modem's native speed is a modest 300 baud—modest, but no slower than that used most commonly for personal computers.

We talk to the smart modem in ordinary ASCII character codes, so it is relatively easy for us to issue commands, and it is also easy for us to understand any messages that the modem has for us. Normally we use a special communications program to supervise the modem. One such program is included in the BASIC cartridge as the TERM command; another is the popular PC-Talk program. We can enter modem commands directly from the keyboard or we can use our communications programs to send commands to the modem.

When we want to send a command to the modem, we begin with a special character, CHR$(14), which can be keyed in simply as Ctrl-N. From the keyboard, Ctrl-N is the easiest way to begin the command; from a BASIC program, CHR$(14) is the easiest way to generate the special character. Whenever the modem is receiving data from us, it continually looks for this special code. When it finds it, the modem expects commands to follow, and it interprets any data that follow this character as modem commands.

Modem commands are given in a line beginning with CHR$(14) and ending with a carriage return, CHR$(13). Anything between those two characters is taken by the modem as a set of commands. The command data are not acted on immediately as they come in. Instead, the modem stores the data until the command line is complete. After the carriage-return character, CHR$(13), is encountered, the modem carries out the commands it has been given.

Several different commands, separated by commas, can be given in a single command line; Ctrl-N is not needed for each command, since this character really marks the beginning of a line of commands, and not the beginning of individual commands.

Each modem command begins with a single letter of the alphabet. Although the commands have full, descriptive names, such as Answer, to help us keep track of them, only the first letter of the command matters to the smart modem, and Answer and Abracadabra would both be interpreted as the same command. So each command begins with a letter that identifies it; if it needs any parameters, they follow, separated by spaces. For example, to get the modem to dial a number, we would give it a command line like:

<Ctrl-N> DIAL 213-399-3948 <Carriage Return>

The modem would dial that number, reaching my office in Venice, California. The hyphens in the telephone number are for our convenience; the smart modem is smart enough to ignore them.

As another example of how we might use modem commands, let's suppose that we have our telephone line connected both to our PCjr's smart modem and also to a speakerphone. If we're working at the computer and the telephone rings, we can tell the modem to answer the phone and then switch to voice mode (so the modem doesn't generate its screeching carrier tone). This command would do the trick:

<Ctrl-N> PICKUP <Carriage Return>

After the modem answers the telephone and switches to voice mode, we can use the speakerphone to talk to the caller. Using the modem like this to answer the telephone is no big deal, but it does show what can be done. Using the modem to dial, and redial, our calls is another handy way to use a modem with our PCjr.

Let's now go over the main points of the various modem commands, giving a brief description of what each can do. We won't go into full detail about how these commands work, because communications is a very rich and complicated subject and will be covered more fully in *Mastering the IBM PCjr Home Computer.*

Modem Commands

There are 20 different commands for the smart modem; they are listed below in alphabetic order:

■ ANSWER—Answers the telephone when it rings.

■ BREAK—Sets the communications break time. It takes one numeric parameter, which specifies the time in tenths of a second.

■ COUNT—Controls the number of times the telephone rings before the modem will answer when it is in automatic answering mode. The reason for not having the modem answer on the first ring is to give you a chance to answer the telephone yourself if you want to.

■ DIAL—Dials telephone numbers. Dialing is the most complex of all the smart modem's commands because of all the things that it must handle, including two kinds of dialing (touch-tone and pulse), waiting for dial tones, and so forth. All in all, the dialing features of this modem are quite impressive.

■ FORMAT—Controls the communications mode, or format, which will vary with the computer at the other end of your connection. The format command sets the parity, character size, and stop bits. The default mode is number 3, which is even parity, 7-bit characters, and one stop bit. Figure 14-1 is a table of the complete format options.

■ INITIALIZE—Resets the modem to its normal operating modes.

■ HANGUP—Disconnects the telephone.

■ LONG—Sets the messages that the modem generates to long or short. Long, or verbose, messages, such as CONNECT, are easily understandable by people, while short, or terse, commands are single-digit codes, such as 1, which are easier for programs to recognize.

■ MODEM—Forces the modem into active mode, ready to use.

■ NEW—Changes the code that marks the beginning of a command line. The numeric parameter is the ASCII character code for the new code. The default code, Ctrl-N, is ASCII 14.

■ ORIGINATE—Places the modem in originate mode, as opposed to answer mode. These modes are the two fundamental ways that two computers can operate when they are talking through a telephone line. Usually, one expects to originate calls, and the other expects to answer calls.

■ PICKUP—Takes the telephone off the hook electronically and places it in voice mode.

■ RETRY—Tells the modem to redial the last phone number without having to repeat the details of the dialing.

■ SPEED—Sets the modem's operating speed. There are two speed rates: 0 sets the modem to operate at 110 baud, which is terribly slow and not used much for computers any more; 1 sets the speed to 300 baud, which is much better, although experience will teach you that 300 baud is only barely adequate for most computer use.

■ TRANSPARENT—Tells the modem that the next several bytes are to be sent in transparent mode, which means that they are to be sent exactly as they are. Transparent transmission is essential for sending binary data; that is, any computer data that aren't coded into ASCII characters. If you want to send a copy of a program in its COM or EXE format, you will need to use transparent mode to do it, so that the bytes being sent aren't interpreted or modified in any way. This command takes one numeric parameter, which specifies the number of transparent bytes that follow.

■ VOICE—Switches to voice mode on the telephone line. This is the opposite of the MODEM command.

■ WAIT—Makes the modem wait for a period of time.

■ XMIT—Makes the modem transmit data while in the voice mode.

■ ZTEST—Tells the modem to test the communications operation.

Bear in mind that all these commands are passed to the modem through the RS-232 communications line, in the same way that other information is sent through this data path. As we'll see in the next section, the ROM-BIOS services that support communications have nothing to do with the smart modem —it needs no special support, and that is part of what makes it smart. Instead, it is controlled by the high-level commands we, or our programs, give it.

ROM-BIOS COMMUNICATIONS SERVICES

As it does for every active part of the PCjr, the ROM-BIOS programs provide supporting services for the RS-232 serial port. These services were originally designed for the PC and were intended to support the many uses of a serial port, including communications at rates beyond the capabilities of the PCjr's special smart modem.

There are four ROM-BIOS services for the serial port, all invoked with interrupt 20 (hex 14). As usual, the services are numbered from 0. Because the other IBM personal computers can have several communications ports attached to them (even though our PCjr can't), each of these services needs a number to indicate which port is being used; for us, it's always port 0, known to DOS and BASIC as COM(1), COM1, or AUX.

■ *Service 0* is used to set the communications parameters of baud rate, parity, stop bits, and character size. Take care not to confuse these communications parameters with the modem's parameters, which are set by the FORMAT and SPEED commands. We're talking about the same communications parameters, but this service controls how the ROM-BIOS will send data out the serial port, while the modem commands will set how the modem works. We're talking about the same items, but controlled in two different places.

When this service is used to set the communications parameters, all four parameters are combined into a single byte. The three high-order bits, bits 5 through 7, contain the code giving the baud rate; bits 3 and 4 specify the parity; bit 2 indicates the number of stop bits; and finally, bits 0 and 1 indicate the character size. These four parts can be combined into one byte, by this formula:

$$\text{COMM.PARMS} = \text{BAUD.CODE} \times 32 + \text{PARITY} \times 8 + \text{STOP.BITS} \times 4 + \text{CHAR.SIZE}$$

Each of the four parameters is coded in its own way, as you can see in the following figures. The baud rate is specified as shown in Figure 14-2; Code 111 is 4800 for the PCjr and not 9600 as it is for the PC. Parity is specified as shown in Figure 14-3; stop bits are specified as shown in Figure 14-4; and character size is specified as shown in Figure 14-5. Thus a byte with a value of hex 4E (01001110) would indicate a baud rate of 300, odd parity, two stop bits, and 7-bit characters.

Bits (7,6,5)	Numeric Value	Baud Rate	Notes
000	0	110	The slow rate for the PCjr's modem
001	1	150	
010	2	300	The default faster rate for our modem
011	3	600	
100	4	1200	Often used for computers; maximum PCjr rate if asynchronous input is going on at the same time as keyboard input
101	5	2400	
110	6		
111	7	4800	9600 for the PC/XT

Figure 14-2. Baud rate codes for bits 5 through 7

Bits (4,3)	Numeric Value	Parity
00	0	None
01	1	Odd parity
10	2	None
11	3	Even parity

Figure 14-3. Parity codes for bits 3 and 4

Bit 2	Numeric Value	Stop Bits
0	0	1
1	1	2

Figure 14-4. Stop-bit codes for bit 2

■ *Services 1 and 2* are used to receive and send a single character along the communications line. A status code is returned in the AH register, indicating the success or failure of the operation. If AH is 0, the operation was successful;

201

Bits (1,0)	Numeric Value	Character Size
10	2	7 bits
11	3	8 bits

Figure 14-5. Character-size codes for bits 0 and 1

Register	Bit	Meaning	Norton Comments
AH	7	Time out	No result within allowed time
AH	6	Shift register empty	
AH	5	Holding register empty	
AH	4	Break detected	
AH	3	Framing error	That's sorting out characters
AH	2	Parity error	
AH	1	Overrun error	Data lost due to speed
AH	0	Data ready	
AL	7	Line signal detected	
AL	6	Ringing	
AL	5	Data set (modem ready)	
AL	4	Clear-to-send signal	We may transmit data
AL	3	Delta receive line signal detect	Got that?
AL	2	Trailing edge ring detector	We're in deep water
AL	1	Delta data set ready	Clearly this is technical
AL	0	Delta clear to send	Communications is complicated

Figure 14-6. Communications status codes

if AH is not 0, bits 1 through 4 and 7 will indicate the problem, as explained in service 3.

■ *Service 3* provides a communications status report, including the information provided by services 1 and 2, plus quite a bit of other information. Register AX (or registers AH and AL, to look at it another way) is used to return the status codes. Although you have to be something of a communications expert to make use of these codes, they can be interesting to study. The status of the communications line is given in the AH register, while the status of the modem is given in the AL register. Figure 14-6 shows how each bit of the status code is used.

If anything was needed to convince you that communications is a complicated, specialty subject, these status codes should do the job. One main reason why communications is so messy is because it is vulnerable and exposed. Within the guts of a computer, the designers are fully in charge, and any operating errors can usually be hidden from civilians like you and me. With communications, it's a different game. Communications goes on in the outside world, over cables and telephone lines that aren't under the control of our computer's designers. Worse than that, telephone lines are more vulnerable to all sorts of problems, from electrical surges to bird droppings, than the inside of a computer. You'll rarely have a thunderstorm or bird droppings inside your PCjr, but the same can't be said for the telephone system.

All this adds up to the fact that the messy details of communications can't be swept under the covers as easily as details of computer design and operation, and that explains why the communications status codes are so complicated.

CHAPTER

15
SUPER SOUND

Sound is an integral part of the
connection between our computers
and us, but it is one that is often
neglected. In this chapter, we'll look
at Junior's ability to make sounds:

old sounds—using the same techniques as the PC and XT—and new sounds —using the Texas Instruments sound chip.

OLD SOUNDS

When the IBM PC was first announced, many observers noted that it did not break much new ground in personal computing. The PC did, however, combine the finest elements of microcomputers to achieve a breakthrough in overall quality. That breakthrough is as true for sound as for anything else.

Since all the IBM personal computers can make sounds on a built-in speaker in the same way, we'll first cover this shared skill. This common means of making sounds is important to our understanding of the PCjr, both because it is one of Junior's abilities and because it represents the only kind of sound that our programs can use that will work on all IBM personal computer models.

Each of the IBM personal computers has a small speaker about two inches, or five centimeters, in diameter. It isn't intended for accurate sound reproduction, like the speakers in a hi-fi system; rather, this little speaker is meant to be a simple, inexpensive way to produce simple sounds.

Sounds are waves of pressure in the air, and sound-recording equipment imitates these waves by using varying electrical signals to represent the varying pressure in the air. The task of a speaker is to translate these electrical signals into sound waves—air-pressure waves. In a hi-fi the electrical signal, like the sound itself, is made up of very complex variations in *amplitude* (strength or loudness) and *frequency* (tone or pitch). Although this is the way sound is produced by our hi-fi, it is not the way it is produced by our computer. Our computer sends a simple and pure voltage to its speaker. When the voltage is on, the speaker pulses in; when the voltage is off, the speaker pulses out. If we turn the voltage on and off once, we get a single cycle of sound. If we repeat the process of pulsing the speaker in and out 440 times a second, we get a pure sound at the frequency of 440, which is the musical note A.

Unlike a hi-fi, our computer's speaker has no volume control; a constant voltage level is fed to the speaker, so there is no intended variation in loudness; it varies only because of the speaker's limitations. Even high-quality speakers are slightly inaccurate in their response to the electrical signals sent to them, so it is understandable that the inexpensive speaker used in our PCjr varies quite a bit in how loudly it sounds at different frequencies. This is a by-product of the speaker design, and is not something we can control. In terms of the signal given to the speaker, there is no variation in volume.

The simple program in Figure 15-1 demonstrates the speaker's volume at different frequencies. To see the effect of this program on your PCjr, you must be sure the speaker is active.

```
 10 PRINT "Demonstrating the speaker's volume ";
 20 PRINT "at various frequencies"
 30 PLAY "MF"
 40 ' start with 37, the lowest frequency allowed
 50 FREQUENCY = 37
 60 PRINT INT (FREQUENCY)
 70 SOUND FREQUENCY, 5
 80 FREQUENCY = FREQUENCY * 1.1
 90 ' end with 32767, the highest frequency allowed
100 IF FREQUENCY < 32767 GOTO 60
```

*Figure 15-1. A program to demonstrate the
speaker's volume at various frequencies*

We can generate sounds on the speaker in two ways. First, we can write a program to generate the on/off signals that pulse the speaker in and out. When this method is used, the program controls the exact timing of each pulse and can potentially produce complex sounds. Second, we can use the PCjr's programmable timer to generate the on/off signals at a precise frequency. When this method is used, a pure tone is generated and the computing power of the PCjr isn't tied up in generating speaker pulses. We'll see how to use each of these methods and how they can be combined, but first we need to pause for some technical background.

How the Computer Produces Sound

The speaker is supervised by the programmable peripheral interface, or PPI, chip that we mentioned in Chapter 2. As with most other parts of the PCjr, the speaker is manipulated by controlling values sent to a specific port. The port used for the speaker is port number 97 (hex 61). Whenever data are sent to, or read from, this port, the PPI acts on the information by sending the appropriate signals to the appropriate device. Only two of port 97's eight bits are used by the speaker, the low-order bits numbered 0 and 1. The other bits for this port are used for other purposes, including the cassette interface and the keyboard, so it is important that we don't disturb them when we are working with the speaker.

The lowest bit, bit 0, controls whether the timer signal is used to drive the speaker. If we set this bit to 0, the speaker can be controlled fully by a program. The second bit, bit 1, controls the pulsing of the speaker. If we successively set this bit on and off, the speaker will be pulsed in and out and will produce a

```
100 ' demonstrate producing sounds
110 '
120 OLD.PORT = INP (97)
130 '
140 PULSE.IN = (OLD.PORT \ 4) * 4
150 PULSE.OUT = PULSE.IN + 2
160 OUT 97, PULSE.IN
170 OUT 97, PULSE.OUT
180 GOTO 160
```

Figure 15-2. A program to demonstrate sound production

sound. When sounds are made like this, it is done in assembly language, so it can be done as fast as necessary to produce the desired frequency. To illustrate, we can do the same thing in BASIC, although our program won't be quick enough to make a high-pitched sound. The program is shown in Figure 15-2.

If you run this program, you will find that it produces a low sound. Notice that in line 120 we get the existing value of port 97. So that we can leave the non-speaker bits undisturbed, in line 140, we calculate a value that is the same as the existing port 97, but with the two speaker bits off. In line 150, we calculate the same thing with bit 1 on. (Bit 1 has a binary value of 2, so we add 2.) Then in lines 160 and 170, we alternately send the two calculated values to the speaker port to produce the sound.

A real assembly-language program to produce sounds would work like this, with two things added: There would be a deliberate delay between each pulse in and out, and there would be a count or something similar to end the program when it had run long enough. If the program wanted to produce a varying sound, it could vary the delay between pulses. With clever programming, varying the delay could even produce chords.

A second method of producing sounds uses the programmable timer to generate the desired frequency. This frequency can then be fed continuously into the speaker, so that the computing power of the 8088 is free to go on with other work while the sound continues. A program that uses the timer to generate sounds is given in Figure 15-3.

As shown in Figure 15-3, before we can use the timer, we have to program it to produce the right frequency. The timer starts with a base frequency of 1,193,180 cycles per second. To get the frequency we want, we give the timer a count value called a divisor. The timer counts the cycles of its base frequency until the count matches our divisor, then it produces a signal, and it starts

```
100 ' demonstrate use of timer to make sounds
110 ' from Exploring the IBM PCjr Home Computer
120 ' authored by Peter Norton, 1983
130 '
200 ' load the programmable timer
210 '
220 ' calculate our divisor
230 '
240 ' calculate the full divisor
250 DIVISOR = 1193180! / 440
260 ' calculate the low-order byte
270 LO.DIVISOR = DIVISOR MOD 256
280 ' calculate the high-order byte
290 HI.DIVISOR = DIVISOR / 256
300 '
310 ' send the values out
320 '
330 OUT 67, 182                    ' preparatory signal
340 OUT 66, LO.DIVISOR             ' low-order byte
350 OUT 66, HI.DIVISOR             ' high-order byte
360 OUT 97, (INP (97) \ 4) * 4 + 3
370 '
400 ' switch the timer frequency on and off
410 '
420 OLD.PORT = INP (97)
430 '
440 FREQUENCY.ON = (OLD.PORT \ 4) * 4
450 FREQUENCY.OFF = FREQUENCY.ON + 3
460 OUT 97, FREQUENCY.ON
470 FOR I = 1 TO 128 : NEXT I      ' kill some time
480 OUT 97, FREQUENCY.OFF
490 FOR I = 1 TO 128 : NEXT I      ' kill some time
500 GOTO 460
```

*Figure 15-3. A program to produce sound using
      the programmable timer*

counting over again. So, to get the frequency of 440 cycles per second, the program first calculates our divisor like this:

```
250 DIVISOR = 1193180! / 440
```

Sending a divisor "program" to the programmable timer is oddly complicated. It's done in three steps. First, we prepare the timer to receive a divisor by sending the value 182 (hex B6) out to port 67. (This value is not arbitrary: Each of the bits in this byte has a special meaning to the timer and when the combination of bits necessary to prepare it is set, the value of the byte is 182.) Then we send the divisor itself to port 66, but we send it in two parts: the low-order byte of the divisor (calculated in line 270), then the high-order byte (calculated in line 290). Sending these two parts of the divisor completes the three steps of loading the timer, and the timer begins generating the frequency we asked for. Here is how we would do this in BASIC:

```
240 'calculate the full divisor
250 DIVISOR = 1193180! / 440
260 ' calculate the low-order byte
270 LO.DIVISOR = DIVISOR MOD 256
280 ' calculate the high-order byte
290 HI.DIVISOR = DIVISOR / 256
300 '
310 ' send the values out
320 '
330 OUT 67, 182                    ' preparatory signal
340 OUT 66, LO.DIVISOR             ' low-order byte
350 OUT 66, HI.DIVISOR             ' high-order byte
```

Once the timer is loaded and a frequency is generated, we can turn the sound on and off by setting the speaker bits. To make use of the timer frequency, we have to set both of the speaker bits on. While line 150 in our earlier program (Figure 15-2) adds 2 to set just bit 1 on, we now need to add 3 to set both bits on (because the binary values of bit 0 and bit 1 are 1 and 2, respectively).

```
360 OUT 97, (INP (97) \ 4) * 4 + 3
```

For a trick example, we mimic lines 100 through 180 of Figure 15-2, but this time, instead of pulsing the speaker with each OUT statement, we'll be activating and deactivating the use of the timer frequency. These new program lines, combined with lines 240 through 350 above, will do the trick:

```
400 ' switch the timer frequency on and off
410 '
420 OLD.PORT = INP (97)
430 '
440 FREQUENCY.ON = (OLD PORT \ 4) * 4
450 FREQUENCY.OFF = FREQUENCY.ON + 3
460 OUT 97, FREQUENCY.ON
470 FOR I = 1 TO 128 : NEXT I       ' kill some time
480 OUT 97, FREQUENCY.OFF
490 FOR I = 1 TO 128 : NEXT I       ' kill some time
500 GOTO 460
```

That pretty much covers the sound capabilities that are common to all the IBM personal computers. Now we'll move on to the PCjr's very special, new sound abilities.

NEW SOUNDS

Junior is much more oriented toward games and entertainment than the other IBM personal computer models. This shift of focus led to the development of the PCjr's two most dramatic new features—its extended graphics modes, which we covered in Chapter 13, and its new sound capabilities.

For business, financial, and word-processing use, a computer doesn't need a lot in the way of sound, and the PC's original sound abilities have provided much more than most programs have tried to use. For arcade-style games, though, a lot more sound is needed. Enter the Texas Instruments SN76496A sound generator chip, our PCjr's sound superstar.

The TI sound chip adds three main new capabilities to the PCjr's ability to produce sound. First, it has *attenuation*, or volume control, so it can produce sounds at 15 distinct levels. Second, it has three voices, meaning that it can produce three different tones, each with its own, distinct attenuation. And third, it has an additional noise voice that can be used to produce sounds like jets and bombs. Let's start with the attenuation, or volume control.

Attenuation

Each voice on the TI sound chip has its own attenuation, controlled by four bits referred to as A0 through A3. Each bit controls a separate attenuation level, which is measured in *decibels*, or *dB*. When each bit is set on, the sound is attenuated (that is, reduced) by the specific amounts shown in Figure 15-4.

Bit	Attenuation (in dB)
A0	2
A1	4
A2	7
A3	15.5

Figure 15-4. Reduction of volume produced by setting on bits A0 through A3

The four separate levels can be combined in any way to produce 15 distinct volumes. When all four bits are set on, the sound is turned completely off, rather than being attenuated a total of 28.5 dB, as you might think from Figure 15-4. When all four bits are off, the sound is at its full volume. You will notice that the attenuation is roughly doubled with each successive bit, giving us a fairly smooth spectrum of volume levels.

Understanding completely the arithmetic of the sound chip's attenuation involves some messy mathematics, more than we can explain here. For those technically inclined, we'll just briefly note that sound energy is measured in a logarithmic scale, and each decibel is one-tenth of a unit in the logarithmic measure. Since we're referring to attenuation on our TI sound chip, a higher dB number means a softer sound. But, when BASIC refers to volume levels, it reverses the scale to something more natural for us: A higher volume number means a louder sound (but a lower attenuation number inside the TI sound chip).

Because of the complications in how the attenuation levels are set, it is simpler for us to choose the sound levels that our programs will use by experimentation than by trying to calculate what they ought to be.

Tone

The tone of each voice, sometimes called its pitch or frequency, is controlled by a 10-bit binary number, which our programs provide to the sound chip. The sound chip uses this number, just as the programmable timer we discussed does, as a counting base, in effect dividing our controlling number into the clock frequency. In detail what the TI chip does is this: It starts with the clock frequency of 1,193,180 cycles per second, and reduces it by a factor of 16, to get a frequency of about 74,576; this frequency is counted against our 10-bit controlling count, and each time it matches, the TI chip generates an on or off signal, alternately. Each pair of on and off signals gives us one sound cycle, one count in the sound frequency. That's the mechanics of it, but we can simplify the arithmetic for our own use. If we divide 37,287 by the 10-bit controlling number, we get the frequency that it generates, and vice versa. These formulas show the relationship:

FREQUENCY = 37287 / CONTROLLING NUMBER
CONTROLLING NUMBER = 37287 / FREQUENCY

As a 10-bit number, the controlling number can range from 1, which gives a frequency of 37,287, well above ordinary hearing, to 1,023, which gives a frequency of 36.4. This range (36.4 to 37,287) is almost the same as the range allowed in BASIC (38 to 32,767) before the sound chip was added to the PCjr.

NF0	NF1	Noise Frequency
0	0	$1,193,180 / 512 = 2330$
0	1	$1,193,180 / 1024 = 1165$
1	0	$1,193,180 / 2048 = 583$
1	1	Borrowed from voice 3

*Figure 15-5. Noise-generator frequencies produced by
NF0 and NF1 bit combinations*

Besides the three pure voices, the TI chip also has a noise-generating voice. The noise voice can work two ways and is controlled by a bit known as the FB bit. When FB is 0, a periodic, or cyclic, noise is generated; when FB is 1, a continuous "white noise" is produced.

Two bits, known as NF0 and NF1, control the frequency at which the noise generator works; this frequency is equivalent to its pitch. Three of the four possible combinations of NF0 and NF1 set an independent noise frequency based on the timer; the fourth combination borrows the frequency from the third of the three pure voices. The NF0 and NF1 bit settings are shown in Figure 15-5.

When control information is loaded into the sound chip, it is preceded by three bits, known as R0 through R2, which identify the parameter being set. The code values used are shown in Figure 15-6. As with almost everything else, programs control these parameters through ports.

R0	R1	R2	Parameter
0	0	0	Voice 1 frequency control number (10 bits)
0	0	1	Voice 1 attenuation (4 bits)
0	1	0	Voice 2 frequency control number (10 bits)
0	1	1	Voice 2 attenuation (4 bits)
1	0	0	Voice 3 frequency control number (10 bits)
1	0	1	Voice 3 attenuation (4 bits)
1	1	0	Noise voice control (4 bits, 3 used)
1	1	1	Noise voice attenuation (4 bits)

Figure 15-6. Parameter identification bits

One of the unusual things about the use of sound on the IBM personal computers is that there is no support for it in the ROM-BIOS. For all the other basic operations that our programs might request, there are service routines in the BIOS to help with the work and provide conventional ways of getting things done. But for sound, there is no special ROM-BIOS support. Although there is no great need for supporting routines, since it is relatively easy for programs to control sounds directly, it is still surprising that this one area is left completely alone by the ROM-BIOS.

SOUND TRICKS USED IN BASIC

Before we finish up on sound, there is one interesting trick that BASIC performs, which you might want to know about.

In the fundamental setup of the IBM personal computers, the same timer that can be programmed to produce a sound frequency is also programmed to produce a clock interrupt once for each 65,536 main clock cycles, or roughly 18.2 times each second. This clock interrupt is called a clock tick in the PCjr manuals. The ROM-BIOS keeps track of clock ticks so it can calculate the current time and date; DOS and BASIC also make use of the clock tick for timekeeping.

On each clock tick, the ROM-BIOS increments its clock count and also generates a special clock-tick interrupt for use by programs that need to keep track of the passage of time. One natural use for this clock-tick interrupt is BASIC's music-in-the-background. With music-in-the-background, BASIC is doing two things at once: It is carrying out our program, and it is also playing whatever tune is required. The trick to doing this can be used by any assembly-language program.

So that you can understand how the trick works, we'll describe the most straightforward way for BASIC to use the clock-tick interrupt for music-in-the-background.

When we give BASIC some music to play in the background, BASIC translates our music string into a form in which it can be used. This form is probably a simple table of frequencies, with the duration of each note recorded as a number of clock ticks. The first note is started, and then BASIC sets up an interrupt handler to be activated by the clock-tick interrupt. As each clock-tick interrupt occurs, the interrupt handler subtracts one from the count of the current note. If the count has reached zero, the interrupt handler starts the next note going. Then, whether a new note has been started or an old note continued, the interrupt handler returns control of the computer to the BASIC interpreter, which is carrying out the rest of our BASIC program.

The scheme just described is the normal way to do such things, but BASIC adds a special twist to the process. In order to be able to play music more precisely, BASIC needs to receive clock-tick interrupts faster than 18.2 times a second. So BASIC changes the clock programming to produce ticks four times as fast as normal. But, since the ROM-BIOS expects to keep track of time with the ordinary clock rate, BASIC filters out three out of four ticks, so that the ROM-BIOS experiences clock interrupts at the normal rate.

In the usual mode of operation, the original clock interrupt is handled by the ROM-BIOS which, in turn, hands clock-tick interrupts to any program that wants them. BASIC turns the process around. Since the clock interrupt is occurring four times as often as usual, BASIC sets the interrupt vectors so that the clock interrupt comes to BASIC first. Then, on one of every four clock interrupts, BASIC passes control to the ROM-BIOS, just as if the BIOS had received the interrupt in the first place. The ROM-BIOS does its job of adding one to the count of clock ticks, and then generates the clock-tick interrupt. Programs like BASIC are supposed to work in response to the clock-tick interrupt, but BASIC is clever enough to reverse the process, with no harm done.

In case you are confused by any of this, let's diagram it for more clarity. First, here is the normal way things happen:

1. The clock runs at 1,193,180 cycles each second.

2. Based on a controlling count, the clock generates a clock interrupt, interrupt number 8, 18.2 times a second.

3. The ROM-BIOS receives the clock interrupt (number 8), increments its tick count, and then generates a clock-tick interrupt, interrupt number 28, hex 1C.

4a. If no program has asked to use the clock-tick interrupt (by setting an interrupt vector), control returns to the ROM-BIOS, which returns control to whatever was happening before the original interrupt 8.

4b. If a program has set the clock-tick interrupt vector, then control passes to that part of the program, which will do whatever needs to be done. If BASIC operated this way (as described above), BASIC would check to see if a note had played long enough. When the program's tick subroutine is done, control is returned just as described in item *4a.*

Now, that is what normally happens. But when BASIC is running music-in-the-background, here is how it goes:

1. The clock still runs at 1,193,180 cycles each second. No change.

2. Based on a controlling count that is four times as fast, the clock generates a clock interrupt, interrupt number 8, 72.8 times a second.

3a. BASIC receives control of the clock interrupt, simply because BASIC has reset the interrupt vector for interrupt 8. BASIC now does its own work (checking if a note is finished, etc.) and then, for every fourth clock cycle, passes control to the ROM-BIOS just as if the interrupt number 8 had led directly there.

3b. The ROM-BIOS receives control as if from interrupt 8, increments its tick count, and then generates a clock-tick interrupt, interrupt number 28 (hex 1C). The ROM-BIOS has no way of knowing that BASIC is running, and that there is no need for a clock-tick interrupt 28.

4. There is no special interrupt vector set for the clock-tick interrupt, so control immediately returns to the ROM-BIOS, which returns control to whatever was happening before the original interrupt 8—which is the regular part of the BASIC program.

All this fancy footwork allows BASIC to operate with a faster clock so that it can play music for more accurate lengths of time. This is a trick that we are very unlikely to use ourselves, but learning about it gives us more insight into what can be done with sophisticated programming for the IBM personal computers.

16
POUNDING ON THE KEYBOARD

One of the most interesting and ingenious parts of the IBM personal computers is the keyboard. The keyboard of our PCjr is more ingenious still, so for this chapter we have an especially fascinating subject.

There is a certain amount of irony to the fascination of the keyboard, though. For all the other parts of the PCjr there are two strong reasons for learning how they work. First, sheer curiosity—the desire to understand these little marvels. Second, to gain practical understanding that can be put to use in our programs. The first reason is just as true for the keyboard as it is for the other parts of the PCjr. However, the second reason isn't. It turns out that it is very unwise for our programs to snuggle up to the keyboard, which effectively puts a damper on the uses to which we might put our knowledge.

To understand what I am talking about, we need to make a short digression into a realm that is very interesting all by itself—the subject of the intimacy of software and hardware, and where our own programs can decently fit.

INTIMACY, GOOD AND BAD

Our PCjr, like most computers, requires very smart, very intimate software in order to work well. In a sense, the hardware is only half the design of a computer; the intimate software is the other half of the design. Ordinary programs, like the BASIC programs that you or I might write, aren't based on the detailed inner workings of the computer; these programs aren't intimate with the computer.

The ROM-BIOS programs *are* intimate. They reflect a very deep understanding of the inner workings of the computer—and the computer depends upon them. Some things in the workings of a computer are best handled by physical circuitry; others are best handled by programs. The role of ROM-BIOS programs is twofold: partly to handle the work that is best done with programming, and partly to act as a translator and go-between, uniting our own programs and the computer's hardware.

Thanks to IBM's policy of an open system design, we know most of the details of how the PCjr's circuitry works, and we have nearly complete listings of the ROM-BIOS programs, as well. So if we want or need to, we can make our own programs work as closely with the hardware as the ROM-BIOS does. Whether or not we program this way depends on a number of things.

First, do we really need to penetrate through the ROM-BIOS and get right down to the hardware? For some tasks, we might need to, and for others we might not. For example, many successful IBM personal computer programmers—myself included—have found that it really is necessary to bypass the ROM-BIOS and get directly to the hardware in order to manipulate the display screen efficiently. For other parts of the equipment, there is less practical reason to bypass the ROM-BIOS. The diskette BIOS programs, for example, do not need to be bypassed, except when we are working with copy-protected diskettes. Likewise, few programmers have found any real need to bypass the

ROM-BIOS programs for the keyboard, since they usually provide everything we need.

The other factor that decides whether many programs will need to work intimately with the hardware is safety. It can be very risky for programs to bypass the ROM-BIOS since, in effect, going around the BIOS is subverting half of the design of the computer. Two main factors decide how unsafe it might be to bypass the ROM-BIOS and work directly with the hardware. First, if our programs work intimately with the hardware, will they interfere with the BIOS's work with the hardware? Second, how likely is it that the hardware will be changed, and thus make our programs obsolete?

As it turns out, working directly with the display hardware is relatively safe in both regards. For the keyboard, however, it was evident from the first introduction of the IBM PC that having our programs work directly with the keyboard could severely interfere with the workings of the ROM-BIOS. Moreover, when the PCjr was announced with a keyboard that operated in a thoroughly different way than the PC's keyboard, it became clear that any program that was tied to the PC's keyboard hardware was likely not to work on the PCjr and vice versa.

The PCjr keyboard differs significantly from the keyboard common to the PC and XT, yet both keyboards share a great deal of the same design philosophy; they also appear functionally the same to our programs. In the next section, we'll look at what is common to both IBM personal computer keyboards, before we look at the differences.

COMMON GROUND

The common philosophy and the common operation of the IBM personal computer keyboards divide neatly into three parts: What the keyboard knows; what the ROM-BIOS acts on; and what our programs experience.

What the Keyboard Knows

The IBM personal computer keyboards do not, repeat not, have any sense of the meaning of the keys we press. From the point of view of the keyboard, each key has an identifying number, known as its *scan code*. The PC and XT keyboards have 83 keys, with scan codes numbered from 1 to 83; our PCjr has only 62 keys, with scan codes from 1 to 62. The keyboard knows when we press each key and also when we release each key. To the keyboard, the pressing and releasing of each key are separate events, each experienced and acted on independently of any other keyboard action.

When a key is pressed, the scan code uses the key's ordinary code—for example, 30 for the A key. When the key is released, the same scan-code byte also has bit 7 set on, which is equivalent to adding 128 (hex 80) to the scan code of the key that was pressed.

Let's suppose that we type a lowercase a. The keyboard experiences a press of scan code 30, then a release of scan code 158. Suppose we want an uppercase A. We press the shift key and then the A key; then we release them. The keyboard experiences a press of scan code 42 (one of the shift keys) and then a press of scan code 30 (a), followed by the release of scan codes 170 and 158.

As we type, the keyboard has no knowledge of the meaning of each key; it certainly does not keep track of the shift key to change the meaning of the A key. When a key is pressed or released, the keyboard signals the event to the rest of the computer by generating an interrupt and then transfers the scan code of the key that has been pressed or released.

What the ROM-BIOS Acts On

The ROM-BIOS is alerted to each key action by the interrupt that the keyboard generates. Acting on the interrupt, the ROM-BIOS gets the scan code from the keyboard, and then figures out what the key action means.

The ROM-BIOS keeps track of everything that is needed to understand each key action. For example, if a shift key has been pressed, but not yet released, then the ROM-BIOS notes that we are in the shift state—the state that distinguishes A from a.

This business of keeping track of the shift state is more complicated than you might at first think. For example, the Caps-Lock key reverses the meaning of the shift key for the alphabet part of the keyboard, but not for the rest of the keys. Then there are the special shift states: Ctrl and Alt (meaning control and alternative).

By taking everything into account—the current key and the effect of prior keys, such as the shift keys—the ROM-BIOS programs translate each key action into its meaning. If a key action means a keyboard character, such as the letter A, the ROM-BIOS generates that character code and stores it in a *buffer*, ready for a program to read. According to the ground rules for IBM personal computers, programs are supposed to ask for keyboard characters when they want them, rather than the ROM-BIOS interrupting them when the characters are ready. Since the computer does not control when we can pound on the keyboard and when we can't, a place is needed to store the keyboard characters that the ROM-BIOS generates as a result of our pounding. For this purpose, the ROM-BIOS maintains a buffer with room for 15 characters. If, as often happens, the program that is running stops what it's doing to wait for us to type something in, the keyboard buffer will be kept empty—the program will read information out of the buffer as quickly as we type it in. But if the program isn't reading keyboard information, or if it is acting too slowly on the information, the buffer can start to fill up. When the buffer is full, the ROM-BIOS has no choice but to discard any new, incoming data. To alert us to this problem, the ROM-BIOS beeps the speaker in complaint.

In addition to generating keyboard characters from scan codes, the ROM-BIOS must also look for three special key combinations. One is the Ctrl-Alt-Del combination, which is used to request that the computer reboot, or reload its control program. Another is the pause combination, which is accomplished by Alt-Num Lock on the PC keyboard and Fn-Q on the PCjr keyboard. When the ROM-BIOS comes across the pause combination, it holds control of the computer, except for interrupt handling, until another key is pressed. In effect, the keyboard service routines make the computer pause or halt. In actuality, the computer keeps running at full speed, but it just executes the ROM-BIOS control program, waiting for a keystroke, instead of executing any of our own programs.

The third of the special keys that the ROM-BIOS looks out for is the print-screen combination, Fn-P on the PCjr, shift-PrtSc on the PC and XT. When these keys are encountered, the ROM-BIOS keyboard routines act on them, running the print-screen interrupt handler (which we went over in detail in Chapter 7).

Everything that we have said so far about what the ROM-BIOS acts on is equally true for the PCjr and the PC and XT models, even though they have different keyboards. Junior's different keyboard adds some extra twists to the ROM-BIOS, which we'll come to shortly.

What Our Programs Experience

As a result of our pounding on the keyboard, our programs experience a series of characters, each coded into two bytes. Two bytes are needed because there are more keyboard-character possibilities than will fit into one byte. First, there are the ordinary ASCII characters, coded CHR$(0) through CHR$(127), and the extended ASCII characters, coded CHR$(128) through CHR$(255). Then there are the characters needed to indicate all the special keyboard keys, such as the cursor arrow keys and the function keys.

The keys we press are reported to our programs in an interesting way. As we mentioned, two bytes are used to report each character; we will call these two the main byte and the auxiliary byte.

When the main byte is not 0, then the BIOS is reporting an ASCII character, CHR$(1) through CHR$(255), and not a special key, like the cursor keys. The ASCII character code is in the main byte, while the auxiliary byte contains the scan-code for the key that was pressed.

A few ASCII characters can be keyed in more than one way, and a program

Auxiliary Byte	Key Combinations
3	Null character
15	Enter
16 through 25	Alt-Q, W, E, R, T, Y, U, I, O, P
30 through 38	Alt-A, S, D, F, G, H, J, K, L
44 through 50	Alt-Z, X, C, V, B, N, M
59 through 68	Fn-1, 2, 3, 4, 5, 6, 7, 8, 9, 0 (functions 1 through 10)
71	Home
72	Up arrow
73	PgUp
75	Left arrow
77	Right arrow
79	End
80	Down arrow
81	PgDn
82	Ins (insert)
83	Del (delete)
84 through 93	F11 through F20 (shift-F1 through F10)
94 through 103	Ctrl-F1 through F10
104 through 113	Alt-F1 through F10
114	Fn-E or Ctrl-Fn-P
115	Ctrl-Left arrow
116	Ctrl-Right arrow
117	Ctrl-End
118	Ctrl-PgDn
119	Ctrl-Home
120 through 131	Alt-1, 2, 3, 4, 5, 6, 7, 8, 9, 0 −, = (keys 2 through 13)
132	Ctrl-PgUp

Figure 16-1. Auxiliary-byte value of special key combinations

can look at the auxiliary byte to distinguish which way was used. Normally, this isn't a good thing for a program to do, but if any of our programs need to know exactly how a character was keyed in, this is the way they can find out. One of the 256 ASCII codes, CHR$(0) can't be keyed in, for the simple reason that 0 in the main byte is used to signal a special key, rather than an ASCII character. You might think that it could be a problem that we can key in every character but one; however, in practice, that's no problem at all.

So the main byte can also contain CHR$(0) to report that a special key was used. In this case, the auxiliary byte contains a value that indicates which special key was pressed. The special keys include the function keys, the various shifts of the function keys, the cursor arrows, the keys such as Home and End, the use of Ctrl with some keys like Home, and the use of Alt with the alphabet keys. Figure 16-1 gives the auxiliary-byte value that represents each of these special keys.

There are some things worth noting about all these keyboard characters. One is that each key potentially has four meanings (even more on the PCjr keyboard, as we'll see in the next section). The four meanings come from the key itself, and then from the key used with the ordinary shift or with the special Ctrl and Alt shifts as shown in Figure 16-2. Not all combinations of keys and shifts have a meaning, though, and the ROM-BIOS just ignores meaningless combinations, treating them as if we hadn't pressed any keys at all.

Ordinary Key	Uppercase Shift	Ctrl Shift	Alt Shift
a	A	CHR$(1)	
b	B	CHR$(2)	
c	C	CHR$(3)	
d	D	CHR$(4)	
e	E	CHR$(5)	
f	F	CHR$(6)	
g	G	CHR$(7)	
h	H	CHR$(8)	
i	I	CHR$(9)	
j	J	CHR$(10)	
k	K	CHR$(11)	
l	L	CHR$(12)	
m	M	CHR$(13)	
n	N	CHR$(14)	
o	O	CHR$(15)	
p	P	CHR$(16)	
q	Q	CHR$(17)	
r	R	CHR$(18)	
s	S	CHR$(19)	
t	T	CHR$(20)	
u	U	CHR$(21)	
v	V	CHR$(22)	
w	W	CHR$(23)	
x	X	CHR$(24)	
y	Y	CHR$(25)	
z	Z	CHR$(26)	
1	!		
2	@		

(continued)

Figure 16-2. The shift states of each key

Ordinary Key	Uppercase Shift	Ctrl Shift	Alt Shift
3	#		
4	$		
5	%		
6	^		
7	&	CHR$(30)	
8	*		
9	(		
0	)		
Enter	Enter	CHR$(10)	
Space	Space	Space	Space
Esc	Esc	Esc	
Tab	Reverse tab		
-	—	CHR$(31)	
=	+		
Backspace	Backspace	CHR$(127)	
[	{	CHR$(27)	Vertical bar
]	}	CHR$(29)	Tilde
;	:		
'	"		Reverse quote
,	<		
.	>		* (2nd asterisk)
/	?		Reverse slash
Ins	0		
Del	.		
Up arrow	8		
Left arrow	4		
Right arrow	6		
Down arrow	2		

Figure 16-2. The shift states of each key (continued)

For the alphabet keys, all four shift combinations work. Upper- and lowercase shifts work, of course, producing characters in the ordinary ASCII character set. The Alt-letter combinations all produce some of the special characters that are reported in the auxiliary byte. The Ctrl-letter combinations are particularly interesting. They all produce ASCII characters, in alphabetical order from CHR$(1), produced by Ctrl-A, through CHR$(26), produced by Ctrl-Z.

The codes for the complete set of characters and special keys are generated by the ROM-BIOS, but different programming languages vary in the way they handle the codes. BASIC, for example, takes a mixed approach to the special keys. When we use ordinary BASIC input statements, BASIC hands over the regular ASCII characters and filters out any special keys. Some of the special keys can be acted on specially, with the ON KEY statement. However, we can use the BASIC INKEY$ function to get directly to the ROM-BIOS coding for keyboard characters. If the INKEY$ function returns a string one byte long, it is reporting an ordinary or extended ASCII keyboard character. If INKEY$ returns a 2-byte string, the first byte in the string is the ROM-BIOS's main byte and will always by CHR$(0), and the second byte is the auxiliary byte and will indicate which special key was pressed.

So far, we have seen the philosophy and operating details that are common to all the IBM personal computer keyboards. Now, it is time to look at their differences.

OLD AND NEW KEYBOARDS

To start with, two dramatic differences set the PCjr keyboard apart from the keyboard used by the PC and XT. First, there is a different number of keys—62, instead of 83. Second, the keyboard can "talk" to the computer by infrared light as well as by a wired connection. Let's start with the infrared connection.

New and Old Connections

The infrared connection works on the same principle used by remote controls for television sets. The keyboard contains a pair of transmitters, which generate infrared light with a coded message in it. The computer contains an infrared receiver, which can detect the light and decode the message. The message buried in the infrared light contains the interrupt signalling a key action and the scan code of the key.

Infrared light is used both for the PCjr's keyboard and TV remote controllers because it has just the right combination of properties. It is invisible to our eyes; its transmitters and receivers can be built relatively cheaply; and finally, it bounces very well. One of the problems with remote controls, including our keyboard, is getting a reliable signal from the sender to the receiver. Infrared light is relatively good at bouncing off walls, ceilings, and furniture, so there doesn't necessarily have to be a direct line-of-sight between sender and receiver. Of course, it is still quite easy to disrupt the signal passing through the air, but infrared signals are more reliable than other methods.

To deal with the possibility of interference in the infrared signal, the PCjr's ROM-BIOS contains some special programming that isn't needed by the PC's wired keyboard. This special programming checks, as much as possible, for lost or scrambled data—and if it detects any problem, it lets out a special beep to alert us.

Because of the potential problems with an infrared signal, the PCjr's keyboard can also be connected to Junior's system unit with a cable. When the cable is attached, the keyboard's infrared transmitter is disconnected, and the electrical signals in the wires replace the infrared light. The wired connection has several advantages: It can't be disrupted by passers-by or by another PCjr's keyboard.

Old and New Keys

In the effort to hold down the cost of the PCjr, the number of keys on the keyboard was reduced. While the original PC keyboard has 83 keys, the PCjr's keyboard has only 62 keys. Figures 16-3 and 16-4 show the two keyboard layouts, with the keys that exactly match highlighted.

One of the most important design requirements for the PCjr was functional compatibility with the PC, so that most PC programs could be used on our PCjr. This means that every usable key and key combination on the PC has to exist on the PCjr, or the PCjr has to have a key combination that will produce an equivalent function. To make this possible, a new key has been added to Junior, the Fn (function) key.

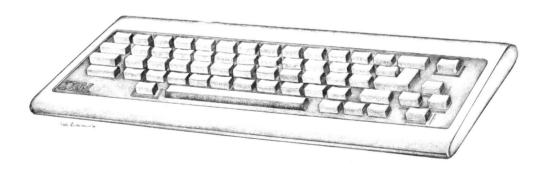

Figure 16-3. The PCjr keyboard: one unique key

The PCjr's keyboard has 21 fewer keys than the PC's, but 22 PC keys are actually missing. The new Fn key adds one to the PCjr's key count:

(83 PC keys) − (22 missing) + (1 added) = (62 PCjr keys)

The 22 extra keys on the PC keyboard are: 10 dedicated function keys, labeled F1 through F10; another 10 keys on a numeric keypad (also containing a few special keys, like Home and End); and finally, two keys with special, rarely used characters (vertical bar and backslash on one, reverse quote and tilde on the other).

The PCjr's Alt shift key and special Fn key are used in combination with other keys to serve the same purpose as most of the missing keys. For the F1 to F10 function keys, Fn is pressed, followed by one of the digit keys. (The zero key, naturally, serves for F10.) Twelve other Fn combinations, used to replace parts of missing keys, are shown in Figure 16-5.

Five special Alt combinations give us the four rarely used, special characters from the two rarely used character keys, plus the second asterisk that appears with PrtSc on the PC keyboard. These combinations are shown in Figure 16-6.

Three of these special key combinations are strange, because they mimic duplicate keys on the PC keyboard. The PC keyboard has two asterisks, two

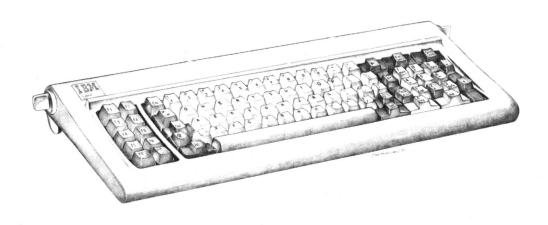

Figure 16-4. The PC keyboard: 22 unique keys

Fn Plus	Replaces
B	Break (Ctrl-Break on PCs)
Q	Pause (Ctrl-Num Lock on PCs)
E	Echo (Ctrl-PrtSc on PCs)
P	Shift-PrtSc
S	Scroll Lock
N	Num Lock
Up	Home
Down	End
Left	Page Up
Right	Page Down
−	− on the numeric keypad of the PC
=	+ on the numeric keypad of the PC

Figure 16-5. Fn key combinations
that replace missing PC keys

Alt Plus	Replaces
/	\ (Reverse slash)
'	` (Reverse quote)
[	¦ (Vertical bar)
]	~ (Tilde)
.	* (The other asterisk)

Figure 16-6. Alt key combinations
that replace missing PC keys

minus signs, and two plus signs, all of which are produced on the PCjr with the combinations you have just seen. This duplication would not seem strange, since the PCjr is intended to mimic the PC exactly, but for the fact that 11 other duplicates aren't mimicked. The PC keyboard has 10 duplicate digits and a duplicate period that the PCjr keyboard doesn't reproduce. This is one area in which PCjr has a very minor functional difference from its bigger brothers.

In the last section, we mentioned three special keys or key combinations that the BIOS looks for: print-screen, pause, and reboot. The PCjr has these and several more special combinations.

■ *Alt-Ctrl-Caps Lock* is used to tell the ROM-BIOS to click when a key is pressed. While the PC keyboard makes a nice, mechanical click when the keys are pressed, the PCjr's keyboard does not click. If a silent keyboard bothers you, you should know that the ROM-BIOS for the PCjr is capable of making a clicking sound through the speaker when a key is pressed and that this is the key combination that toggles the clicking on or off.

■ *Alt-Ctrl-Ins* asks the ROM-BIOS to carry out the diagnostic programs that are built into the PCjr.

■ *Alt-Ctrl-right arrow* and *Alt-Ctrl-left arrow* are two other special key combinations used with the PCjr to adjust the display screen. Alt-Ctrl-right arrow shifts the display screen right; Alt-Ctrl-left arrow shifts it left. These keys are used to adjust the PCjr's display generation to the TV set or monitor that you are using. The DOS command MODE also provides this function, but these two key combinations allow us to shift the screen even if we aren't using DOS.

Besides the physical layout of the keyboards and the way keys are mimicked, there is also a difference in the way the ROM-BIOS and the keyboards work together.

The ROM-BIOS's Additional Workload

In the PC keyboard there is a small microprocessor, the Intel 8048, that gives the keyboard some smarts. This microprocessor enables the PC keyboard to test itself when power is turned on, to check continually for stuck keys, to generate automatic repeat-key action (called typematic by IBM), and also to buffer up to 20 key actions. If the computer has temporarily masked the interrupts, the PC keyboard can buffer 20 key actions—the equivalent of 10 keys being pressed and released—and can then report key actions to the computer by means of regular interrupts when the computer is once again able to process them. The computer reads data out of the keyboard's buffer by using the keyboard ports, 96 and 97 (hex 60 and 61). Although the keyboard's buffer is usually empty, its presence ensures that nothing is lost if the computer is delayed in handling the interrupts.

Our PCjr's inexpensive keyboard is not smart like that at all. Following the design philosophy of the PCjr, programming in the ROM-BIOS takes the functional place of more expensive hardware, at the price of a slight loss in speed. In the PCjr, the keyboard can't wait for the computer to decide that it is free, so Junior's keyboard generates a non-maskable interrupt, which the ROM-BIOS always acts on immediately.

One of the biggest differences between the PCjr and its more powerful relatives is that, for both the keyboard and the diskette, the ROM-BIOS programs do the work of decoding signals into bits and bytes. Sharing the ROM-BIOS is an area of potential conflict inside the PCjr, because both the keyboard and the diskette expect the ROM-BIOS to give them special and undivided attention. The ROM-BIOS favors the diskette; if the disk drive is in operation, the entire system is masked and keyboard input can't take place (asynchronous communications through the serial port can't take place, either).

The scan codes that the PCjr receives from its keyboard are not the same ones used by the PC keyboard, since the number and use of the keys is different. So another of the additional tasks of the PCjr's busy ROM-BIOS is translating PCjr scan codes into the equivalent PC scan codes, to maintain as much compatibility as possible between Junior and the other IBM personal computers.

There is one more PC-keyboard function that the PCjr's ROM-BIOS must take care of—the automatic repeat-key action. In the PC keyboard, the 8048 microprocessor checks to see if any key is being held down and then generates any necessary repeat-key action. It waits a certain amount of time before generating the first repeat action in case the person at the keyboard has slow fingers, but after that, it waits a shorter time between each automatic repeat action. In the PC keyboard, every key repeats automatically, and the PC's ROM-BIOS takes responsibility for filtering out the keys that aren't meant to repeat, such as the shift keys.

In the PCjr the ROM-BIOS keeps track of how long each key has been pressed and generates the repeat-key action as needed. Interestingly enough, the delay before repeat-key action starts is a variable, which our programs can modify, as we'll see in the next section.

ROM-BIOS KEYBOARD SERVICES

In this section, we'll take a look at the services that the ROM-BIOS provides for our programs, and then we'll see some tricks that we can play with keyboard control.

The keyboard services are all invoked with interrupt 22 (hex 16); there are just three simple services.

■ *Service 0* reads the next available keyboard character and stores it in the AX register. The main byte is stored in the AL part of the register, and the auxiliary byte is stored in AH. If the ROM-BIOS is holding a character in its buffer, this service will read that character immediately. If not, the service will wait until a keyboard character is generated, do its work, and then return control to the program that asked for the service.

■ *Service 1* allows a program to see if keyboard input is ready without being suspended if there is none. This service is very important for programs that want to respond to the keyboard, but continue running when there is no keyboard input. The BASIC function INKEY$ is using this service when it reports no key is ready. Service 1 sets the zero flag on to indicate that a character is available. The interrupt handler then copies the character into AX so that a program can inspect it. The character is also still in the ROM-BIOS buffer, so the next service 0 or service 1 will see the same character.

■ *Service 2* is used to report the shift-key status. The ROM-BIOS keeps track of the current status, and programs can use this service to find out what it is. Using the information returned by the service, they might reinterpret the meaning of some characters (sometimes effectively ignoring the shift keys).

This brings us to the record of what information the ROM-BIOS keeps about the keyboard, and how our programs might make use of it.

KEEPING TABS ON THE KEYBOARD

Certain locations in low memory are used by the ROM-BIOS for data that it needs. This low-memory area begins at segment paragraph hex 40. Among the data kept here are two bytes used for the shift flags, kept at offset memory locations hex 17 and 18. We can read these bytes in a BASIC program with these statements:

```
100 DEF SEG = &H40
110 KB.FLAG.0 = PEEK (&H17)
120 KB.FLAG.1 = PEEK (&H18)
```

The first byte records the current shift state (reported by service 2), while the second byte records which shift keys are actually pressed and still held down.

The coding of these bytes is shown in Figure 16-7. Except for the two bits noted, these control bytes apply to all models of IBM personal computers.

One of the things that can be done with these bytes is to change the controlling bits. Since the ROM-BIOS takes the coding of these bits as gospel, if we change the coding, we change the workings of the keyboard. One popular use for this idea is to have a program put the keyboard into Caps-Lock state; surprisingly, many BASIC programs do this. As an example, the following program will set the Caps-Lock bit, whether it was on or off.

```
130 KB.FLAG.0 = PEEK (&H17)           ' get existing flag
140 KB.FLAG.= KB.FLAG.0 OR&H0040' turn on Caps-Lock
150 POKE &H17, KB.FLAG.0              ' put value back
```

The PCjr also has a third control byte, byte 2, located at offset hex 8C. We can inspect this byte with the BASIC statement:

```
160 KB.FLAG.2 = PEEK (&H8C)
```

Figure 16-8 shows this byte's coding.

The ROM-BIOS's keyboard-character buffer is located at offset hex 1E and contains 15 pairs of bytes of currently buffered keyboard data. It would be unwise for our programs to mess around with these data, but it is interesting to know where they are.

Rather than the next character being shifted up as the character before it is taken out of the ROM-BIOS buffer, the buffer is used in a continuous circle, so pointers are needed to indicate both the current head and the current tail of the buffer contents. These pointers are two 2-byte words stored just before the buffered characters. When the pointers are equal, the buffer is empty.

Here is one final note about where the ROM-BIOS keeps keyboard information. While the PC keyboard generates its own repeat-key action, in the PCjr the BIOS is responsible for repeating keys, so the last key pressed has to be kept in memory. You'll find it at offset hex 89.

There are a lot more tidbits like this in the memory locations used by the ROM-BIOS, but we won't pore over them all, partly so you will have some

Byte	Bit	Use
0	0	Right shift pressed
	1	Left shift pressed
	2	Ctrl pressed
	3	Alt pressed
	4	Scroll Lock active
	5	Num Lock active
	6	Caps Lock active
	7	Ins (insert) active
1	0	Not used
	1	Clicking combination (Alt-Ctrl-Caps Lock) pressed (PCjr only)
	2	Keyboard click on (PCjr only)
	3	Hold state active (No program allowed to run)
	4	Scroll Lock pressed
	5	Num Lock pressed
	6	Caps Lock pressed
	7	Ins (insert) pressed

Figure 16-7. Coding of the two shift-flag bytes

Byte	Bit	Use
2	0	Put char operation
	1	Initial delay in repeat-key
	2	Half-rate delay in repeat-key (After first)
	3	Typematic repeating off
	4	Fn function lock
	5	Fn function pending (Function key was pressed)
	6	Fn function break
	7	Fn function flag

Figure 16-8. Coding of the third control byte

more to explore on your own, if you are so inclined. (If you are, the information is laid out in the ROM-BIOS listing in the *Technical Reference* manual.)

And that completes our tour through the keyboard.

17
OTHER
CONNECTIONS

When the PC was first released, it had the ability to use cassette tapes for data storage, joysticks for game control, and light pens for interactive graphics. Sadly, little was done with any of these three and, in fact, the cassette interface was even dropped from the XT model.

Now our PCjr has revived interest in all three of these neglected connections. In this chapter we'll look at each of them and see how they are used.

CONNECTING WITH THE CASSETTE

The most inexpensive home computers have usually relied on audio cassette recorders for data and program storage. When IBM designed the PC, they wanted it to be as universal and complete a small computer as possible. A computer cannot be used very effectively without a way to read and write data, and the *cassette interface* provides a cheap and reasonably efficient way to store data without the expense of a diskette system.

The virtue of the cassette interface is that it can be used with a very ordinary, inexpensive, cassette recorder—no special, fancy, or expensive equipment is needed, just a modest connecting cable. The disadvantage of the cassette, though, is that it is slow and clumsy. It takes a long time to read and write data; there is no random access—to find data, the computer has to read a tape sequentially, looking for the right information; and even manual intervention (pushing the rewind button) is required to rewind the tapes.

IBM's original support for the cassette interface was half-hearted at best, and given the disadvantages of cassettes, I don't suppose we can blame them. Their eyes were on the computer user who could afford a diskette-based system. Our PCjr model, though, has an entirely different focus from its predecessors. It makes more sense to use a cassette recorder with an inexpensive home machine, and so the cassette interface has been revived.

What were originally provided for the PC's cassette interface were four simple ROM-BIOS services and the ability, in BASIC, to SAVE and LOAD programs or read or write data with the cassette. In the PCjr, the cassette interface has the same support it had on the PC.

If any of our programs use the cassette interface directly, they will make use of these ROM-BIOS cassette services. The ROM-BIOS services for the cassette interface are invoked with interrupt number 21 (hex 15). There are four simple services.

■ *Service 0* turns the cassette motor on, just as the BASIC statement MOTOR 1 does. *Service 1* turns it off, like the BASIC statement MOTOR 0.

■ *Services 2 and 3* read or write data on cassette. Data are always stored in blocks of 256 bytes, and these services can read or write any number of blocks with one service call.

As a minor point of interest, the ROM-BIOS routines for both the PCjr and the PC do the work of decoding signals into bits, and then into bytes, and finally into 256-byte blocks of data. The process of having a program, instead of hardware, decode bit signals is called *bit nibbling*. All cassette data are handled by the ROM-BIOS in this way, even on the PC model. Our PCjr's ROM-BIOS also decodes signals for the diskette drive and the keyboard, while the other models of IBM personal computer use special circuitry to perform this tedious task for those components.

PLUGGING IN THE JOYSTICK

The next of the connections we want to look at is the joystick. Joysticks are used almost exclusively with games and educational software and have not been used much on the PC and XT. For both these models, we have to buy a *games adapter card* and also the joysticks themselves. Since our PCjr features games, it is natural for the supporting circuitry, the equivalent of the PC's games adapter card, to be built right in. All we need to use joysticks on the PCjr are the joysticks themselves and programs that take advantage of them.

Oddly enough, there is no support programming for the joysticks in the ROM-BIOS. Instead, any program that needs joystick information reads this information from port 513 (hex 201) and decodes it. The BASIC programming language includes two functions, STICK and STRIG to decode joystick data. To understand how BASIC decodes the joystick data, we need some background information.

Joysticks are made up of two elements: the *lever* or stick itself, which is used to move a playing piece around the screen, and the *triggers*, which are used as firing buttons. The triggers are purely on/off switches, while the sticks indicate a position, showing how far they have been moved.

Joysticks, like the IBM joysticks sold for the PCjr, usually have two trigger buttons and a stick that can move freely in all directions. The position of the stick, at any moment, is like a point on a two-dimensional graph. We need two numbers to describe the stick's position, like the two graph coordinates. So each IBM-style joystick has two trigger switches and two position values. With a pair of joysticks, there is a total of four triggers and four position values, which is the most that the PCjr, or a PC's game adapter, can handle.

There is another way to use four buttons and four positions, with what are called *game paddles*. A paddle is essentially half a joystick; it has one button and its lever moves in only one dimension. A one-dimensional control can't be used to move a playing piece freely in two dimensions, but it can be used to steer left and right, or as a throttle control. The one main advantage that paddles have for us is that four people could be playing at once with paddles, where only two at a time could use joysticks. I don't know many uses for paddles with the PCjr, but you'll find them mentioned occasionally, so you ought to know about them.

Programs read information about the joystick in an interesting way. To begin the process, a program sends any value out through the joystick port, 513.

Bit	Information Source	Paddle	Joystick
0	Relative position 0	A	A, x-coordinate
1	Relative position 1	B	A, y-coordinate
2	Relative position 2	C	B, x-coordinate
3	Relative position 3	D	B, y-coordinate
4	Trigger 0	A	Button A-1
5	Trigger 1	B	Button A-2
6	Trigger 2	C	Button B-1
7	Trigger 3	D	Button B-2

*Figure 17-1. Coding of bits in the value read
from the joystick port*

This value has the sole purpose of nudging the computer so that it will send information about the joystick back. The program then immediately reads the data byte sent back through that port. Each of the eight bits in this byte is dedicated to one of the eight information sources, the four triggers and the four position indicators. The bits are used as shown in Figure 17-1.

The way joystick information is transmitted is curious and interesting. For the triggers, a single bit, indicating whether or not the button is pressed, is all that is needed. One reading of the data byte at port 513 is enough to give the program this information; the trigger bits will be set to 1 if the trigger is released, and 0 if the trigger is pressed—just the opposite of what you might expect.

However, for the position indicators, we need a range of values to indicate the range of possible positions. The program finds out the relative position by the unusual means of successively reading the port. When the program starts the process by sending a value out through port 513, all the relative position bits are set to 1. Over a period of time (about one millisecond), each of these bits is independently reset to 0, with the amount of time to reset being in proportion to the relative position of the joystick lever. Our program keeps reading port 513 until each of the four relative position indicator bits has been reset to 0. The program can calculate the position of the joystick or paddle either from the exact time that it took each bit to be reset, or from a relative value obtained from the number of times it had to read the port until the value of each bit changed.

There is no absolute range of values for the joystick positions; if we move two different joysticks all the way in some direction, they are likely to report different position values just because of minor electrical variations. Programs that use joysticks normally adjust, or scale, the position values to match their needs. It's common, for example, for a program to adjust the working scale of the joystick so that the limits of the joystick movement correspond to the edges of the display screen.

The programming necessary to read the joystick port and calculate these positions is slightly tricky, but it can be done in assembly language by a knowledgeable programmer. If we are writing in BASIC, however, it is easier, since the work of sampling and interpreting the joystick information is done for us by the STICK and STRIG functions.

LIGHTING THE LIGHT PEN

The light pen is the last of the three neglected connections that has gained importance on the PCjr. Light pens are mostly used in sophisticated graphics applications, where a combination of the light pen and the right software allows us to draw interactively on the display screen.

Actually, the light pen is not an instrument for writing, but for reading. We do not draw directly with the pen, we simply point with it. A light pen provides a way for the computer to find the exact location we are pointing to on the display screen.

A light pen has a light-sensing tip and some sort of trigger that is used to indicate when we want to use the pen. The trigger might be pressed by our fingers, or it might be at the tip of the pen and be pressed automatically when we push the pen against the display screen. When the pen is activated, the ROM-BIOS support programs for the display screen can tell exactly where on the screen the pen is pointing, down to the exact pixel location—which of the 200 scan lines the pen is on vertically, and which of the 160, 320, or 640 column locations it is on horizontally. All that the ROM-BIOS support programs do is to report when the light pen is active, and where it is.

A program can use a light pen to have items selected from a menu of choices, or it could change a drawing on the screen to reproduce the movements of the light pen. With this last application, the light pen seems to draw on the screen, though actually a graphics program does the drawing. The program takes its cues from the light pen, and as a result it seems to us as if the pen is writing directly on the screen.

A light pen works by sensing when the display screen's scanning electron beam hits it. It immediately sends a signal that tells the computer its location on the screen. For the pen to be successful, the phosphor on the screen has to respond very quickly to the electron beam. Many display screens have high-persistence phosphors, which hold their image and reduce the amount of flicker on the screen, but a light pen can only work with quick-acting, low-persistence phosphors. If you expect to make any use of light pens, you need to make sure that they will work with the sort of display screen you will be using.

To support the light pen, there is a single ROM-BIOS service, one of the group of video services invoked with interrupt 16 (hex 10). For the light pen, service 4 indicates if the pen is triggered and, if it is, returns the row and column position of the pen.

As for everything else in the PCjr, the BASIC language provides the means to use the light pen, with the PEN function and statement. If we are programming in BASIC we can use these features of the language; otherwise, we must use an assembly-language connection to get access to the ROM-BIOS service for the pen.

18

THE PRINTER ADAPTER AND FURTHER CONNECTIONS

As we've seen, the PCjr is full of sockets
where all sorts of interesting equipment
can be connected. Each of these sockets
has a single, dedicated purpose, except
for one on the side of the system unit,
the I/O channel connector.

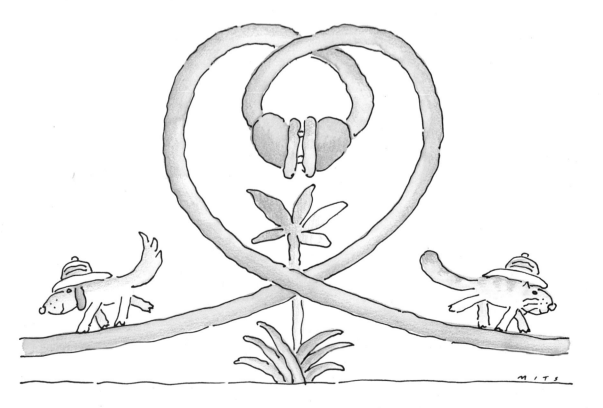

The I/O channel connector is the one open-ended connection to the PCjr. To understand the I/O channel connector, we need to learn about what is called *bus architecture*.

TAKING THE BUS

There are two main ways to wire the parts of a computer together. One is to make specific, special-purpose connections: If part A needs to talk to part B, we can run a wire, or several wires, between the two parts. There are some real disadvantages to using this kind of special-purpose connection. For one, if there are lots of parts, we can end up with a complicated rat's nest of wiring; for another, adding a new part, or allowing for an optional part, can be very complicated.

The solution to these problems is provided by the other main way of connecting computer parts: a bus. A bus is not a dedicated connection between two parts; instead, it is like a telephone party line. It is a shared set of wires, with a set of rules for using it. The wires in the bus include power connections, data transmission lines, and ways of determining whether the party line is busy or free to use.

When one part of the computer needs to talk to another through a bus, it does roughly the following: First, the initiating part checks to see if the bus is in use; if the bus is free, the part sends out a signal indicating what it wants, or which part of the computer it wants to talk to. Then it waits for a reply. If a reply comes, fine; but if there is no reply, it may mean that an optional part has not been installed.

Bus architecture is complicated, and it takes more work and time to use a bus than it does to use a dedicated, wired connection, where you know who is on the other end of the line. Still, in spite of this complexity, if more than a few parts use the bus, the end result is much simpler than all the dedicated wires would be.

The greatest advantage of a bus, though, is that it is open-ended and flexible. With a well-designed bus, all sorts of equipment can be plugged into the computer, including equipment that did not even exist when the computer was originally designed.

The IBM PC uses a bus for virtually all its optional parts. Each PC and XT has a number of expansion slots that are simply connections to the bus. Any suitable equipment can be plugged into an expansion slot, including all the basic options, such as memory expansion, the diskette drive adapter, the printer adapter, and much more.

Our PCjr is a little different because it has dedicated, plug-in connections for all the main options: memory expansion to 128K, the smart modem, the diskette drive adapter, the joysticks, the light pen, and the cassette. The PCjr does, however, have the PC's bus in the form of its I/O channel connector. While the main parts of the PCjr do not connect to the bus, as they do on the PC and XT, our Junior still has a bus that can be used for many purposes.

The first use of the I/O channel connector is for attaching the PCjr's printer adapter. However, the printer adapter or any other part that connects to the I/O channel can carry the connection through to its far side, so that more parts can be connected, one plugging into the other.

Mechanically, the PCjr's bus is quite different from that of the PC. The PCjr's bus has only one plug where one part can be connected (though, as I've said, another part can be connected to that, and so on); the PC's bus, on the other hand, has several connections and normally only one part is plugged into each. Electronically, though, the PCjr's bus and the PC's bus work in exactly the same way. With each bus, one or more optional parts can be connected, and as soon as a part is plugged in, it becomes an active component of the computer.

THE PRINTER ADAPTER

IBM's main use for our Junior's I/O channel connector is as a plug for a printer adapter.

As we mentioned in our discussion of the serial port in Chapter 14, there are two ways to connect a printer to a personal computer. One way is to use the RS-232 serial port, and the other is to use a special *parallel printer adapter* plugged into the I/O channel connector. Either outlet can be used successfully to drive a printer, but there are some advantages to using a parallel connection. For one thing, connecting a printer to our RS-232 port ties up the port and prevents us from using it for other things, particularly communications. The main reason, though, for connecting a printer to a parallel printer adapter is because the parallel connection is specially designed for efficient printer use. With a parallel printer adapter, we can drive a printer faster and use less computing power while we are doing it.

The main thing that distinguishes a parallel printer connection from the serial port is the amount of data being transmitted. The parallel connection transmits data a full byte at a time—there is a separate line for each of the eight bits in a byte, so the bits are sent out at the same time, in parallel. A serial port sends the bits out one at a time, and they have to be assembled into bytes at the receiving end.

Having said that, I have to acknowledge that, for a personal computer and particularly for a small home computer like our Junior, there is little practical difference between using the RS-232 port and using a parallel printer adapter plugged into the I/O channel connector. While it is true that a parallel connection can transmit data much faster than a serial port, either one is fast enough to run the sort of printers that we usually use with personal computers. For most people, the factors that decide which to use are based on two very simple questions: Is the printer set up for a serial connection or a parallel connection? (The inexpensive IBM Compact Printer uses the serial interface, while the popular Epson® and IBM matrix printers use the parallel interface.) Do you want to keep your RS-232 serial port free for another use? Usually, but not always, the less expensive choice is to use the serial port, and the higher performance choice is to use the parallel connection.

The parallel printer adapter connects to the PCjr's I/O channel connector and has a parallel printer plug to accommodate the cable to the printer. This parallel connection is often called a *Centronics interface*, after the name of the company that developed and popularized it. The Centronics interface is very much the standard printer connection for small computers, both microcomputers, like our PCjr, and much larger minicomputers.

ROM-BIOS PRINTER SERVICES

The ROM-BIOS in our PCjr provides all the primitive services needed to operate a printer. A printer is a very simple device (from the point of view of the computer that uses it, if not the mechanic who has to repair it!), so there are only three BIOS services. Since the PC and XT can have more than one printer attached to them, these services call for specification of a printer number: printer 0, 1, or 2. Our PCjr normally can have only one printer (it is rare for any personal computer to have more than one printer, anyway), so our programs always have to specify printer number 0. Interrupt number 23 (hex 17) is used to invoke all three of these ROM-BIOS services.

■ *Service 0* is used to print a single character. This is the main working service for the printer.

■ *Service 1* is used to initialize the printer adapter, to ensure that it is set and ready to use. This service also returns a single-byte status code, with each bit dedicated to reporting on one particular aspect of the printer. The bit codes are shown in Figure 18-1.

■ *Service 2*, the last of the printer services, reports the status of the printer. It returns the same 1-byte status code as service 1.

All these services are the same for the PCjr as for the other IBM personal computer models, but the PCjr adds one particularly useful twist for those of us who connect our printers to the serial port rather than the I/O channel connector.

Bit	Meaning
0	Time out—the printer did not complete an operation in a reasonable amount of time
1	This bit is unused
2	This bit is unused
3	The printer reports an I/O error—something went wrong
4	This printer is selected
5	The printer reports it is out of paper
6	Acknowledge
7	The printer is busy (0 = busy, 1 = not busy)

Figure 18-1. Coding of the printer status byte

The PC and XT have to be told that the printer is actually connected to the serial port. Each time we turn one of them on, we have to specify that the printer is connected to the serial port. Even worse, sometimes just switching from one program to another can mean we have to tell the computer, yet again, that the printer really is connected to the serial port. Our PCjr makes life easier.

The ROM-BIOS printer service routines for the PCjr go to the trouble of checking to see if a parallel printer adapter is plugged into the I/O channel connector. If it is not, the ROM-BIOS automatically reroutes printer output to the serial port. This behind-the-scenes service is an enormous convenience and it makes the use of the serial port for a printer much more practical. (It is particularly tailored to the needs of PCjr owners who use the inexpensive IBM Compact Printer.)

This extra routine is just one indication of the care and thought that went into Junior's design. Scrutiny of the PC has paid off in improvements to our PCjr, and this automatic use of the serial port for the printer is just one example of how good our Junior is.

FURTHER CONNECTIONS

When IBM released the original PC, it was accompanied by a handful of options, all designed to fit into the PC's expansion slots (which are the equivalent of our PCjr's I/O channel). While IBM's PC options were fine, they didn't suit everyone's needs. A host of very nimble companies began creating add-on boards in a much wider variety than IBM had provided. After a while, it began to appear that, while IBM was doing a terrific job of designing and making computers, these after-market manufacturers were responding even better than IBM to the changing needs for options and add-on boards.

Possibly because of this, IBM initially created only one use for the PCjr's I/O connector bus, the parallel printer adapter. In effect, IBM has left the uses and extensions of Junior's I/O channel connector to the ingenuity of all the suppliers of IBM personal computer equipment.

So, IBM hasn't defined what the further connections for the PCjr will be. Instead it has left the way open for outside suppliers to define the shape Junior will take. The possibilities are as unlimited for the PCjr as they are for the PC and XT—it all depends upon the needs of PCjr owners.

What we do know is that the PCjr's open bus, in the form of the I/O channel connector, makes it possible to add any number of new parts and options. These can take the same form as Junior's parallel printer adapter, which plugs into the I/O channel connector and passes access to the connector on to the next piece of equipment. Or, they can also take the form, used by the PC and XT, of an expansion cabinet that would plug into the I/O channel connector and would contain slots for expansion boards. Each of these expansion slots would be electronically connected to the PCjr's I/O channel. Both of these approaches to adding new options to the PCjr are functionally the same—they are just two ways of wrapping the operation up. Options that work like the parallel printer adapter have to have their own cabinet parts to contain them, while an expansion cabinet provides a single enclosure that can be used by several naked option boards.

Whatever form additions to the PCjr take, they will use the I/O channel connector as a bus connection to Junior's main circuitry. And the PCjr's bus places no limits on the wonders that we can add to our computers.

19
HIDDEN GOODIES IN THE ROM-BIOS

Much of the wonder of the IBM personal computers is embodied in their ROM-BIOS programs. This is even more the case with Junior than it is with its more expensive relatives, since in the PCjr quite a lot of expensive hardware has been replaced by ROM-BIOS software.

So far in this book, we have covered the programming in the ROM-BIOS topic-by-topic, as we have covered each of the features and subject areas of the computer. That approach is actually best, since the ROM-BIOS lives to serve the working parts of the computer.

Now, though, the time has come to look at the glories of the ROM-BIOS and the miscellaneous goodies that are tucked away inside. As we have done throughout the book, we'll begin with the interesting stuff that the PCjr shares with its relatives, the parts of the ROM-BIOS that are common to all members of the IBM personal computer family. After that, we'll look at what is new and special about the ROM-BIOS in the PCjr.

THE BENEFITS OF BROWSING

Almost everything that can be learned about the ROM-BIOS can be found in Appendix A of the PCjr's *Technical Reference* manual, which gives a complete assembly-language listing of the ROM-BIOS. This listing is useful to study for quite a few reasons. First, it includes the comments of IBM's programmers, and these provide the best clues to what is going on inside the ROM-BIOS. Second, comparing the hexadecimal machine-language code and the assembly-language instructions gives us a feel for the instruction set of the 8088 micro-processor that our PCjr uses. Browsing through the hexadecimal coding quickly teaches you which instructions are long and which are short, how numbers are stored, and so forth.

A third reason for studying the ROM-BIOS assembly listing is to learn more about assembly language. No matter what your level of interest and expertise in assembly language, the ROM-BIOS in IBM's *Technical Reference* manual can help you a lot. If you are contemplating trying your hand at assembly language, this listing should give you some idea of what is involved and help you discover quickly if assembly language is within your present ability as a programmer. If you are starting out in 8088 assembly language, you will learn quite a bit from this listing; but be forewarned: While the body of the ROM-BIOS program-ming is similar to programs you might write, the overhead parts—the begin-ning and end of a program and the parts that tell the assembler what to do—are rather different. Finally, if you are experienced in assembly language and want to learn some advanced methods, the ROM-BIOS provides you with a wealth of tricks and examples.

A fourth benefit of studying the ROM-BIOS listing is to learn about the data areas used by the BIOS. All programs need a place to keep the data they work with, and the ROM-BIOS is no different. Since ROM is, by definition, read only memory, the storage area for the data used by the ROM-BIOS has to be located in ordinary RAM.

A small area of 256 bytes, located at segment paragraph hex 40, or absolute addresses hex 400 through hex 4FF, is reserved for use by the ROM-BIOS. If you want your programs to inspect (PEEK) or change (POKE) system information, these ROM-BIOS storage locations will be of real interest to you. We have discussed some of the ROM-BIOS data to be found here, such as the keyboard control bytes, but I am not going to pore over the rest of the data in this ROM-BIOS storage area in detail, since it is not really of general interest. If you want to learn more, you can find the data at the beginning of the ROM-BIOS listing.

There is, finally, a fifth reason to study the ROM-BIOS listing: to discover the odds and ends of interesting programming, tables of information, and routines that are buried in the BIOS. That is what this chapter is about, so let's begin looking at these goodies.

OLD GOODIES

The first ROM-BIOS programs used are the power-on self test, or POST routines. The POST tests various parts of the computer when the power is first turned on. As I have said, it is not a thorough set of diagnostics, because a complete diagnosis would take much too long to run. The tests carried out by the POST are a compromise between the desire to check out the computer and the desire to get down to work with no delay. Because the POST routines are tied very closely to the hardware, they differ considerably in detail from one model of IBM personal computer to another. In concept, though, they are the same for all the machines. You have to have a very deep interest in the PCjr's hardware to go over these routines in detail, and some of them are difficult to figure out. We'll cover the highlights, and leave the rest for you to explore, if you are interested.

One of the POST routines, called PODSTG, tests a block of storage. While all the IBM personal computers need to have this test performed, oddly enough the test is quite different for each model. In our PCjr, the routine can check up to 32K bytes at a time and it can be called several times to check more memory. It also has the special virtue of testing for a "warm start." If the routine is being used during a power-up, it will do its full read/write test; on a warm start, as when we press the Ctrl-Alt-Del keys, this routine cuts the test short and just sets memory to zero, ensuring that no data that could confuse our programs are left in memory.

Other parts of the POST check the working of the 8088 by testing flags, registers, and jump instructions. The POST routines are also responsible for initializing many of the programmable parts of the electronic circuitry; they take care of the starting settings for such things as the TI sound generator chip, the video control, and the disk control.

Boot and Reboot

Another interesting part of the ROM-BIOS is the *bootstrap loader,* which reads in a self-loading program, such as the DOS operating system. This bootstrap routine does one thing, yet serves several purposes. It is used when we power up the computer; it is also used when we do a Ctrl-Alt-Del warm start; and finally, it can be used by any program that wants to restart the computer. So that the bootstrap loader can be available for all these purposes, it has been set up as an interrupt handler. To cause a reboot of the system, all a program has to do is invoke interrupt 25 (hex 19).

Now, why would a program want to reboot the system? Rebooting certainly isn't an ordinary operation, but there are some special occasions when it might be needed. For example, some copy-protected programs reboot when they have detected tampering, as a sort of punishment. Other copy-protected programs, such as Microsoft Flight Simulator, don't operate with DOS; instead they have, in effect, their own individual operating systems. When such programs finish running, it is reasonable for them to automatically reboot the computer, so that we can work with DOS or something else.

While the principles of the bootstrap loader are the same, the details vary from model to model of IBM personal computer. As we have already seen, the PC tries to read a control program from its first diskette drive; if that doesn't work, it fires up the built-in ROM-BASIC. The XT (or a PC upgraded to XT specifications with a hard disk) tries to boot first from a diskette, then from the hard disk, and then it finally goes to the ROM-BASIC.

Our PCjr enriches this process considerably. First, it checks the universal starting point, the diskette. Next, it allows a cartridge to take control. Finally, it goes to ROM-BASIC (or any cartridge that replaces the ROM-BASIC, such as the BASIC cartridge).

The Disk Base Table

The next interesting part of the ROM-BIOS is the disk base table. The disk base is a short table of controlling parameters for the diskette drives. The interrupt vector for interrupt 30 (hex 1E) normally points to this table in ROM, but it can be changed, if necessary, to point to another table in ordinary memory, effectively replacing the original table.

After the original release of the PC, IBM changed its mind about what the controlling parameters for the diskette drives should be, and so all releases of the operating system after DOS 1.00 have replaced this table with an updated version. However, to help maintain strict compatibility, the disk base table built into the ROM has stayed the same. This continues to be true for our PCjr, except for one minor change. In the other models, the diskette drive circuitry works directly with the computer's memory in what is called *direct memory access*, or *DMA*. As we saw in Chapter 10, instead of data being transferred directly, our PCjr uses ROM programming to transfer data between memory and diskette, and so DMA is not used. As a consequence, there is one minor difference in the disk base table in the PCjr's ROM-BIOS: The second byte is 03, rather than 02, indicating that DMA is not used.

Equipment and Memory

The next two items in the ROM-BIOS are even more interesting. There are two special interrupt service routines that can tell our programs about the equipment and memory attached to our computers. These routines are invoked with interrupt 17 (hex 11), which gives the list of equipment on the computer, and interrupt 18 (hex 12), which gives the amount of RAM in the computer. In both instances, the information is gathered by the POST routines when the computer is powered up, and the record is kept in the ROM-BIOS storage locations. Later, when either of these interrupt routines is activated, they refer to the record in memory.

This may seem like a curious way to do things, but there is an important reason for collecting this information in this particular way. If these two routines checked on the equipment and memory directly, they could only report on the equipment and memory that were actually present. By using a record left by the POST routines in memory, these two service routines gain an extra element of flexibility, since a program could, if necessary, change the record of the equipment or amount of memory available and thus override the hardware. Obviously, we could not make equipment or memory magically appear or disappear simply by changing the record, but we could, if we wanted, manipulate the record of equipment and memory. For example, we could set aside some memory for a special use or deactivate a defective piece of equipment. In general, software should always be as much in charge of the computer as possible, and this indirect way of manipulating the equipment and memory helps accomplish that goal. Now, let's look more closely at interrupts 17 and 18.

Interrupt 17 (hex 11) reports on the equipment attached to the computer. This equipment report is general and only takes into account the main equipment designed into the original PC model. The report is given in one 2-byte word, with the equipment coded as shown in Figures 19-1, 19-2, and 19-3.

Bits	Meaning
0	Diskette-drive indicator—0 if no diskette drives, 1 if there is a diskette drive.
1	Not used.
2-3	Memory on the system board, in 16K increments, minus one. For technical reasons, these bits are always 11 on the PCjr, with or without the memory expansion.
4-5	Initial video mode, coded as shown in Figure 19-3.
6-7	Number of diskette drives, minus one; if we have a disk, these bits are 00.
8	DMA chip present in system (new to PCjr, unused in other models); this apparently relates to some PCjr features yet to come.
9-11	Number of RS-232 ports, from 0 through 7; for the PCjr this is 1.
12	Game adapter attached (optional on a PC or XT; built into the PCjr).
13	Serial printer attached (not used for PC and XT models).
14-15	Number of printers attached (handled differently for the PCjr).

Figure 19-1. Coding of the equipment bytes returned by interrupt 17

Bit 2	Bit 3	Amount of Memory on System Board (in K)
0	0	16
0	1	32 (Used on early PCs; now obsolete)
1	0	48
1	1	64 (The minimum for the PCjr)

Figure 19-2. Coding of bits 2 and 3 of the equipment bytes

Bit 4	Bit 5	Initial Video Mode
0	0	Unused
0	1	40 × 25, black-and-white, using color adapter
1	0	80 × 25, black-and-white, using color adapter
1	1	80 × 25, black-and-white, using monochrome adapter

Figure 19-3. Coding of bits 4 and 5 of the equipment bytes

Interrupt 18 (hex 12) reports the amount of memory in the system in 1K units, so that the answer can be given in one 2-byte word. For our PCjr, this report subtracts the amount of memory set aside for the display screen; so, for example, if we had 64K and, as usual, 16K were in use by the display screen, this interrupt service would report 48K of memory. On an ordinary PC, the total amount of memory would be reported, since memory is not normally set aside for any purpose on a PC.

Various parts of the system programs, the DOS operating system, BASIC, and some other clever programs make use of these equipment and memory-size reporting routines to gather information about the environment in which they are working.

Graphics Characters

The next interesting part of the ROM-BIOS we can look at is the graphics character table, which we mentioned in Chapter 13. When the computer's display is in text mode, the characters are generated by the display circuitry. But in graphics mode, characters have to be drawn. The drawings that represent the first 128 characters, from CHR$(0) through CHR$(127), are in a table in ROM. The video services refer to this table whenever they are asked to draw characters (or read characters off the screen) in graphics mode. This table is in a fixed location in ROM, at address F000:FA6E. The location of the table was incidental in the PC, but it is now carefully maintained at that address in case any programs refer to it. (Programs aren't supposed to do that sort of thing—it is most unwise; but since some do, IBM maintained compatibility by keeping the table in the exact same location.)

Time of Day

Next, let's look at the time-of-day routine. As we have mentioned, the timer circuitry for the computer produces a clock-tick interrupt every 18.2 seconds. The ROM-BIOS keeps a count of the ticks, and other programs can calculate the actual time of day from this count. To do so, of course, they need a point of reference, and so a count of zero is considered to be midnight. Any routine that reports the time of day, such as the BASIC TIME$ function, translates the tick count into the appropriate time. Likewise, anything that sets the time, such as the DOS TIME command or BASIC TIME$ statement, translates the time into the corresponding tick count.

The ROM-BIOS doesn't keep track of the date, but it assists date-keeping by resetting the tick count to zero at midnight and keeping a record of the fact that it did so. When any program requests a time-of-day count, a special signal is also given if midnight has been passed since the last time-of-day request.

Routines that read the time are supposed to check this and change the date when it happens. However, the ROM-BIOS does not keep track of more than one passing of midnight, so, if you leave your PCjr running unused through two midnights and then ask for the date, the date you are given will be incorrect. Though not exactly major, this defect was an oversight in the design of the ROM-BIOS.

The time-of-day services are invoked with interrupt number 26 (hex 1A). Service 0 is used to get both the tick count and the midnight-was-passed signal, and service 1 is used to set the tick count.

As part of the timer support, the ROM-BIOS contains the interrupt handler for interrupt 8, the clock interrupt. As we've mentioned before, the timer interrupt handler, in turn, generates a clock-tick interrupt, interrupt 28 (hex 1C), to alert our programs to each tick of the clock. However, unless our programs have set an interrupt vector for this service, nothing happens.

Besides maintaining the tick count and generating the clock-tick interrupt, the clock-interrupt service has one additional task. The motor of the diskette drive is deliberately left running for 37 ticks (about two seconds) after the diskette is used, in case it is needed again right away. The clock-interrupt routine has the job of counting down from 37 to 0 to measure the time the drive has been left running; when the count expires, a diskette-drive routine is called to turn the motor off. Each time the diskette is used, this count is again reset to 37, to keep the motor running for another two seconds.

Miscellany

Now, let's look quickly at a collection of unrelated, but interesting, ROM-BIOS routines. As odd as it may at first sound, there is a need in several places for an interrupt-handling routine that does nothing. Here is an example: When our programs aren't using the clock-tick interrupt, the vector for interrupt 28 has to point to a do-nothing routine. To provide this facility, the ROM-BIOS contains a dummy return service, which consists of nothing more than an IRET, or interrupt return, instruction. This IRET dummy return can be used whenever it is needed.

Another part of the ROM-BIOS, which we already took a close look at in Chapter 7, is the print-screen routine. This is the routine that is activated whenever we press the PrtSc key. In order to make the service available to any program, it is set up as an interrupt handler, invoked with interrupt 5. Using an interrupt number this low is rather unusual, but there it is.

The interrupt vector table at the beginning of RAM memory has to be set up when the computer is turned on, so that the 8088 will know where to go when an interrupt occurs. This table doesn't automatically appear by itself. One of the jobs of the POST start-up routines is to set the initial interrupt vectors, from values kept on ROM. Later, of course, programs can change the vectors, but their initial values are set at start-up time, from the ROM.

There is one more miscellaneous part of the ROM-BIOS that we have already looked at: the release marker, which indicates which version of the ROM-BIOS is being used. The release marker is kept at the very top of memory, in location F000:FFF5. The dates vary with revisions to the ROM. You can check yours using the method in Chapter 7.

The only remaining byte in the ROM-BIOS is a data check-sum at the very highest byte of memory. This byte is used to test for damage to the ROM-BIOS, and it is set to whatever value is needed to confirm that the ROM-BIOS is intact. With each change to the ROM-BIOS, no matter how minor, this byte is reset to the appropriate value.

What we have seen so far is all the odds and ends in the ROM-BIOS that are common to all of the IBM personal computers. Next, we'll look at what is completely new for the PCjr.

NEW GOODIES

There are just a few things that are completely new and special in the ROM-BIOS for the PCjr.

More Characters

The first item we'll discuss has to do with characters in graphics mode. You'll recall that the standard ASCII character set uses only 128 of the 256 byte codes, and that the family of IBM personal computers uses the remaining 128 codes for some special characters, including the wonderful box-drawing characters. When the computer is in text mode, all these characters can be used. In the original PC design, the first 128 ASCII characters were incorporated into a table of drawings that allowed the computer to produce them in graphics mode. However, the extra 128 characters could only be used in graphics mode if we ourselves created a special table of drawings for them.

What is quite new and special to the newest member of the IBM family is that Junior's ROM-BIOS gives us a default table of the other 128 characters. This new table is still accessed through the interrupt vector for interrupt 31 (hex 1F), so we can also build our own table of drawings and access it by resetting the interrupt vector. This makes it practical to combine graphics effects with the full range of 256 character shapes. Given this possibility, it would be silly for any PCjr program not to take advantage of the graphics modes.

Pretty Colors

The second new and special item in the PCjr's ROM-BIOS is an interesting display routine, which shows the IBM logo and generates color bars that show each of the display attributes. This routine is rather pretty, but it is also practical, since it gives us a way to check the colors on our display screen. Unfortunately, this routine isn't designed for external use like the print-screen routine—it is not accessed by an interrupt, so our programs can't take advantage of it—but still, it is nice to know about it.

20
GETTING
PROGRAM ACCESS

As I said way back in the Introduction,
this book is about understanding
the principles and inner workings of
the PCjr. This knowledge is worthwhile
in itself, because it is interesting and
it enhances our ability to use this
wonder computer effectively.

But there are practical reasons for knowing about the inner workings of the PCjr, and the most important of them is putting this knowledge to use in our own programs.

MAKING CONNECTIONS

BASIC stands out as a language for programming the PCjr because it includes facilities for most of what is special about all the IBM personal computers, and what is uniquely special about the PCjr. BASIC has many virtues, and its supreme virtue in relation to the IBM PCjr is that so much of Junior can be directly controlled by BASIC programs.

BASIC, though, isn't for everyone. In fact, few of the best-selling, "serious" programs for the PCjr—spreadsheets, word processors, and the snappiest games—are written in BASIC. So, if you want to write a best-seller, or you just need to use the PCjr's special features in your own way, you need to know about program connections.

A program connection is the way one program talks to another. This connection can be as simple as using a subroutine in the same language you are using, or it can be as complex as an interconnection, an interface, between one programming language and another. Or, and this is of special interest to us, it can be a connection to the ROM-BIOS services.

There is no end to the exotic things you might want to do in programming your PCjr, but the main reason most of us need to break out of the facilities offered by our programming language is to get more direct control of the computer—either to manipulate its memory (one of the best ways to manipulate the memory-mapped display screen) or to use one of the built-in ROM-BIOS services. Our goal in this chapter is to see how this is done. You will then be able to write programs in the programming language of your choice and break out of that language when you need to connect with the BIOS or other programs. If you are doing major program development, this ability will be one of your most important resources.

If you are not yet comfortable as a programmer, don't despair. Push on, even if the going does get tough. At the very least, you will get an idea of what can be done with the magic of your PCjr. And in the best of all possible worlds, this chapter will spur you on to learn more, so that you, too, can fiddle around, exploring the IBM PCjr.

There is an endless number of ways to combine programming-language connections. We won't try to cover them all here. Instead, we'll lay out the main principles and cover the one thing you are most likely to need: a quick connection to the ROM-BIOS through an assembly-language connection. We'll see the specifics for three programming languages: BASIC, Pascal, and

C. We'll cover these three languages because they are probably the most important languages for the PCjr and because their differences highlight most of the variations in assembly-language connections that languages require.

Since there are different versions of programming languages, let's get specific here. The BASIC we'll be using is the official IBM BASIC, created by Microsoft; either interpreted or compiled BASIC can be used. The Pascal is the IBM compiled Pascal, also written by Microsoft. Don't confuse this with UCSD Pascal®, or Digital Research® Pascal/MT+. The C—and there are many C compilers available—we'll be discussing is Lattice-Microsoft C, created by Lattice, adopted and sold by Microsoft.

The programs produced by all three of these compilers work beautifully on the PCjr, but only two of the three compilers can be used to develop programs on the PCjr itself; the Pascal compiler requires more memory to compile than Junior provides; but many programs compiled on a PC could then be run on a PCjr. We'll cover the rules for this Pascal compiler anyway, for two reasons: It's the only Pascal supported by IBM to produce PCjr programs; and it is a good illustration of a standard variation on how to connect with assembly language.

The tools you will need for this task are your own programming language—C, Pascal, the BASIC compiler, or the BASIC interpreter—the DOS operating system with its LINK program, and the IBM Macro Assembler program. In addition, you will need to know how to operate your programming language, the Macro Assembler, and LINK; and you'll need some sophistication in programming techniques, since this is advanced material. With that in hand, let's proceed.

THE GENERAL RULES

Programs cannot work with one another unless they follow some rules, or conventions, for making connections and passing information back and forth. An understanding of these rules is essential for anyone working with the mechanics of making the connections. Once the connections are established, they can be used freely without much technical know-how.

Although these connections are among the most important technical programming issues, the designers of computers and programming languages usually allow a great deal of latitude in how things are done. These programming-interface connections ought to be universally designed, but oddly enough, this rarely happens. So, there is no one simple way we can make programming connections—we have to handle them case-by-case for each programming language, and sometimes for each purpose, as well. Luckily for us, while there is this kind of chaos, it doesn't reign supreme. Beneath all the variations in how programming connections can be made, there are some common, underlying principles that are handled very consistently in the IBM personal computers. That's what we'll discuss in this section.

A Typical Connection

When program A makes use of subroutine B, there are some things that have to be taken care of. Let's list what they are, and then go over the list item by item, to see what the general principles are and how they can vary. So, what has to be looked after, when programs connect?

- Program A has to be able to find its way to subroutine B.

- Subroutine B must be able to find its way back to program A.

- Program A may need to pass parameters to subroutine B.

- Everyone has to know how many parameters there are.

- Parameters have to be put somewhere.

- Program A may want to protect the parameters from being changed.

- On the other hand, program A may *need* to have the parameters changed by B.

- Subroutine B may need to pass information back.

- The information may be simple or complex.

- There may be more than one piece of information.

- Subroutine B needs to know what supporting framework it is getting from A.

- Subroutine B may need workspace.

- Everyone needs to know how to behave; B must know what it is allowed to do and what must be preserved.

- And, who cleans up when subroutine B has finished?

Let's now go over these things item by item and see how they are handled by the IBM personal computers, and also see when there is more than one way to do things.

- *Program A has to be able to find its way to subroutine B.* Finding the way to a subroutine can be done two ways in the PCjr's Intel 8088 microprocessor: via a CALL instruction, or via an interrupt. Interrupts, however, are reserved for

260

privileged, system-type operations. Ordinary programs use the CALL instruction; that is what all our programming languages use, so this is universal for program connections. However, there are two varieties of CALL—FAR and NEAR.

You'll recall from our discussion of the 8088's memory addressing that there is a code segment register, CS, that locates programs in memory. If all the parts of a program are known to be contained within 64K of memory, the CS register need not be reset when passing from subroutine to subroutine; this is done with the NEAR CALL instruction. But if a subroutine is, or might be, outside the current 64K block addressed by the CS register, the CALL instruction must have a fully segmented address for the subroutine that is being called; this is done with a FAR CALL instruction.

C uses only NEAR CALLs; this is more efficient, but it restricts the total program size. BASIC uses only FAR CALLs. Pascal uses both NEAR and FAR.

■ *Subroutine B must be able to find its way back to program A.* Finding the way back to a program is always done with the return instruction, RET, but there are both NEAR and FAR returns, so it matters to the called subroutine whether it was called NEAR or FAR. Normally, an assembly-language subroutine is set up to handle the return one way or the other, but it is possible for the subroutine to have both kinds of return and to choose between them on the basis of a signal passed by the calling program. (The last item, cleaning up, also influences the exact nature of the subroutine's RET instruction.)

■ *Program A may need to pass parameters to subroutine B; everyone has to know how many parameters there are.* Most commonly, a subroutine has a fixed number of parameters, and these must always be given, even if some of them are not used. There are ways to handle a variable number of parameters, but the cleanest and most common working rules call for a rigidly fixed number of parameters, agreed upon between caller and callee. C provides a way to handle a variable number of parameters; BASIC and Pascal don't.

■ *Parameters have to be put somewhere.* Parameters are always passed through the stack, either directly or indirectly. There are two main ways to do this. Either the value of the parameter itself is placed on the stack or the address of a memory location holding the value is placed on the stack. Several things influence which way is used. Generally, if the value is a single byte, or a word, or a pair of words (such as a segmented address), it *may* be placed on the stack. If it is larger than two words (four bytes), it is never placed on the stack; instead its address is. The called program absolutely must know which method is being used, so this arrangement is made when the subroutine is designed.

BASIC never places values on the stack; Pascal and C can place either the value or its address on the stack, and they let us control which. BASIC and C always use relative offset addresses when putting parameter addresses on the stack. Pascal lets us choose between offset and fully segmented addresses.

■ *Program A may want to protect the parameters from being changed.* If the calling program wants to ensure that its original copy of the parameter is not changed, it protects the location of the original. If the parameter value is passed on the stack, this protection is automatic; if an address is passed on the stack, the caller must copy the original value and pass the address of the copy—a clumsy and expensive operation.

BASIC, which only puts addresses on the stack, provides no protection for the original value; Pascal very explicitly allows us to protect values; C gives us control but, to protect values, we have to know some C tricks.

■ *Program A may need to have the parameters changed by B.* When A needs to have B change a parameter, the parameter passed on the stack *must* be an address of the original value. This is the flip side of the last item. The called subroutine changes the value by modifying what is stored at the specified memory address.

BASIC always lets us change a value; Pascal gives us control; C tricks allow control, too.

■ *Subroutine B may need to pass information back; the information may be simple or complex.* Because of the complex and seemingly screwy rules that BASIC follows, there is a complicated set of special rules for returning values to a BASIC program. For all other languages, a simple, general principle applies: If the value being returned is a single byte, it is returned in the AL register; if it is two bytes, the full AX register is used. For more complex values, which are less common, other rules are used. When this is the case, often the simplest thing to do is return the value not as a function (which could use AX for the value), but return the value in one of the parameters. This method is safe and reliable for all languages. And, frankly, since there is a method that works for all languages, you would be wise to use it to avoid having to change your techniques when you change languages.

■ *There may be more than one piece of information.* If there is more than one piece of information to be returned back to program A, pass it back through several parameters. This is a standard technique common to all programming languages.

■ *Subroutine B needs to know what supporting framework it is getting from A.* This supporting framework involves such fundamental things as how the segment registers are set and whether there is a stack that can be used. In general, the segment registers are just as they should be: CS has the right code segment; DS points to the location of the calling program's data; SS and SP are set up with the caller's own stack, and the called program can usually continue to use the caller's stack. Unfortunately, there is no practical way to know how much working space is available on the stack, but there is usually enough for ordinary purposes.

This segment register and stack setup is standard among programming languages. BASIC warns, however, that only 16 bytes of available space are guaranteed on the stack, so a nervous subroutine can set up its own stack if it wants. The ES register might have anything in it, though BASIC sets it to the same location as the DS; the SS register is usually independently set, but, again, BASIC sets it to the DS location.

■ *Subroutine B may need workspace.* A subroutine usually uses the stack for its working storage, if the needs are reasonable—say, less than 64 bytes. If more storage is needed, the subroutine should set up its own data space in memory. The kind of assembly-language interface routine we are working toward needs very little storage, so the stack should be just dandy for current purposes.

■ *Everyone needs to know how to behave; B must know what it is allowed to do and what must be preserved.* There are simple ground rules for what can and can't be done.

The segment registers should be preserved. Some languages do not mind having the extra segment register, ES, changed, but it is better to play it safe. If any segment register is modified, the original should be preserved (by being passed on the stack with a PUSH and later restored with a POP). One other very important register to preserve, under most circumstances, is the BP (base pointer) register; most programs use BP to keep track of a location on the stack (usually the location of their parameters). So our interface routines ought to preserve BP. BASIC, however, does not require this.

All the working registers, AX, BX, CX, DX, DI, and SI can be changed freely, as can all the flags. The convention is that a calling program does not expect its working register values to be preserved.

Interrupts can be suspended (though it is usually not a good idea, except briefly when segment registers are changed), but must be turned back on before returning.

The caller's stack also has to be preserved, although just how that is done is part of the clean-up rules we are coming to.

■ *Who cleans up when subroutine B has finished?* This is one of the most interesting topics of all. Cleaning up the mess mostly means removing bits and pieces from the stack. There are four things that might be cluttering up the stack when a subroutine is finished. First, there are parameters. Second, there is the return address from the CALL instruction. Third, there might be register values saved with PUSH instructions. And finally, there might be some working storage for the subroutine.

All subroutines are expected to remove their working storage from the stack. Saved register values are removed automatically when the values are restored into their registers by POP instructions. Likewise, the return address of the caller is restored automatically by the RET instruction. The matter for debate is the set of parameters. Most programming languages expect the called subroutine to remove the parameters from the stack—the caller puts them on, the callee takes them off. This is done as part of the RET instruction. For example, if 10 bytes of parameters were put on the stack, a subroutine would end with the instruction RET 10.

This rule applies to BASIC and Pascal, but it does not apply to C. The rules used by C have the caller eliminate the parameters after a subroutine has returned. C is set up to make it easy to pass a variable number of parameters to a subroutine, instead of a fixed number. Although the called subroutine has a way of finding out how many parameters were passed (after all, it has to know) and so could clean up the stack itself, C considers it simpler and safer to have the calling program do it.

These are the main rules and programming conventions for connecting one program to another. Of course, if we are programming strictly within one language, such as Pascal, these details are handled for us, though it is interesting for us to know about them. But if we have to write assembly-language programs that can be called by other languages, we need to know and work with these rules in our assembly code.

Our main objective here is to see how to build assembly-language interface routines so that our high-level language programs can get to the ROM-BIOS or to the DOS services. The next section will show outlines of the assembly code needed and also illustrate a typical connection to the ROM-BIOS.

A TYPICAL ROM-BIOS CONNECTION

What we'll be building here is an assembly-language interface routine to connect to the ROM-BIOS. We'll build it up, piece by piece. At various points, we'll have to assume that we're doing one thing or another—so what we put together will not be a finished tool that you can use. It will be a collection of all the elements you need to create your own interface routines. If you plan to go on and do this yourself, you should have some ability to do assembly-language programming for the 8088. The elements of our interface routine are so simple, though, you do not have to be proficient in assembly language to make it work.

In fact, with some intelligence and pluck, you can build your own interface routines successfully, even if you don't know any 8088 assembly language.

I know that this is true from my own experience. When I first started using the IBM Macro Assembler, I knew nothing about 8088 assembly language and had not learned half as much as this chapter is teaching you. Yet, my first assembly-language interface routine (which was intended to let Pascal programs read specific parts of a diskette) worked on my third try, and the whole process took no more than 45 minutes. That is how easy it can be, even for a beginner at assembly language.

Now, to work. Let's start with the overhead outline of the assembler source code, with no working program parts. Here it is, with the assembler code in CAPITALS and comments in lowercase:

```
INTERFACE SEGMENT 'CODE'
                         ; this defines an assembler
                         ; SEGMENT, and marks it as CODE,
                         ; so it will be linked with other
                         ; programs. The name INTERFACE
                         ; is arbitrary.

PUBLIC MEMSIZE           ; this makes the subroutine
                         ; (MEMSIZE) that follows
                         ; visible, or public, to the
                         ; world. Without it, LINK could
                         ; not connect the subroutine to
                         ; its users. Our name, MEMSIZE
                         ; is arbitrary

MEMSIZE PROC FAR         ; this begins a procedure, a
                         ; subroutine itself. FAR or NEAR
                         ; should be specified—recall
                         ; that your programming language
                         ; may require you to use one or
                         ; the other. MEMSIZE is the name
                         ; of the subroutine; it could be
                         ; any name your language can use

; the body of the program would fit in here

MEMSIZE ENDP             ; this tells the assembler we're
                         ; at the end of the MEMSIZE
                         ; subroutine

INTERFACE ENDS           ; this tells the assembler we're
                         ; at the end of the INTERFACE
                         ; segment
```

265

```
END                    ; this tells the assembler we're
                       ; done, entirely
```

That is the assembler overhead, for the most part. The segment can contain as many subroutines as we want, each enclosed in PROC-ENDP statements.

Be sure to make each PROC either NEAR or FAR according to your language requirements. The exact coding on the SEGMENT statement depends on the conventions used by the programming language. We can usually find this out by studying how the language categorizes object modules (which are the form programs take after they have been compiled or assembled, but before they have been linked). We can usually learn what we need to know either from the language's documentation, or by poring over the map that is produced when we link a program. The SEGMENT statement we showed here applies to Pascal. For C, you need to include a GROUP statement, something like this:

```
PGROUP GROUP PROG
INTERFACE SEGMENT   BYTE PUBLIC 'PROG'
```

All of that is needed, but the noticeable difference from Pascal is that the named type is PROG, instead of CODE. Check the examples in your own programming-language manual to get this sort of thing straight; that's where I've always found out about these details, and that's where you should look, too.

There is one more bit of overhead we ought to mention. Although our example here will not involve any logic and branching, others might. Many of the ROM-BIOS services indicate success or failure with a flag, such as the CF flag, and our assembly-language routines will need to test that flag and branch on it. Even though these branches don't need or use the CS segment register, the assembler insists on knowing about the CS value. So to solve this problem, we insert an innocuous statement, following the SEGMENT statement, like this:

```
ASSUME CS:INTERFACE
```

So far, what we have seen is the assembler overhead, which generates no machine code at all. Next we'll look at the program overhead—the part of the program that takes care of beginning and ending, but not the part that does our specific work. Here is the standard code for that:

```
PUSH   BP    ; we save the caller's BP—this is important to
             ; the caller; we're about to create our own BP
```

```
MOV    BP,SP ; we move the current stack pointer, SP, into
             ; the base pointer, BP, so that we can look at
             ; our parameters on the stack

; our working instructions would be here

POP    BP    ; now we restore our caller's BP

RET    0     ; now we return to our caller; the assembler
             ; automatically makes this a NEAR or FAR
             ; return. If we are to take parameters off
             ; the stack, we replace the "0" with the
             ; number of bytes—usually two for each
             ; parameter (check in your case). For no
             ; parameters, or for the C language, we use
             ; zero
```

The setting of BP is what enables us to get at the part of the stack holding our parameters. We'll come to that shortly. First, let's complete one subroutine by asking it to perform the simplest kind of ROM-BIOS interface—a straightforward interrupt service with no parameters. Interrupt 18 (hex 12), which gives us the size of memory, will serve nicely. To get this service, we just do this:

```
INT    12H   ; request interrupt hex 12—memory size
```

This one short instruction is the working body of our subroutine. As it turns out, this ROM-BIOS service returns its value, the size of memory, in the AX register. This is the standard place to return it to our caller, so we don't need any more code at all.

In case you've lost track of any of the pieces, look at Figure 20-1 to put it all together.

One of the most complicated things we have to consider in our interface routine is how to get our hands on parameters. The BP is set to the current location in the stack, above which will be our parameters. But we need a little help to know what is there. The stack will have our parameters on it, probably with two bytes for each. (Even 1-byte parameters take up two bytes on the stack. Usually, only a segmented address from Pascal takes up more than two bytes.) The stack will also have the return address of the caller, which will be two bytes for a NEAR PROC and four for a FAR PROC. Finally, it will have the BP value we originally pushed. Figure 20-2 is a diagram of the stack contents, in the case of a FAR subroutine with 2-byte parameters. For a NEAR subroutine, each parameter would be two bytes closer to BP.

```
INTERFACE SEGMENT  'CODE'
          ASSUME   CS:INTERFACE
          PUBLIC   MEMSIZE
MEMSIZE   PROC     FAR
          PUSH     BP
          MOV      BP,SP
          INT      12H
          POP      BP
          RET      0
MEMSIZE   ENDP

INTERFACE ENDS
          END
```

Figure 20-1. An assembly-language interface routine to access
ROM-BIOS interrupt 18 (hex 12)

Now, what order are the parameters in? The Microsoft convention is to push the parameters in the order they are written, and this means that the receiving subroutine finds them in the reverse order: BP + 6 would be the last parameter, BP + 8 would be next to last, and so forth. C, which you'll recall was written not by Microsoft, but by the folks at Lattice, goes the other way. It pushes the parameters in the reverse order, so that the receiving subroutine finds them on the stack from first to last.

For an example of how this is done, let's use our assembler interface to set

Location	Contents
BP	Caller's saved BP
BP + 2	Return address (offset and segment offset only for NEAR)
BP + 6	One parameter (B + 4, if NEAR)
BP + 8	Another parameter
BP + 10	Yet another parameter

Figure 20-2. Stack contents for a FAR PROC
with 2-byte parameters

the time-of-day tick count. Before invoking this service, which is service code 1, interrupt 26 (hex 1A), we would have to hand it the parameters—the tick count. This ROM-BIOS service expects to get the parameters in registers CX and DX. We can move them there from the stack, like this:

```
MOV    DX,[BP +  8]    ; move the second parameter into DX
MOV    CX,[BP + 10]    ; move the first parameter into CX
```

The expression [BP + 8] means this: Take the value in BP, add 8 to it, and then, as indicated by the brackets, take the resulting value as a relative offset address to find and grab a value from memory. And that value is the one that the instruction moves into the DX register. Next, we would invoke the ROM-BIOS service, like this:

```
MOV    AH,1            ; service code 1: set the clock
INT    1AH             ; invoke interrupt hex 1A
```

Now, the way we grabbed the parameters assumed that the values themselves were on the stack. Suppose that their addresses were on the stack instead, as they are in BASIC and can be with Pascal and C. Here is what we would do to get them:

```
MOV    DX,[BP + 8]     ; move the address into DX
MOV    DX,[DX]         ; move the value that DX points to
```

The same maneuver would load the CX register.

```
MOV    CX, [BP + 10]
MOV    CX, [CX]
```

If we are modifying a parameter, the process is reversed. Suppose that, instead of using the ROM-BIOS service that sets the tick count, we used the service (interrupt hex 1A, service code 0) that tells us the tick count. After we got it, we would want to pass it back to our parameters. We would do that in a way similar to the way we set the tick count, but with the movement reversed:

```
MOV    AH,0            ; service code 0: read the clock
INT    1AH             ; invoke interrupt hex 1A
MOV    AX,[BP + 8]     ; move the address into AX
MOV    [AX],DX         ; move the value from DX to memory
MOV    AX,[BP + 10]    ; move the address into AX
```

```
MOV      [AX],CX        ; move the value from CX to memory
```

Before, we performed the trick of using CX and DX to hold first an address and then a value; here, we need some other place to hold the address, and so we use AX, which is conveniently available.

We've now covered all the main points of writing a working, assembly-language interface to the BIOS, but there are still two more small items to cover: saving more registers and branching on the flags.

Some of the ROM-BIOS services that we might use call for setting segment registers, which should be preserved. If we have to save any registers, we do it on the stack, with some PUSH instructions. Just for illustration, here is what we would do to save both DS and ES:

```
PUSH     DS
PUSH     ES
```

This would be done just after the two start-up instructions:

```
PUSH     BP
MOV      BP,SP
```

When we are through, we need to restore the registers. This has to be done in the reverse order, so we would finish with instructions like this:

```
POP      ES
POP      DS
POP      BP
```

with the return instruction, RET, immediately following.

Also, as we have mentioned, some of the ROM-BIOS services use flags to signal success or failure. Our high-level languages can't see these flags, so we need to translate them into visible values—for example, a 1 in AX for success, and a 0 in AX for failure.

For a specific example, let's use the diskette services: the carry flag (CF) is 0 on success, and 1 on failure. We cannot just move the CF flag into AX, but we can branch on it, like this:

```
        MOV      AX,0           ; set to failure code,
                                ; for the moment
        JC       RETURN         ; if carry flag is set, skip over
                                ; success code
        MOV      AX,1           ; set to success code
RETURN:                         ; label for jump-if-carry
                                ; instruction
        RET                     ; return to caller
```

With all that, you now have all the parts and examples that you need to build your own, custom interface routines. To finish up, we will look at the specific rules used by the programming languages BASIC, Pascal, and C.

THE RULES FOR BASIC

BASIC has its own, rather complicated rules for many of the things that are particular to BASIC, such as the way string and floating-point values are passed back from functions. We will not cover them here, for they belong in a book of tricks for BASIC, such as *Mastering the IBM PCjr Home Computer.* Our goal here is simply to connect BASIC to assembly-language routines so it can interface with the ROM-BIOS, so we can hold to the simple stuff.

Here are the variations that apply for BASIC. First, all calls are FAR, so the interface routine must be declared FAR. The parameters are all passed as the relative offset addresses of the actual parameter values. The parameters are pushed onto the stack in the order they are written, so the interface routine will find them in reverse order, as mentioned above.

Most parameters that you might want to pass are simple integers, which you can declare in BASIC with the % suffix. Using either string parameters or floating-point (single- and double-precision) numbers is just asking for extra grief in your assembly-language coding.

Recall that BASIC sets ES, DS, and SS to the address of its data space. With interpreted BASIC, everything is kept in this space. If your assembler program needs to know the current DEF SEG value, it is in the CS register, controlling the code location of our assembler subroutine.

The subroutine is responsible for clearing the parameters off the stack; if there are X number of parameters (each of which, remember, takes two bytes), use a RET 2 * X instruction.

If you are using the BASIC compiler, be aware of the special differences in calling external routines. While interpreted BASIC uses the CALL statement to use assembler routines that are poked or loaded (with a BLOAD instruction) into memory, compiled BASIC does this with CALL ABSOLUTE. Compiled BASIC uses the CALL statement the same way most languages do, calling the program by name and using the linker to combine programs and subroutines.

And, finally, if you find any of this confusing, don't forge blindly ahead. This is a tricky technical area; study it carefully until you understand what's going on, and then go ahead—again, carefully.

THE RULES FOR PASCAL

Of all the languages available for the PCjr, Pascal is probably the richest and best organized. Certainly it gives us the most control over the way a connection is made to assembly-language interface routines. Here are the particulars on how to connect Pascal to an assembler interface.

Pascal is set up to use both NEAR and FAR calls, but all external routines—including assembly interfaces—are treated as FAR. As with BASIC, parameters are pushed in the order written, so an interface routine should look for them in reverse order. Again as with BASIC, the subroutine must clear parameters off the stack with its RET instruction.

Either parameter values or their addresses may be placed on the stack. We can also choose whether the addresses are relative to the DS register or are complete segmented addresses. When a subroutine is declared in Pascal, its parameters are declared, either with or without the VAR option. With VAR, the subroutine is given the address of the parameter, so that it can be changed. In this case, VAR places the address of a variable on the stack. If an S is added, making the option VARS, Pascal passes a segmented address, instead of just a relative offset address. For each VARS parameter, four bytes are placed on the stack: the segment paragraph first, then the relative offset.

When VAR is not specified in Pascal, we are telling Pascal to protect our data from change. This means that Pascal must make a copy of the data and let the subroutine have access to the copy. When the parameter value is a byte or a word—normal for routines interfacing with the ROM-BOS—the value itself is placed on the stack. With a longer or more complex parameter, Pascal copies the value to somewhere in memory, and then passes the address of the copy as a parameter on the stack. This is obviously inefficient and adds unnecessary overhead to the program.

Pascal expects the results of word or byte functions to come back in the AX or AL registers, so our subroutines can freely use them to return values. For more than one value, or longer values, pass the information back to your Pascal program through a VAR parameter.

For an example of the Pascal side of the connection with assembly language, here is how we would declare and use the MEMSIZE routine we developed above:

```
FUNCTION MEMSIZE : WORD;
  EXTERNAL;

X := MEMSIZE;
WRITELN ('The size of memory is ', X, ' K-bytes');
```

A routine named READ_TICKS, which reads the tick count, might be declared like this:

```
PROCEDURE READ_TICKS (VAR LOW_COUNT, HIGH_COUNT : WORD);
```

```
EXTERNAL;
```

```
READ_TICKS (X,Y);
```

Similar methods can be used to interface to any ROM-BIOS or DOS service routine.

THE RULES FOR C

The same basic operations can be performed with C, but there are differences in the rules—partly because of the nature of C, and partly because the C compiler was written by a company other than Microsoft, and so some different approaches were taken to technical issues.

All calls are made as NEAR in C, and the caller, not the called subroutine, is responsible for clearing parameters off the stack. So, while there is enough similarity to the way BASIC and Pascal operate to allow the use of identical interface routines, C requires coding that matches its own calling conventions.

As mentioned before, C pushes parameters onto the stack in reverse order, so that the receiving routine finds them in the order they were written. Like Pascal, C can pass either the address or the value of a parameter; and, again like Pascal, it can pass only 1- or 2-byte values directly on the stack. However, like BASIC and unlike Pascal, C passes only relative offset addresses, not segmented addresses.

In Pascal, the distinction between passing an address and passing a value is made in the declaration. Since C does not have subroutine declarations, we specify whether the address or the value is to be passed when the parameter is given. This is how it is done. If a variable, constant, or expression appears as the parameter, like this:

```
READ_TICKS (LO_COUNT,HI_COUNT)
```

then the value is passed on the stack. But, if a variable name is given with & before it, the address is passed on the stack:

```
READ_TICKS (&LO_COUNT, &HI_COUNT)
```

By the rules of C, you could call a parameter both ways—but, of course, the subroutine would be expecting to find either a value or an address on the parameter stack, so we would have to make sure we did it whichever way the subroutine expected.

And that finishes our short tour through assembly-language connections to the ROM-BIOS. It also ends our exploration of the IBM PCjr.

APPENDICES

This group of five appendices includes
a glossary, suggestions for further
reading, a description of the
Norton Utilities, a table of the
extended ASCII characters, and
the 8086/8088 instruction set.

A
GLOSSARY

Address

A number that locates and identifies each 1-byte memory location. Our computer's addresses are 20 bits, too big for 16-bit calculations; so addresses are divided into a segment and a relative part, two 16-bit words that are combined to produce a 20-bit address.

Address register

Any of nine special registers used in specifying memory addresses. Four registers are used to specify the segment part of an address: the CS register for the code segment; DS for the data segment; SS for the stack segment; and ES for an extra data segment. Five registers are used to specify the relative or offset part of an address: IP (also called PC) for the instruction pointer, used with CS; SP for the stack pointer and BP for the base pointer, used with SS; DI and SI for the source and destination indexes, used with DS. These registers are dedicated to addressing; the general registers (AX, BX, CX, and DX) can also be used for relative addresses.

Amplitude

The strength or loudness of a sound.

Apage, or active page

A parameter of the BASIC SCREEN command that controls which display page receives any output from the program.

Application program

An informal term used to distinguish programs, such as a word-processing program or an accounting program, that help us do things other than run the computer. Programs that help with running the computer, such as DOS and BASIC, are called systems programs.

ASCII, ASCII text

ASCII, the American Standard Code for Information Interchange, sets a standard way to store characters—letters of the alphabet, punctuation and such—in computers. ASCII text, or just text, is information, like the words you're reading here, stored in a computer following the ASCII coding scheme. Standard ASCII consists of the most common, standard characters. Extended ASCII adds additional characters to standard ASCII, to enrich its possibilities.

Assembler

A systems program that translates assembly-language source code programs into machine-language code. A compiler does the same for languages other than assembly, such as Pascal or BASIC. We use the term assembler exclusively for assembly language, and compiler for other languages; otherwise, the terms mean the same. Assemblers and compilers are one kind of language translator; interpreters are another.

Assembly language

A form of programming language very close to machine language. It uses words, such as ADD, to represent machine-language codes, such as hex 83C207. When we speak informally, assembly language and machine language are sometimes used to mean the same thing—the computer's own detailed instructions. Assembly language is in a form that people can read; machine language is in a form the computer can execute.

Asynchronous

One of two main ways that computers can communicate. The convention for asynchronous communications is known as RS-232C. Data are passed serially, which means bit-by-bit, and the transmission of the data is asynchronous—the sender and receiver don't expect bits to appear at certain precise times. Compare *synchronous*.

Both asynchronous and synchronous are called serial communications and can be used to talk over telephone lines, to other computers, or to a printer. There is another, more efficient way to talk to a printer from our PCjr called parallel communications.

Attenuation

Volume control; measured in decibels (dB).

AX

One of several general-purpose, or scratch-pad, registers. The others are BX, CX, and DX, and their halves AH and AL, BH and BL, etc. See *scratch-pad register.*

BASIC

A programming language that is very widely used with small computers. Our PCjr, like the other IBM personal computers, has a simple version, called Cassette BASIC built into it; the BASIC language cartridge has a richer version of BASIC. These versions of BASIC are interpreted; there is also a compiled version of BASIC.

BASICA

Advanced BASIC. The BASIC cartridge contains both ordinary BASIC and advanced BASICA. In the original IBM personal computers, BASIC and BASICA were two distinct diskette programs; the distinction is less significant in the PCjr's cartridge BASIC. There is no difference between BASIC and BASICA in the PCjr.

Batch command file

A diskette file that contains several DOS commands, which can be performed in a combined operation. Batch files are identified by the file-name extension BAT. AUTOEXEC.BAT is a batch command file.

Baud

The speed of a communications line, equivalent to one bit transmitted each second.

Binary

A number system based on powers of two. Binary numbers are written with only two symbols, 1 and 0. Binary numbers are used to represent high and low voltage inside the computer.

BIOS

The Basic Input/Output System, a set of programs that intimately control the computer's operation, especially input and output. There is a ROM-BIOS, built into our computers, that is an integral part of the machine. Another BIOS, which builds on the services provided by the ROM-BIOS, is a part of DOS.

Bit

A binary digit.

Bit nibbling

The process of having a program, instead of hardware, decode bit signals.

BLOAD format

A disk file format used by BASIC. The data in a BLOAD-format file are the exact image of what is in memory, but BASIC adds a header and a trailer to the file to indicate what is what. The BASIC commands BLOAD and BSAVE read and write data in this format.

Boot, boot record

To start up the computer, particularly to load in the programs that supervise the computer's operation. Turning the computer on, or pressing the Ctrl-Alt-

Del key combination will boot up the computer. Diskettes contain a boot record, a short program used to start up the disk operating system, DOS.

Bootstrap loader

A program that starts up the computer, particularly from a diskette. This program looks to the diskette for a boot record. If there is no disk drive, it transfers control to Cassette BASIC.

Bootstrap program

The program that starts up the computer's operation. When referring to diskettes, the bootstrap program is the boot record. When referring to the computer's built-in ROM programs, this program is the one that initializes the computer, and then tries to activate a boot record from diskette.

BP

The base pointer register, used to locate parts of the stack (as is the SP).

Buffer

A section of memory set aside to assist in I/O operations. Typically, a buffer is used to cushion the difference between the amount of data that a program wants to work with, and the amount of data that the I/O device, such as a diskette, works with.

Bus

The collection of wires that makes up a common signal channel for the computer's information. The bus is a "party line" that allows many parts of the computer to share a general-purpose communication channel. On our PCjr, the I/O channel connector on the right side (where the printer adapter attaches) is a bus connection. On the PC and XT, the expansion slots are each connections to the bus.

Bus architecture

The computer design philosophy that uses a general-purpose bus instead of many special-purpose connections for the parts of the computer to talk to each other.

BX

One of several general-purpose, or scratch-pad, registers. The others are AX, CX, and DX, and their halves AH and AL, BH and BL, etc. See *scratch-pad register.*

Byte

Eight bits, treated as a single unit. A byte is the common unit of computer memory, and each byte in memory has its unique address. A byte can hold a single character, coded in ASCII, so the terms byte and character are sometimes used interchangeably.

Cartridge

A plug-in unit which contains a program permanently recorded in read only memory (ROM). Also called a software cartridge.

Cassette BASIC

The version of BASIC that is built into the PCjr. IBM calls it Cassette BASIC (although it has little to do with cassettes). I sometimes call it ROM-BASIC, since it's built into the ROM, just like the ROM-BIOS.

Cassette interface

A connection for use with a cassette recorder; it provides a cheap and reasonably efficient way to store data.

Cathode ray tube

See *CRT.*

Centronics interface

One of two standard schemes for passing signals from a computer to a printer; also called a parallel interface, or parallel connection. The other is the serial, or RS-232, connection. The PCjr's printer adapter, which attaches to the right side of the system unit, provides a Centronics parallel interface. The IBM graphics printer and the Epson printers use the parallel interface; the IBM Compact Printer uses the serial interface.

Character generator

A device built into the display circuitry that does the work of making the characters that ASCII codes represent appear on the screen.

Clock signal

A signal used by the 8088 to regulate and synchronize its operation. In the PCjr, the clock runs at 4.77 MHz, or slightly less than 5 million clock cycles each second.

Cluster

The unit of storage allocated to a file by DOS. As a file grows and needs more space, DOS allocates the space piece-by-piece, in clusters. For single-sided diskettes, a cluster consists of a single sector; for double-sided diskettes, there are two sectors in a cluster.

Code segment

The area of memory where the current program is located. The CS register is used to indicate the location of the code segment.

Color/graphics adapter

One of two display adapters used by the PC and XT; the other is the monochrome adapter. Our PCjr has the equivalent of a color/graphics adapter built into it. The monochrome adapter displays only characters and not pictures (graphics), and cannot produce colors. Our PCjr does not use the monochrome adapter.

COM, COM file

One of two diskette formats for executable programs; the other is EXE. This format is identified by the file-name extension COM. The COM format is more compact than the EXE, and provides less program support. A COM file is essentially an exact image of a program, as it appears in memory. Note that BASIC programs are neither COM nor EXE, since they are not executable (they must be interpreted by the BASIC language program). Compare *EXE*.

Command interpreter

A key part of DOS, which accepts our commands and acts on them. The command interpreter is stored in the diskette file named COMMAND.COM. Occasionally the command interpreter is overwritten by an application program and must be reloaded into memory when that program ends; this is why we may wish to copy COMMAND.COM onto many of our diskettes.

Compiler

A systems program that translates high-level languages, such as Pascal, into machine-language code. An assembler does the same for assembly language, so assembler and compiler mean much the same. Compilers and assemblers are one kind of language translator; interpreters are another.

Composite video

A display signal that combines the three color signals (red, green, and blue) into one.

Copy protection

A scheme to prevent diskettes from being copied.

CRT

Cathode ray tube; the type of display screen ordinarily used for television sets and computer display screens. The term CRT is usually used just to mean the computer's display screen.

CS

The code segment register, used to indicate the general section of memory where a program is currently located.

CX

One of several general-purpose, or scratch-pad, registers. The others are AX, BX, and DX, and their halves AH and AL, BH and BL, etc. See *scratch-pad register.*

Data segment

The area of memory currently being used for a program's miscellaneous data. The DS register is used to indicate the location of the data segment.

DEBUG

A powerful, complex program included as part of the DOS operating system, intended as a working tool for advanced programmers. It enables us to explore memory, disks, programs, and data.

Decibel (dB)

A scientific measure of how loud sound is, or of how strong sound-related signals are. The term is also used in the opposite sense, to indicate how much a sound signal has been reduced, or attenuated. Decibels are of interest to us when we consider the technical details of the PCjr's TI sound generation chip.

Demodulation

The translation of telephone signals into computer signals; the opposite of modulation, which translates the other way. A modem does both translations, so that a computer can be connected to the telephone system.

Diagnostic routines

Programs that test the keyboard, the diskette drive, and so forth for malfunctioning. They are divided into two groups: a complete, interactive set of diagnostics incorporated into a separate part of the ROM and used during manufacturing, and the simple, quick, but essential diagnostics performed by the ordinary ROM-BIOS when the machine is turned on.

Direct memory access (DMA)

The process by which diskette drive circuitry works directly with the computer's memory. Our PCjr works with its diskettes by bit nibbling, rather than by DMA. This is one reason why Junior is slower than its bigger brothers.

Directory

An item stored on the diskette containing a record for each file on the diskette, giving the file's name, size, location, and so forth. Each diskette has a root, or main directory; with DOS 2.00 and later versions, each diskette can also have subdirectories. The root directory is kept in a fixed, standard location at the beginning of each diskette; a subdirectory is stored like any other file. The root directory is fixed in size and limits the number of files it will keep track of; subdirectories have no size limit. Subdirectories are always attached to a parent directory, which can be either the root directory or another subdirectory.

Disassembling

The process of translating the machine-language form of a program into assembly code; so named because disassembling reverses the process followed by an assembler when it translates assembly language into machine language. The DEBUG program can disassemble (or unassemble) other programs, with the U-unassemble command.

Disk operating system

See *DOS*.

Diskette

A disk of magnetic recording material, which can be used to record computer information. Diskettes are the most common way of storing information for personal computers. Diskettes and cartridges are the two main ways to bring programs to our computers. To use diskettes with our PCjr, we must have the diskette drive, and usually DOS as well.

Diskette drive

The recording and playback machinery needed to use diskettes. The enhanced model of PCjr comes with a diskette drive.

Diskette drive adapter

The circuitry that controls a diskette drive. When a computer has several diskette drives, they are usually controlled by a single adapter. The PCjr's adapter will only allow one diskette drive.

Display

One of many terms for the visual screen on which the computer shows its results. A computer's display screen is very similar to the screen of a TV set, and a TV can be used as a computer display screen. Display screens are also sometimes informally called terminals.

DOS

The Disk Operating System, which provides the facilities needed to make the PCjr a complete working computer. Programs need an environment, an operating framework, in which to work. The task of the disk operating system is to provide the framework, the working environment that programs need to get their work done. The operating system does three main things: task management, memory management, and storage management. The DOS that we use on the PCjr is also called PC-DOS, to distinguish it from the closely-related version, MS-DOS. PC-DOS is specifically adapted to the IBM personal computers; MS-DOS is used on many different computers. Both are by Microsoft.

DOS functions, interrupts, and services

These are tasks carried out by DOS to assist the operation of programs. They are used, for example, to read or write information on diskettes. They are divided into two groups, technically known as functions and interrupts; in this book, the two together are informally referred to as DOS services.

DOS-BIOS

The BIOS programs that are specially written to support DOS. The DOS-BIOS builds on the PCjr's built in ROM-BIOS.

Double density

The recording density used by our PCjr's diskettes. Other densities, such as single and quad, are not used on Junior.

Double precision

One of several formats of numbers used by BASIC. Double-precision numbers are accurate to about 14 decimal places.

DS

The data segment register, used to indicate the general section of memory where a program's data are located.

Dummy interrupt handler

An interrupt-handler program that does nothing, in effect causing an interrupt to be ignored.

DX

One of several general-purpose, or scratch-pad, registers. The others are AX, BX, and CX, and their halves AH and AL, BH and BL, etc. See *scratch-pad register.*

ES

The extra segment register, used mostly to supplement the DS register.

EXE, EXE file

One of two diskette formats for executable programs; the other is COM. This format is identified by the file-name extension EXE. The EXE format is less compact than the COM, and it includes features that allow for extra program support. Note that BASIC programs are neither COM nor EXE, since they are not executable (they must be interpreted by the BASIC language program). Compare *COM.*

Expansion slot .

A general circuit connection that allows additions to be plugged into a computer. The PC and XT each contain expansion slots, but our PCjr does not. However, the PCjr's I/O channel connector makes it possible to attach expansion slots.

Extended ASCII

The full character set used by the PCjr. It consists of standard ASCII plus many additional characters.

External commands

Commands to DOS that are not incorporated into the command interpreter. Several commands, such as DIR and TIME, are internal, or part of the command interpreter. DOS tries to find the programs to carry out external commands by looking to cartridges, and to the files on a diskette.

File allocation table (FAT)

A table, recorded on each diskette, used to indicate where each diskette file is located and which part of the diskette is free for new information.

Fixed disk

One of several terms for a high-capacity storage disk, such as the one built into the XT model of IBM personal computer. Our PCjr does not normally use this kind of disk.

Flag, flag register

One of several bits in the PCjr's 8088 microprocessor used to control key operations, such as whether interrupts are acted on or suspended. The 8088's flags act independently, but can be treated as a group by accessing the flag register. The term flag is also used in a general way to mean any bit or other signal used as control information.

Flippy diskette

A variety of diskette that can be recorded on both sides, but is used as if it were two separate, single-sided diskettes. To use the second side, you turn the diskette over.

Floating-point numbers

A format of numbers that allows a very wide range of numbers. Most programming languages use floating-point numbers; BASIC uses them under the two names single precision and double precision (both are types of floating point). Floating-point numbers may not be precise. Fixed-point numbers, such as integers (or whole numbers), are precise, but cannot take on the wide range of values of floating-point numbers.

Formatting

The preparation of a new diskette for use with the computer. Formatting is the writing of reference, or framework, information on the diskette that identifies each diskette sector.

Frequency

The tone or pitch of a sound.

Game paddle

Essentially, half a joystick; a paddle has one button and its lever moves in only one dimension.

Game adapter card

The supporting circuitry for joysticks, games, and educational software. Our PCjr includes a built-in game adapter; it is an extra feature for the PC and XT.

General registers

The registers that programs can use for any needed purpose, as opposed to the address registers, which are dedicated to addressing memory. There are four 16-bit general registers, AX, BX, CX, and DX. Each of these is also divided into two 8-bit half registers, AH and AL, BH and BL, CH and CL, and DH and DL.

Hard disk

One of several terms for a high-capacity storage disk, such as the one built into the XT model of IBM personal computer. Our PCjr does not normally use this kind of disk.

Hardware

The physical parts of a computer. Compare *software*.

Head

The magnetic, read-write part of the diskette drive. Heads move in and out to go from track to track of the diskette.

Header

Information recorded at the beginning of a file or section of memory, used to identify information that follows. For example, each software cartridge has a header that identifies the cartridge's contents. Likewise, the BLOAD format has a header that gives key information about what follows.

Hex

Short for hexadecimal.

Hexadecimal

A number system based on powers of 16. Each hex digit represents four binary digits. We need 16 symbols to write in hex: the same ten we use for decimal numbers (0 through 9) and the symbols A through F to represent the values 10 through 15.

Immediate addressing

A form of machine-language instruction in which the address of some data is included in the instruction itself. An instruction can use immediate addressing, or it can refer to an address register, which holds the data's address.

Index hole

A small opening on a diskette jacket that is used by the diskette drive to find a matching hole on the diskette itself. This index hole indicates the beginning and end of a track of data on the diskette.

Instruction set

The machine-language instructions that are particular to a microprocessor, such as our PCjr's 8088; the repertoire of detailed commands that the computer can carry out. Aficionados of computers can debate endlessly the merits of one instruction set over another.

Integer

A whole number, as opposed to a floating-point number.

Interleaving

A technique in which multiple circuits separate out and control adjacent memory locations. Interleaving allows computer memory to act as if it worked much faster than it really does.

Internal commands

Commands to DOS that are incorporated into the command interpreter. Several commands, such as DIR and TIME, are internal, or part of the command interpreter. When we give DOS a command, it checks first to see if it is internal, before searching for an external command.

Interpreter

A program that carries out, or executes, another program by looking at the program as we've written it, and then performing each step in turn; as opposed to a compiler or an assembler, which translates a program into machine language (that can later be used, or executed). An interpreter figures out what needs to be done as the program is being used, which makes it slower than a compiled program, where the figuring out is done in advance. The BASIC cartridge contains an interpreter for the BASIC language. When we use BASIC, we're normally using the BASIC interpreter to carry out, or interpret, a BASIC program. (There is also a compiled form of BASIC, which can be much faster.) The most popular interpreted languages are BASIC, Logo, and Forth. Languages such as Pascal are usually compiled, rather than interpreted.

Interrupt

A signal to the computer to drop what it is doing, and pay attention to some important event. When we press a key on the computer's keyboard, an interrupt is generated, telling the computer that a key has been pressed (and it should then find out which one, and act on it). The idea of interrupts allows our computers to go about their business efficiently, and still respond instantly to something that needs attention.

Interrupt handler

A program that responds to an interrupt, and figures out what needs to be done about it. Each basic type of interrupt has its own interrupt handler, custom-tailored. For example, there is one that responds to keyboard interrupts; another oversees the diskette drive. Some interrupt handlers deal with external events (as in the keyboard and diskette drive); others respond to internal interrupts, which are generated by programs. The DOS interrupts, for example, are used to provide services to programs; the handlers for these interrupts are a part of DOS. When an interrupt vector has done its work, it returns control of the computer to what was being done when the interrupt occurred.

Interrupt vector

The address of an interrupt-handler program. When an interrupt occurs, it has a number that identifies what type it is; this number is used to look up an interrupt vector in a table of these addresses. Control of the computer is then given to the interrupt handler.

I/O channel connector

A bus-type connection on the right side of the PCjr's system unit. The parallel printer adapter plugs into this connector. This connector can also be used to add new options to Junior. It is the equivalent of the expansion slots in the PC and XT.

IP

The instruction pointer register, also called the PC, program counter. The IP gives the offset, within the code segment (pointed to by the CS register), that indicates just which part of a program is being executed. IP and CS together control the flow through a program.

Joystick

A plug-in device used almost exclusively with games and educational software. Joysticks are made up of two elements: the lever or stick itself, which is used to move a playing piece around the screen, and the triggers, which are used as firing buttons.

K

Short for kilo, the metric word for 1,000. When used with computers, K represents a binary number whose exact value is 2 to the 10th power, or 1,024. When we use the term K, we are usually referring to how many bytes of storage there are in memory or on disk; so K usually means 1,024 bytes, and not just the number 1,024 itself.

Keyboard Adventure

A program built into each PCjr, which makes a game of learning how to use Junior's keyboard.

Label, on diskettes

A directory entry that identifies the diskette internally the same way paper labels identify it externally.

Light pen

A hand-held probe that, when touched to the computer's display screen and used with the right programs, can be used to draw on the screen and do other things.

LINK

A program that is part of DOS and translates object code into the EXE executable format. Compilers translate our source code into machine language; for technical reasons, though, they put it into a form called object code, which is not completely ready to use. LINK can combine several pieces of object code and put it into the ready-to-use format of an EXE file.

Loader program

A part of DOS's command interpreter, COMMAND.COM, that loads a program into memory.

Machine language

The detailed form of computer programs, in the format that the computer can actually carry out. Sometimes machine language and assembly language are informally spoken of as if they were the same thing. Actually, machine language is what the computer carries out, and assembly language is its near-equivalent, in a format that we can understand.

Memory

Where computer information is stored. The term memory is used in many informal ways, but it usually refers to the general-purpose storage inside a computer, where programs and data are kept while they are being used. This memory is properly called random access memory, or RAM, which shouldn't be confused with read only memory, or ROM, which is permanently recorded. Memory is organized into 8-bit bytes, and each byte of memory has its own address. Large amounts of memory are usually spoken of in terms of K, or multiples of 1,024 bytes.

Memory-mapped display

The use of memory to control what is on the display screen. Any display-related change to the memory causes an immediate change to the display screen; a very fast and very efficient way to operate a display screen.

Microprocessor

The active, working part of a computer that carries out programs is called the processor. When a processor is miniaturized into a single computer chip, like our PCjr's 8088, it is called a microprocessor.

Modem

A translator between computer signals and telephone signals. A modem modulates computer signals into telephone signals, and demodulates them in return; it gets its name from these terms.

Modulation

Translation from computer signals to telephone signals; part of the basic work of a modem. Compare *demodulation*.

Module

A general term for a functional part of a computer. It's used most often to refer to a part of a program. Usually a program module is designed to perform some distinct task in a general-purpose way, so that it can be used by many different programs that need that particular work done. Program modules may be written as building blocks that can be used again and again, but any separate part of a program can be called a module, and sometimes hardware parts are called modules.

Monochrome adapter

One of two display adapters used by the PC and XT; the other is the color/-graphics adapter. Our PCjr has the equivalent of a color/graphics adapter built into it, and it can do essentially everything the monochrome adapter can do. The monochrome adapter displays only characters and not pictures (graphics), and cannot produce colors. Our PCjr does not use the monochrome adapter.

Motherboard

A folksy term for the system board, the part that contains most of the computer's main circuitry and computer chips.

Non-maskable interrupt (NMI)

A sort of fire alarm that can be used to have the computer take some last-minute, desperate steps before trouble sets in, as when the power is failing.

Object code

A particular format of machine-language code. Compilers and assemblers produce object code, which must then be prepared for use by the LINK program. The object code format is designed to make it practical to prepare parts of programs separately, and then later combine them into complete programs.

Offset

The part of a 20-bit, segmented address that refers to any location that is up to 64K bytes away from the segment location. See also *segment*.

Op code

Short for operation code. Machine-language instructions.

Operand

A parameter or specification that completes the details needed to carry out a command or operation. For example, if we give the computer an instruction to ADD, we have to tell it what numbers to add together and where to put the result—these are the operands of the ADD instruction.

Page

A single image of the display screen; part of memory mapping.

Palette

A selection of colors that can be used together on the display screen.

Paragraph

A memory address that is an even multiple of 16. The segment part of a memory address can point to any paragraph; the offset part can then point to any specific byte within 64K of that paragraph.

Parallel interface

One of two standard schemes for passing signals from a computer to a printer; also called a Centronics interface. The other is the serial, or RS-232, connection. The PCjr's printer adapter, which attaches to the right side of the system unit, provides a Centronics parallel interface. The IBM Graphics Printer and the Epson printers use the parallel interface; the IBM Compact Printer uses the serial interface.

Parallel printer adapter

An optional addition to the computer, to provide a parallel printer interface. On the PCjr, the parallel printer interface connects to the I/O channel adapter, on the right side of the system unit.

Parameter

An operand or specification that completes the details needed to carry out a command or operation. For example, if we give the computer a command to FORMAT a diskette, "/S" would be a parameter that tells it to include a copy of the DOS system on the diskette.

Parity bit

An extra bit used to test that other bits haven't been recorded incorrectly. The PC has a parity bit for each byte of memory, but our PCjr doesn't, since memory errors are rare. Parity bits are also used in computer communications, since there is more danger that data will be scrambled when sent over telephone lines.

PC

When we're referring to registers, this is another name for the instruction pointer or IP. Otherwise, PC means the big brother of the PCjr, the IBM Personal Computer.

Pel

One of several terms for a *picture element*.

Picture element

A single dot on the computer's display screen. Also called a *pixel*, or a *pel*. When our computer is in graphics mode, each picture element can be individually colored, lit up, or darkened.

Pixel

Another term for a *picture element*.

Planar

A technical term for the system board, where most of the computer's circuitry is.

POP

One of the two key operations used to save information on the computer's stack. PUSH places data onto the top of the stack; POP removes information from the top of the stack.

Port

The term port is used in several ways. When referring to the detailed operations of the microprocessor, a port is a general way for the microprocessor to talk to other parts of the computer; each part can have a port number, and the processor can pass data to and from them by signaling the port number on the computer's bus. The INP and OUT commands in BASIC refer to these ports. The term port is also used to refer to some of the computer's connections, particularly the RS-232 asynchronous port.

POST

Short for the Power-On Self Test, a test program that is automatically run whenever we turn the PCjr on.

Power transformer

In the PCjr, a separate part that converts high-voltage household current into safer 17-volt current. Power comes to the PCjr's system unit from the external power transformer.

Programming languages

The format used for us to express computer programs. Since the computer's own machine language is so difficult for us to work with, programming languages were created for us to write programs in. There is a distinction between the language itself (BASIC, Pascal, etc.), and the language-translator program that makes the language work on a computer. But people often don't make that distinction. For example, there is BASIC, a particular way to tell a computer what to do; then there is the BASIC language cartridge, which is an interpreter that can carry out programs written in BASIC; finally, there is the BASIC compiler, which can translate programs into object code. When we want to be precise in what we say, we can be careful about indicating just which of these we mean; when we're talking casually, we could refer to any of those three things as BASIC, or the BASIC programming language.

Protected format

A BASIC storage format in which programs are coded to prevent them from being listed. The protected format is roughly the same as the tokenized format but in addition it is scrambled, so that it is not easy to decipher.

PUSH

One of the two key operations used to save information on the computer's stack. PUSH places data onto the top of the stack; POP removes information from the top of the stack.

RAM

See *random access memory.*

Random access memory

RAM; the computer's general-purpose memory, which can be read and also modified. This is what we usually call just plain memory, as opposed to read only memory (ROM).

Raster scan

A way to draw a picture on a CRT, used by TVs and by almost all computer display screens. The flying spot of the electron beam moves in a fixed trace over the entire screen. As the spot is tracing over the screen, it is given the signal to light up, or not light up, each part of the screen. Compare *vector scan*.

Read only memory

Permanently recorded computer memory. Read only memory, or ROM, works much like ordinary memory, but it can't be changed; its contents are safe even when the computer's power is turned off. Our PCjr uses two kinds of ROM: a built-in ROM, permanently installed, which holds the ROM-BIOS and other programs; and the software cartridges, which can be plugged in and removed at will.

Relative offset

See *offset*.

Resolution

The level of detail of a picture; lots of detail is high resolution, not much detail is low resolution. Our PCjr uses three different resolutions. Each has 200 lines of dots, or pixels, from the top to the bottom of the screen. In low resolution, each line has 160 pixel dots across; in medium resolution, 320 pixels; and in high resolution, 640 pixels.

Reverse video

Black (unlit) characters on a white (lit) background. A special "color" used by the monochrome adapter for monochrome characters.

RF (Radio-Frequency) modulator

A device for adapting a video signal for use with a TV set.

RGB

A display signal for the highest-quality picture possible; provides separate signals for each of the three colors that are used: Red, Green, and Blue.

ROM

See *read only memory*.

ROM-BASIC

The version of BASIC that is built into the PCjr. IBM calls it Cassette

BASIC (although it has little to do with cassettes). I sometimes call it ROM-BASIC, since it's built into the ROM, just like the ROM-BIOS.

ROM-BIOS

The BIOS, or control programs, that are built into the PCjr's read only memory. See *BIOS* for more discussion.

RS-232

A standard scheme, used in many computers, for talking between different computer devices. RS-232 is essentially the same thing as a serial or asynchronous port. The RS-232 scheme is used to work with modems, and also with serial printers, such as the IBM Compact Printer.

Scan code

An identifying number for each key on the keyboard.

Scan lines

The lines traced by the electron beam on our display screens. The lines we mentioned when discussing the graphics modes and the three different resolutions are scan lines.

Scratch-pad register

Another term for the general-purpose registers, AX, BX, CX, and DX.

Sector

A block of data on a diskette. The actual space occupied by data records. The number and size of sectors can vary, depending on the operating system. DOS 2.10 uses only one sector size, 512 bytes, and either eight or nine sectors per track.

Segment

The part of a 20-bit, segmented address that refers to any location in a 1,024K byte memory space that is a multiple of 16. See also *offset*.

Segment register

See *address register*.

Segmented address

A memory-addressing scheme used to address a 20-bit address space; that is, to locate any byte out of over a million bytes. Two 16-bit numbers are combined to make up a 20-bit, segmented address. The complete address consists of two parts, the segment and the offset.

Serial port

Another term for the RS-232 port, used to connect to the IBM Compact

Printer to modems, and to other serial devices. The S connection on the back of the PCjr's system unit is a serial port.

Signature

A special code used to help identify a set of data, and to distinguish invalid information. For example, each software cartridge for the PCjr has a signature in its header, which helps verify that the cartridge is properly recorded and is the cartridge we need.

Single sided

Of a diskette drive: with a recording head on one side; of a diskette: capable of storing information on one side only.

Single precision

One of several formats of numbers used by BASIC. Single-precision numbers are accurate to about 6 decimal places.

Software

Computer programs; compare *hardware*, the physical parts of computers.

Sound chip

A chip used for sophisticated sound production. The PCjr's sound chip (SN76469N, made by Texas Instruments) has three voices, each with its own separate attenuation, and a fourth voice for nonmusical sounds, such as explosions.

Source code

Computer programs, in the form that we write them. When we write programs, we write source code; our source code, one way or another, is converted into a running program. For a compiled language such as Pascal, a compiler reads our source code and translates it into object code (machine language, in a special format); the LINK program then converts the object code into a ready-to-use program, in EXE format. For an interpreted language, like our cartridge BASIC, the interpreter reads our source code and then carries it out, step by step.

SP

The stack pointer register, used to locate parts of the stack (as is the BP).

SS

The stack segment register, used to indicate the general section of memory where a program's stack is located.

Start bit

An asynchronous communications parameter needed to separate one character from another and to allow the receiver to get ready for each character.

Stop bit

An asynchronous communications parameter needed to separate one character from another and to allow the receiver to get ready for each character.

Subroutine

A section of a program that is used by other parts of the program to perform some services. Subroutines are usually written so that the same work can be done in different parts of a program, without duplicating the actual working code. But even if a subroutine is only used once, it can be convenient to separate it from the rest of the program. Dividing a program into subroutines can make writing it easier, on the theory of "divide and conquer."

Synchronous

A more sophisticated scheme of serial communications than the asynchronous. With synchronous, both sender and receiver expect bits to appear at precise, predefined times. Our PCjr does not use synchronous communications. Compare *asynchronous*.

Both asynchronous and synchronous are called serial communications and can be used to talk over telephone lines, to other computers, or to a printer. There is another, more efficient way to talk to a printer from our PCjr called parallel communications.

System board

The single circuit board that contains most or all of the key parts that make the computer work. *Motherboard* is a more informal term for the system board, and *planar* is a more technical one.

System diskette

A diskette that has a complete copy of DOS on it, so that DOS can be booted, or started up, from the diskette. Also called a system-formatted diskette, or a DOS diskette. When a blank diskette is prepared for use by being formatted, it can be system formatted or not. Generally DOS can't be added to a diskette that is already in use, unless we reformat it, erasing everything that was recorded on it.

Systems program

An informal term used to distinguish those programs, like DOS and BASIC, that help us use our computers; as opposed to application programs, which serve a purpose beyond the computer.

System unit

The main physical part of the computer, which includes the system board. The PCjr itself consists of the keyboard, the power transformer, and the system unit. Additional parts, such as a display screen, connect to the system unit.

Telecommuting

Working at home and communicating with your employer's computers; commuting to work by computer connection.

TERM

A program in the BASIC cartridge that makes the PCjr act like (emulate) an ASCII terminal, or "dumb" terminal (dumb because it has no sophisticated features).

Terminal

Usually this means a combination of a keyboard and a display screen that are connected to a large computer that might be miles away. In casual talk, any computer display screen could be called a terminal—even the one we use with our PCjr.

Text

Computer data made up of alphabetic characters and such, like the words you are reading here. If our text, like these words, is stored in a computer following the ASCII coding scheme, then we have ASCII text. Informally, the terms text and ASCII are used to mean any written words like these.

Tokenized format

A data format, used by the BASIC interpreter, to store BASIC programs compactly. In the tokenized format, the key words of BASIC, such as LOAD, SAVE, and SCREEN, are replaced with abbreviations, called tokens. When we store a BASIC program on diskette, it is kept in tokenized format unless we ask that it be expanded into its full ASCII-text equivalent, using the "A" option of the SAVE command.

Track

Part of the way data are recorded on a diskette. Each track is a full circle around one side of the diskette; there are 40 tracks on each side of our diskettes. Within each track, data are recorded in eight or nine sectors.

True ASCII

The official, standard ASCII characters, exclusive of the added characters in our PCjr's extended ASCII. There are 128 true ASCII characters, and another 128 in our extended ASCII.

VGA

See *video gate array.*

Video gate array

A special part of the PCjr's circuitry, which helps it mimic the color graphics adapter of the more expensive PC and XT models.

Video graphics character table

A table of data used to produce characters on our computer's display screen. When our PCjr's display is in text mode, the character-generator circuitry does the work of drawing characters on the screen. In graphics mode, software must build drawings of characters out of pixel dots. This table is used by the software, in graphics mode.

Vpage or visual page

Part of the SCREEN command in BASIC, used to control which display page is actually shown.

Winchester disk

One of several terms for a high-capacity storage disk, such as the one built into the XT model of IBM personal computer. Our PCjr does not normally use this kind of disk.

Window

A rectangular part of the whole display screen.

Word

As a computer term, two bytes taken together as a 16-bit unit.

Write-protection notch

An opening on the side of the diskette jacket, which controls whether or not the diskette drive has permission to write on the diskette.

B
FURTHER READING

The most important and useful source
of more detailed information about
the IBM PCjr is IBM's own PCjr
Technical Reference manual.

The *Technical Reference* manual covers a world of information, from circuit diagrams, through controlling commands, to a listing of the ROM-BIOS, the controlling program that makes the PCjr tick.

The PCjr's *Technical Reference* manual isn't the only one of its kind. For each personal computer IBM has introduced, there is a corresponding *Technical Reference* manual. If you want to compare the details of the PCjr with those of the other IBM personal computers, you can check the corresponding sections of the other *Technical Reference* manuals. The information is there, but since differences between models are not well-emphasized, you have to do a little research to discover what those differences are. If you are interested in both the original IBM PC and the XT, you'll find that the XT's version of the *Technical Reference* manual will serve for both machines unless you have to be absolutely certain of differences between the two.

A computer is primarily a collection of smart "chip" components; the smartest of the lot is the Intel 8088 microprocessor, the brains of the PCjr. The most complete technical information about the 8088 is available from its designer, Intel Corporation, Santa Clara, California. In addition, there are two books I can recommend to help you understand this microprocessor. For the best explanation of the philosophy and inner workings of the 8088, turn to *The 8086/8088 Primer* by Stephen P. Morse (Hayden, 1980). Microprocessors usually have a very complicated and convoluted inner structure, and Morse's *Primer* is very good at clarifying the 8088; it certainly did the job for me. For more detailed information about the 8088, but with less explanation, look to *The 8086 Book* by Russell Rector and George Alexy (Osborne/McGraw-Hill, 1980).

If you want to program Junior on an assembly-language level, giving direct commands to the 8088 microprocessor, there are several books that explain assembly-language programming for the IBM personal computers. One such is

IBM PC Assembly Language by Leo Scanlan (Brady, 1983). To learn 8088 assembly language, though, do not look to the manual that comes with the IBM Macro Assembler. The assembler manual is a reference book, not an explanatory tutorial.

To understand the inner workings of the other smart chips in the IBM PCjr, scout a technical book store for any of the electronics "cookbooks" that cover the chips you are interested in. It is here you will find information on such chips as the Texas Instruments SN76489A sound generator, which provides Junior's rich sound-making capabilities.

To understand more of the workings of the DOS operating system, turn to the appendices in the IBM *DOS* manual.

Finally, for a treatment similar to this book, but covering information specific to the original IBM Personal Computer, see my book *Inside the IBM PC* (Brady, 1983).

C
THE
NORTON UTILITIES

Several times in this book, we've
mentioned parts of my software programs
called The Norton Utilities. So that
you'll have a clearer idea of what they
are, here I'll give you a short summary
of the Utilities, and what they do.

Before explaining what these programs are, though, I ought to tell you how they came into being. It may provide some inspiration to anyone dreaming of creating another software success story. Heaven knows, there are still plenty of wonderful opportunities for hit programs for the PCjr.

When I first began playing with my IBM PC, I quickly discovered that there were lots of things I wanted to explore, but none of the programs that were available then helped very much. To satisfy my own curiosity about the computer and especially about the mysteries of the diskettes, I started writing DiskLook, a program designed to make it easy to browse around on a diskette and see what was there.

In the middle of writing DiskLook, I managed to erase the latest version of the program. That left me in quite a pickle—my program was lost. Even though I knew that the data were still recorded on my diskette, I couldn't get to them because DOS considered them erased. This was the inspiration for writing UnErase, the first of a series of programs to help people recover lost data.

After I completed DiskLook, UnErase, and a few more programs like them, I started peddling them in a casual way, hoping to make a few friends and a few dollars as well. I quickly discovered that the educational value of DiskLook—in teaching people about their computers by showing them what was on their diskettes—and the rescue value of UnErase—in recovering lost data files—were making them very popular. There was nothing else that did what they did, and many, many IBM personal computer owners really needed programs like them.

To take advantage of the spreading reputation of these programs, I expanded the original core of four programs into a series of twenty, packaged them, and began promoting them. I didn't want to create a stuffy corporate image for what I was doing, so I put my name and picture on the programs. I wanted to prove that it was still possible for a little guy to win out in the battle for the software marketplace. Eventually, the combination of a good set of programs and some skillful promotion turned these programs into a best-selling series.

Although the heyday of the kitchen-table programmer may be over, it is still possible to create a software success story by yourself. Although microcomputer software has definitely become a big time operation, there is still room for wily individuals, and the appearance of the PCjr has only created more chances for us all. This is the moral of my own tale.

There are twenty programs in the complete Norton Utilities set. Here is a short tour through them:

■ *DiskLook* is the most interesting program in the set. It is designed to show you just about everything there is to know about a diskette; by exploring with DiskLook, you should learn a great deal about how diskettes work. Specifically, DiskLook will give you:

- A graphic map of the complete diskette, showing how various parts of the diskette are used.

- A list of all the files on the diskette (including hidden files), in order by name, size, date, or file attribute.

- The data stored on any part of the diskette; the part can be selected by location on the diskette, or by file; the data are displayed in text format or in hexadecimal.

- For each file, a map of where the file is located, and all the directory information about the file.

■ *UnErase,* on the other hand, is probably the most valuable program in the set. UnErase will reconstruct files that have been erased, or deleted, from a diskette. It is possible to completely recover any erased file, provided no other information has been written on the diskette since the file was erased. If you are careful and conscientious, you'll always have back-up copies of your data, and also never accidentally erase them. But when files do get erased unintentionally, UnErase should be able to get them back.

■ *SecMod*™ is a patching, or "zapping," program, designed to make it easy to make changes to the data stored on a diskette. SecMod allows diskette data to be read, either by the file they belong to, or by their location on the diskette. Changes can then be made to the data in either character or hexadecimal format, and then written back to the diskette.

■ *HardLook*™, *HardUnerase*™, and *HardMod* are special hard-disk versions of these first three programs, designed to meet the special needs of the IBM fixed disk, which is a part of the XT model of IBM PC. These three programs aren't used with the PCjr, but they are part of the full Utilities set.

■ *FileHide*™ is designed to allow us to easily change the hidden-file attribute, and the system and read-only attributes as well. Like DiskLook, UnErase and SecMod, FileHide works interactively, with a full menu screen.

■ *BatHide* performs the same functions as FileHide, but it operates as a batch program, rather than as an interactive program, so that files can be made read-only, or hidden, as an automatic process, using the facilities of batch files.

■ *Beep* is a very simple program that acts like the BEEP statement in BASIC, but it operates as a DOS program. The main use of Beep is to signal when other lengthy programs have ended, so that we know when to return to the computer.

■ *Bload* is to help in the development of assembly-language subroutines for use with BASIC programs. Ordinarily it is difficult to convert assembly programs into the format needed by the BLOAD statement in BASIC. This Bload program performs the conversion automatically.

■ *Clear* clears the computer's display screen, and is similar to the BASIC and DOS commands CLS. Clear is mainly for earlier versions of DOS that did not have the CLS function.

■ *FileSort* is used to sort the file directory of a diskette. FileSort allows us to keep our diskette directories in order by name, extension, size, or date, which can help us keep track of our diskette files.

■ *DiskOpt* is used as part of a process to speed access to diskette files. Like FileSort, DiskOpt rearranges the order of a diskette's directory entries, but DiskOpt's goal is to make diskette use faster, while FileSort's goal is to make the list of files easier to understand.

■ *FileFix*™ is one of the specialized file-recovery tools among the Norton Utilities. FileFix will read each part of each file on a diskette, and report any difficulties. If part of any file is damaged, FileFix will allow us to bypass the damaged parts, so that the rest of a file can be recovered. You can use FileFix routinely to check diskettes for damage, and also to test for some forms of copy-protection.

■ *Label* gives us control over the diskette labels that DOS uses. Although DOS allows us to place labels on diskettes when we format them, DOS does not allow us to add them to existing diskettes, or to change or delete labels. This Label program gives you full control over diskette labels.

■ *Lprint* is a simple print-formatting program, which lists ASCII text files with a heading giving the file name, date, and page numbers. Lprint also gives the line number of each line of text in the file (unless we ask it not to), which can be very useful with some editing programs, such as EDLIN.

■ *ScrAtr* allows us to control the screen attributes, such as the colors of characters that appear on the screen. Any foreground and background colors can be set, and they will remain in effect until they are reset by another program, or by DOS. ScrAtr allows us to choose our own color combinations; for example, my favorites are yellow characters on a blue background and green on black.

■ *Reverse* works like ScrAtr, but it produces one special color combination, black characters on a white background (which is also called reverse video). Some people find reverse video much easier to work with.

■ *SSAR*™ (which is short for Special Search and Recovery) is another file-recovery program. SSAR is designed specifically to recover text data from a diskette that has been damaged beyond ordinary repair. SSAR will read an entire diskette, and transfer all ASCII text data to a file on another diskette.

■ *TimeMark* is used to display the date and time on the screen, and to calculate the elapsed time of an operation. TimeMark is particularly useful for timing lengthy operations; for example, to keep track of how long you work at something.

D
THE CHARACTER SET

NUMBER, dec	NUMBER, hex	SCREEN	PRINTER	NUMBER, dec	NUMBER, hex	SCREEN	PRINTER	NUMBER, dec	NUMBER, hex	SCREEN	PRINTER	NUMBER, dec	NUMBER, hex	SCREEN	PRINTER	NUMBER, dec	NUMBER, hex	SCREEN	PRINTER	NUMBER, dec	NUMBER, hex	SCREEN	PRINTER	NUMBER, dec	NUMBER, hex	SCREEN	PRINTER	NUMBER, dec	NUMBER, hex	SCREEN	PRINTER
000	00			032	20	⑦	⑦	064	40	@	@	096	60	`	`	128	80	Ç		160	A0	á		192	C0	└		224	E0	α	
001	01	☺		033	21	!	!	065	41	A	A	097	61	a	a	129	81	ü		161	A1	í		193	C1	┴		225	E1	β	
002	02	☻		034	22	"	"	066	42	B	B	098	62	b	b	130	82	é		162	A2	ó		194	C2	┬		226	E2	Γ	
003	03	♥		035	23	#	#	067	43	C	C	099	63	c	c	131	83	â		163	A3	ú		195	C3	├		227	E3	π	
004	04	♦		036	24	$	$	068	44	D	D	100	64	d	d	132	84	ä		164	A4	ñ		196	C4	─		228	E4	Σ	
005	05	♣		037	25	%	%	069	45	E	E	101	65	e	e	133	85	à		165	A5	Ñ		197	C5	┼		229	E5	σ	
006	06	♠		038	26	&	&	070	46	F	F	102	66	f	f	134	86	å		166	A6	ª		198	C6	╞		230	E6	μ	
007	07	•	①	039	27	'	'	071	47	G	G	103	67	g	g	135	87	ç		167	A7	º		199	C7	╟		231	E7	τ	
008	08	◘	②	040	28	(	(	072	48	H	H	104	68	h	h	136	88	ê		168	A8	¿		200	C8	╚		232	E8	Φ	
009	09	○	③	041	29	)	)	073	49	I	I	105	69	i	i	137	89	ë		169	A9	⌐		201	C9	╔		233	E9	θ	
010	0A	◙	④	042	2A	*	*	074	4A	J	J	106	6A	j	j	138	8A	è		170	AA	¬		202	CA	╩		234	EA	Ω	
011	0B	♂		043	2B	+	+	075	4B	K	K	107	6B	k	k	139	8B	ï		171	AB	½		203	CB	╦		235	EB	δ	
012	0C	♀	⑤	044	2C	,	,	076	4C	L	L	108	6C	l	l	140	8C	î		172	AC	¼		204	CC	╠		236	EC	∞	
013	0D	♪	⑥	045	2D	-	-	077	4D	M	M	109	6D	m	m	141	8D	ì		173	AD	¡		205	CD	═		237	ED	φ	
014	0E	♫		046	2E	.	.	078	4E	N	N	110	6E	n	n	142	8E	Ä		174	AE	«		206	CE	╬		238	EE	ε	
015	0F	☼		047	2F	/	/	079	4F	O	O	111	6F	o	o	143	8F	Å		175	AF	»		207	CF	╧		239	EF	∩	
016	10	►		048	30	0	0	080	50	P	P	112	70	p	p	144	90	É		176	B0	░		208	D0	╨		240	F0	≡	
017	11	◄		049	31	1	1	081	51	Q	Q	113	71	q	q	145	91	æ		177	B1	▒		209	D1	╤		241	F1	±	
018	12	↕		050	32	2	2	082	52	R	R	114	72	r	r	146	92	Æ		178	B2	▓		210	D2	╥		242	F2	≥	
019	13	‼		051	33	3	3	083	53	S	S	115	73	s	s	147	93	ô		179	B3	│		211	D3	╙		243	F3	≤	
020	14	¶		052	34	4	4	084	54	T	T	116	74	t	t	148	94	ö		180	B4	┤		212	D4	╘		244	F4	⌠	
021	15	§		053	35	5	5	085	55	U	U	117	75	u	u	149	95	ò		181	B5	╡		213	D5	╒		245	F5	⌡	
022	16	▬		054	36	6	6	086	56	V	V	118	76	v	v	150	96	û		182	B6	╢		214	D6	╓		246	F6	÷	
023	17	↨		055	37	7	7	087	57	W	W	119	77	w	w	151	97	ù		183	B7	╖		215	D7	╫		247	F7	≈	
024	18	↑		056	38	8	8	088	58	X	X	120	78	x	x	152	98	ÿ		184	B8	╕		216	D8	╪		248	F8	°	
025	19	↓		057	39	9	9	089	59	Y	Y	121	79	y	y	153	99	Ö		185	B9	╣		217	D9	┘		249	F9	·	
026	1A	→		058	3A	:	:	090	5A	Z	Z	122	7A	z	z	154	9A	Ü		186	BA	║		218	DA	┌		250	FA	·	
027	1B	←		059	3B	;	;	091	5B	[	[	123	7B	{	{	155	9B	¢		187	BB	╗		219	DB	█		251	FB	√	
028	1C	∟		060	3C	<	<	092	5C	\	\	124	7C	¦	¦	156	9C	£		188	BC	╝		220	DC	▄		252	FC	ⁿ	
029	1D	↔		061	3D	=	=	093	5D	]	]	125	7D	}	}	157	9D	¥		189	BD	╜		221	DD	▌		253	FD	²	
030	1E	▲		062	3E	>	>	094	5E	^	^	126	7E	~	~	158	9E	₧		190	BE	╛		222	DE	▐		254	FE	■	
031	1F	▼		063	3F	?	?	095	5F	_	_	127	7F	⌂		159	9F	ƒ		191	BF	┐		223	DF	▀		255	FF		

NOTES

① BEEP
② BACKSPACE
③ TAB
④ LINE FEED
⑤ FORM FEED
⑥ CARRIAGE RETURN
⑦ SPACE

Reprinted from *Personal Computer Age* by permission of CRC Publishing, Copyright © 1982.

E
THE 8086/8088 INSTRUCTION SET

Mnemonic	Full Name	Mnemonic	Full Name
AAA	ASCII adjust for addition	INT	Interrupt
AAD	ASCII adjust for division	INTO	Interrupt on overflow
AAM	ASCII adjust for multiplication	IRET	Interrupt return
AAS	ASCII adjust for subtraction	JA	Jump on above
ADC	Add with carry	JAE	Jump on above or equal
ADD	Add	JB	Jump on below
AND	AND	JBE	Jump on below or equal
CALL	CALL	JC	Jump on carry
CBW	Convert byte to word	JCXZ	Jump on CX zero
CLC	Clear carry flag	JE	Jump on equal
CLD	Clear direction flag	JG	Jump on greater
CLI	Clear interrupt flag	JGE	Jump on greater or equal
CMC	Complement carry flag	JL	Jump on less than
CMP	Compare	JLE	Jump on less than or equal
CMPS	Compare byte or word	JMP	Jump
	(of string)	JNA	Jump on not above
CMPSB	Compare byte string	JNAE	Jump on not above or equal
CMPSW	Compare word string	JNB	Jump on not below
CWD	Convert word to double word	JNBE	Jump on not below or equal
DAA	Decimal adjust for addition	JNC	Jump on no carry
DAS	Decimal adjust for subtraction	JNE	Jump on not equal
DEC	Decrement	JNG	Jump on not greater
DIV	Divide	JNGE	Jump on not greater or equal
ESC	Escape	JNL	Jump on not less than
HLT	Halt	JNLE	Jump on not less than or equal
IDIV	Integer divide	JNO	Jump on not overflow
IMUL	Integer multiply	JNP	Jump on not parity
IN	Input byte or word	JNS	Jump on not sign
INC	Increment	JNZ	Jump on not zero

Mnemonic	Full Name	Mnemonic	Full Name
JO	Jump on overflow	POPF	POP flags
JP	Jump on parity	PUSH	PUSH
JPE	Jump on parity even	PUSHF	PUSH flags
JPO	Jump on parity odd	RCL	Rotate through carry left
JS	Jump on sign	RCR	Rotate through carry right
JZ	Jump on zero	REP	Repeat
LAHF	Load AH with flags	RET	Return
LDS	Load pointer into DS	ROL	Rotate left
LEA	Load effective address	ROR	Rotate right
LES	Load pointer into ES	SAHF	Store AH into flags
LOCK	LOCK bus	SAL	Shift arithmetic left
LODS	Load byte or word (of string)	SAR	Shift arithmetic right
LODSB	Load byte (string)	SBB	Subtract with borrow
LODSW	Load word (string)	SCAS	Scan byte or word (of string)
LOOP	LOOP	SCASB	Scan byte (string)
LOOPE	LOOP while equal	SCASW	Scan word (string)
LOOPNE	LOOP while not equal	SHL	Shift left
LOOPNZ	LOOP while not zero	SHR	Shift right
LOOPZ	LOOP while zero	STC	Set carry flag
MOV	Move	STD	Set direction flag
MOVS	Move byte or word (of string)	STI	Set interrupt flag
MOVSB	Move byte (string)	STOS	Store byte or word (of string)
MOVSW	Move word (string)	STOSB	Store byte (string)
MUL	Multiply	STOSW	Store word (string)
NEG	Negate	SUB	Subtract
NOP	No operation	TEST	TEST
NOT	NOT	WAIT	WAIT
OR	OR	XCHG	Exchange
OUT	Output byte or word	XLAT	Translate
POP	POP	XOR	Exclusive OR

INDEX

Z

PETER NORTON

Peter Norton was raised in Seattle, Washington
and educated at Reed College in Portland, Oregon. Before
discovering microcomputers, Peter spent a dozen years working on
mainframes and minicomputers for companies including Boeing and the Jet
Propulsion Laboratories. After the debut of the IBM PC, Peter was among the
first to buy one. It was then that his exceptional talents for explaining this new
machine came to the fore. Now recognized as the principal authority on the
IBM PC, Peter is the author of the best-selling *Inside the IBM PC* and
creator of the popular Norton Utilities programs which allow the
user to manipulate the "insides" of the IBM PC. Peter is
currently a featured columnist for both
PC and *PCjr.* magazines.

The manuscript for this book was prepared on an
IBM Personal Computer. Submitted to Microsoft Press in
electronic form, text files were processed and formatted using Microsoft Word.

Cover and text design by Ted Mader and Associates; illustrations by Mits Katayama;
figures by Dale Anderson.

Text composition in Caslon 540, with display in Eurostile condensed, by Paul O. Giesey
Typographers, Portland, Oregon, using CCI Book and the Mergenthaler
Linotron 202 digital phototypesetter.

Cover art separated by Color Masters, Phoenix, Arizona. Text stock, 60 lb.
Glatfelter Offset, supplied by Carpenter/Offutt; cover 12 pt. Carolina.
Printed and bound by R.R. Donnelley and Sons,
Crawfordsville, Indiana.